Mediterranean

Mediterranean

bay books

Contents

Introduction

Healthy Mediterranean Cooking

The Mediterranean Sea links Europe, Africa and the Middle East. To follow the Mediterranean model of healthy eating, include in your diet lots of fresh fruit and vegetables, as well as breads, grains and beans. Use olive oil instead of, not as well as, other fats. Eat low to moderate amounts of dairy products. Cook fish and poultry a few times a week and red meat less frequently. Regular exercise is also part of the healthy lifestyle.

THE MEDITERRANEAN DIET

Within the Mediterranean, each country has its own particular cuisine and tends to favour local ingredients. Regions within each country also do this. Indeed, often, areas within regions have their own specialities. So obviously it is just not possible to identify only one Mediterranean diet.

The countries in the region have a similar climate and historical influences and this has meant a reliance on similar kinds of foods. The Mediterranean diet has factors which are common in each of the countries: it is low in saturated fats and high in complex carbohydrates and fibre. The diet is based on cereals (bread, pasta, couscous, burghul, rice), vegetables, fruit and legumes, olives, garlic and herbs. Food is grown locally and is eaten at its freshest and best. These foods make up the core of the diet, while foods from animal sources are used less frequently. Limited availability and the cost of red meat mean that it is generally eaten in small quantities and only a few times per month. Fish, poultry and eggs are used a few times a week. Cheese features prominently in the cuisine in some areas but in most areas dairy products are used in low to moderate amounts, perhaps a few times per week. Red wine plays a large part in the Mediterranean diet but is drunk in moderation and almost always during meals. Spirits are imbibed less frequently.

THE GOOD OIL

Olive oil is the quintessential ingredient that links the diverse Mediterranean cuisines. The flavour, colour and taste varies according to the type of olives used and the climate, soil and area of cultivation. The type and ripeness of the olive influences the colour. Some olive trees are grown to produce olives for eating and some for oil—they are not harvested from the same trees.

Over 30 years ago the Seven Countries Study found that a typical Mediterranean diet resulted in the highest rates of life expectancy. Further studies endorsed by the World Health Organization have shown Mediterranean countries to have the lowest rates of chronic diseases, including coronary heart disease, obesity, diabetes and cancers of the bowel and breast. This applies despite the relative lack of economic wealth in some areas. It seems that the overwhelming

factor in this is a diet low in saturated fats.

We have all become so conditioned to believing that fat is bad that it is difficult for us to believe just how good olive oil is for you. Olive oil is cholesterol-free and is high in oleic acid, a mono-unsaturated fatty acid. Mono-unsaturated fats do not raise blood cholesterol levels the way saturated fats (animal fats and some tropical oils such as palm and coconut oil) do. In fact, the mono-unsaturated fats lower the damaging low-density lipoproteins (LDL) which are responsible for depositing cholesterol in the arteries. This leaves the beneficial high-density lipoproteins (HDL) untouched. Substances present in olive oil also protect LDL cholesterol from oxidation, which is a main feature in the development of coronary artery disease.

Olive oil not only contains large amounts of mono-unsaturated fats (between 55 and 83 per cent) but is also a rich source of antioxidants. Olive oil is also a good source of vitamin E—a powerful antioxidant and disease preventative. Anti-oxidants fight free radicals, elements which can suppress the immune system and may cause heart disease, cancers and ageing.

Why do we need any fat, even if it is olive oil? We need some fat in our diet to help transport essential fat-soluble vitamins A, D, E and K. Also, it makes things taste good. Olive oil helps make the simple Mediterranean foods quite flavoursome. Pasta can be tossed with olive oil and a few other ingredients to give a delicious meal. Olive oil brings out the flavour of other ingredients and is a natural complement to fresh regional produce.

WHAT'S IN A NAME?

'Extra virgin olive oil' is unrefined, has the lowest acidity level and is of the highest quality. Extra virgin olive oil is the first extraction of oil from the olives and the extraction is undertaken without heat or chemicals which may alter the oil. Prices vary considerably.

'Virgin olive oil' is similar to extra virgin but has a slightly higher allowable acidity level.

'Olive oil' is from the second extraction and the olives are heated to make the oil thinner and more easily removed.

'Light olive oil' is made from the filtered combination of refined olive oil and small amounts of virgin olive oil. It is not light in kilojoules, just in texture and taste.

As a general rule, you would use olive oil for cooking, whereas the flavour of extra virgin olive oil is often preferred for salad dressings and drizzling on food such as pasta. However, the choice is a personal one. Contrary to popular opinion, olive oil is also suitable for frying as it doesn't break down when heated and also forms a seal around the food, thus minimizing fat absorption.

With all the studies that have been done regarding the good health of people in the Mediterranean region, it is still not clear how much can be attributed to diet and what part lifestyle plays in the equation. For example, drinking alcohol is generally done in company and with food, even if it's just the things we know and love as meze, tapas, antipasto or hors d'oeuvres. Olive oil is used instead of, rarely as well as, saturated fats. The diet incorporates plenty of fresh and unprocessed foods, with no hidden saturated fats or refined sugars that are evident in some diets.

Also, we should remember that the traditional Mediterranean lifestyle includes a large amount of physical activity. If you make time for daily exercise, you will be sure to reap the benefits.

Mediterranean Pantry

Bocconcini

Burghul

Cedro

Couscous

Feta

BOCCONCINI
A fresh, unripened cheese originally made from buffalo milk but now more commonly made from cow milk. It is often referred to as 'baby mozzarella', and is kept in whey to keep it moist. Young fresh mozzarella will keep in the refrigerator for 2–3 weeks. Change the water it is kept in every 2 days.

BURGHUL
Also known as bulgar or cracked wheat, burghul is a wheat product which has been hulled, parboiled or steamed, then dried and cracked. It is a staple in the Middle East and requires either very little cooking or just soaking. It is available coarse or fine ground.

CEDRO
Also known as citron, cedro originated in north-eastern India before spreading throughout the Middle East and Asia during antiquity. The fruits look like large rough lemons and have a very thick peel and dry flesh with quite a sour flavour. They are now grown especially for their thick peel which is candied. Cedro is available in speciality shops.

COUSCOUS
A staple food of northern Africa, particularly Morocco and Algeria. Couscous is a processed cereal made from semolina and coated with wheat flour. It is used as a high carbohydrate accompaniment to meat and vegetable dishes. Instant couscous is available in supermarkets and cooks in 5 minutes when soaked in boiling water.

FETA
A soft white cheese ripened in brine, giving it a salty taste. Originally made from sheep or goat's milk, feta is now most often made with cow milk. Feta takes its name from the word *fetes,* meaning large blocks or slices, which it is cut into before being ripened and stored in brine. It is the best known of all Greek cheeses and can be eaten as an appetizer, cooked or marinated.

HALOUMI
A salty Middle Eastern cheese made from sheep milk. The name is thought to be one of the few surviving ancient Egyptian words—*ialom.* The curd is heated in whey to boiling, then drained, salted and matured in brine.

HALVA
A Middle Eastern sweet with numerous variations, but most generally made from crushed sesame seeds, sugar and glucose or honey. Flavoured with nuts, fruit, chocolate and spices, halva is made in block form and sold in slices.

KEFALOTYRI CHEESE
A very hard, pale yellow scalded and cured sheep or goat's milk cheese from Greece. The taste and texture are quite similar to the Italian Parmesan cheeses. Kefalotyri has a variety of different uses depending on its age. When young it is used as a table cheese, when six months old it is used in cooking, particularly frying, and when more mature it makes an excellent grating cheese. Parmesan or Pecorino can be substituted.

LENTILS
A legume with many varieties originating from the Middle East with red, green and brown being the most common types. Lentils do not have to be soaked before cooking but they should be rinsed to remove any impurities. Lentils are remarkably high in protein (25 per cent) and low in fat, and are an essential part of any vegetarian diet.

OKRA
A native of Africa, this green curved pod is very popular in the eastern Mediterranean. It is also called gumbo, a name very popular in the United States, and ladies' fingers. It has a very glutinous texture which can be lessened by soaking in lemon juice and salt water before cooking and is a natural thickening agent. Okra is available both fresh and tinned.

PANCETTA
An important ingredient in Italian cooking, pancetta is the unsmoked bacon, from the belly of the pig, that has been cured in salt and spices. It is

Haloumi

Halva

Kefalotyri cheese

Lentils

Okra

Pancetta

usually sold rolled into a sausage shape and cut into very thin slices. Pancetta can be eaten raw or cooked. Bacon can be used as a substitute.

PARMESAN

A hard cow's milk cheese widely used in Italy, either grated in dishes or shaved to garnish. Always buy in a chunk and grate it as you need it rather than using grated packet cheese. Parmigiano-reggiano is the most superior, which is reflected in the price, but is well worth it.

PECORINO

A general name for a wide range of Italian cheeses made from sheep milk. More specifically, the name refers to hard, cooked sheep milk cheeses of central Italy and Sardinia. The most famous of these is Pecorino Romano. Pecorino is available in mild or sharp flavours, or sometimes with added flavours such as peppercorns.

POLENTA

Also known as cornmeal, these ground, dried corn kernels are a staple carbohydrate in Italy. It is most often made into a porridge like mixture with butter and Parmesan or cooked and left to set, then fried, grilled (broiled) or baked. Polenta comes in coarse, medium or fine grains.

POMEGRANATE MOLASSES

Also sold as pomegranate syrup or concentrate. This is the boiled down juice of a sour variety of pomegranate cultivated in Syria and Lebanon. Pomegranate molasses has a sweet and sour flavour and should not be confused with grenadine, a highly sweetened and concentrated syrup used in making beverages.

PORCINI MUSHROOMS

Known as ceps or boletus mushrooms in France, porcini are wild mushrooms used in Italian and French cooking. While sometimes available fresh, they are most common dried. Dried porcini mushrooms need to be reconstituted by soaking in hot water then rinsed thoroughly to remove any grit. Dried porcini have a strong, meaty flavour and should be used sparingly.

PRESERVED LEMONS

A unique flavour popular in northern African dishes, particularly Moroccan tagines. Lemons are packed tightly with salt and sealed in a jar with extra lemon juice and spices such as peppercorns, bay leaves and cinnamon, for up to six weeks. Only the zest is used, so lemons must be rinsed well and have pulp and pith removed before use.

PROSCIUTTO

An Italian ham that has been cured by salting, then drying in the air. Aged for about 8–10 months, it is then sliced thinly and can be eaten raw or cooked. Prosciutto di Parma is the classic Italian ham and is traditionally served as an antipasto and also used extensively in Italian cooking.

PROVOLONE

A golden yellow, mainly southern Italian, cheese with a glossy zest, often moulded by hand into a variety of shapes before being hung to mature. While it is young, provolone is mild and delicate and often used as a table cheese. As it matures, it becomes sharper in flavour and makes an excellent grating cheese.

PUY LENTILS

A tiny, dark green lentil which is regarded as a delicacy in France, their country of origin. They keep their shape and quite a firm texture after cooking and are used most often for salads and hors d'oeuvre. Lentil du Puy are more expensive than other lentils and can be found in speciality shops.

SEMOLINA

The coarse product obtained from the first milling of wheat. Semolina itself is available coarse, medium or fine ground. Often made from durum wheat, it is used in making of pasta, gnocchi and certain puddings or cakes. Semolina is less starchy than other wheat products and results in a lighter texture.

SUMAC

Dried red berries from the Middle Eastern Rhus coriaria or sumac tree containing small, brown, sour seeds. Used mainly in Syria and Lebanon, ground sumac is sprinkled on salads and fish and adds a tangy, citrus flavour. Today it is most common in areas where lemons are still scarce.

Sumac

Semolina

Puy lentils

Provolone

Prosciutto

Parmesan

Pecorino

Polenta

Pomegranate molasses

Porcini mushrooms

Preserved lemons

Tapas and meze

Antipasto

What more delicious way to whet the appetite than with a colourful antipasto platter? The name translates literally as 'before the meal' and the tradition arose from the lengthy banquets of the Roman Empire. These recipes serve 4–8 people, depending on how many dishes you prepare.

CANNELLINI BEAN SALAD

Rinse and drain a 425 g (15 oz) tun of cannellini beans and toss together with 1 tablespoon finely chopped red onion, 1 chopped tomato, 3 sliced anchovy fillets, 2 teaspoons finely chopped basil leaves, 2 teaspoons extra virgin olive oil and 1 teaspoon balsamic vinegar. Season to taste.

ARTICHOKE FRITTATA

Heat 30 g (1 oz) butter in a non-stick frying pan, add 2 small sliced leeks and 1 sliced clove of garlic and cook until soft. Spread evenly over the bottom of the pan. Lightly beat 6 eggs and season with salt and black pepper. Slice 100 g (3 ⅓ oz) bottled artichoke hearts. Pour the eggs into the pan and arrange the artichoke slices on top. Sprinkle with 1 teaspoon chopped fresh tarragon. Cook over low heat until set (this will take about 10 minutes), shaking the pan occasionally to evenly distribute the egg. Place under a hot grill (broiler) to lightly brown the top. Cut into wedges and drizzle with a little lemon juice to serve.

Clockwise from left: Cannellini Bean Salad; Artichoke Frittata; Ricotta Spread; Italian Meatballs; Marinated Mushrooms

RICOTTA SPREAD

Beat 200 g (6½ oz) ricotta with 2 tablespoons lemon juice until smooth and then fold in 3 tablespoons sliced black olives and 1 tablespoon chopped semi-dried (sun-blushed) tomatoes. Pile into a serving bowl and sprinkle with 1 tablespoon chopped chives. Serve with crusty Italian bread.

ITALIAN MEATBALLS

Combine 250 g (8 oz) lean minced (ground) beef, a small grated onion, 1 crushed garlic clove, 40 g (1½/ oz/½ cup) fresh white breadcrumbs, 3 tablespoons chopped black olives, 1 teaspoon dried oregano, 1 tablespoon finely chopped parsely, and salt and black pepper to taste. Mix together thoroughly with your hands. Form teaspoonsful of mixture into balls. Heat a little oil in a frying pan and cook the meatballs in batches until well browned.

MARINATED MUSHROOMS

Wipe 315 g (10 oz) small button mushrooms clean with damp paper towels and cut in half (never wash mushrooms by soaking in water or they will become soggy). Place the mushrooms in a bowl with 3 finely sliced spring onions (scallions) and 1 finely sliced celery stalk, then gently mix together. Stir through 1 crushed garlic clove, 3 tablespoons extra virgin olive oil, 2 tablespoons lemon juice and 1 tablespoon finely chopped chives. Refrigerate for about 4 hours for the flavours to combine, but allow to return to room temperature before serving.

Note: For a delicious mushroom salad, use the same recipe for Marinated Mushrooms but place the mushrooms in the base of a large salad bowl. Top with torn lettuce leaves or a mixture of torn salad leaves and toss well just before serving. You may need to make more dressing (marinade), depending on the amount of lettuce in your salad.

Antipasto

CARPACCIO

Take a 400 g (14 oz) piece of beef eye fillet and remove all the visible fat and sinew. Freeze for 1–2 hours, until firm but not frozen solid (this makes the meat easier to slice thinly). Cut paper thin slices of beef with a large, sharp knife. Arrange on a serving platter and allow to return to room temperature. Drizzle with 1 tablespoon extra virgin olive oil, then scatter with torn rocket (arugula) leaves, black olives cut into slivers and shavings of Parmesan cheese. Serve at room temperature.

PASTA FRITTATA

Cook 300 g (10½ oz) spaghetti in a large pan of boiling water, until just tender, then drain well. Whisk 4 eggs together in a large bowl, then add 50 g (1¾ oz/½ cup) finely grated Parmesan cheese, 2 tablespoons chopped fresh parsley, salt and freshly ground black pepper. Add the spaghetti and toss together until well coated. Melt 1 tablespoon butter in a large frying pan and add the spaghetti mixture. Cover and cook over low heat until the base is crisp and golden. Slide the frittata onto a plate, melt another tablespoon of butter in the pan and flip the frittata back in to cook the other side (do not cover or the frittata will not get a crisp finish). Serve warm, cut into wedges.

16

STUFFED CHERRY TOMATOES

Slice the tops from 16 cherry tomatoes, hollow out and discard the seeds. Turn upside-down and leave to drain for a few minutes. Beat together 50 g (1⅔ oz) each goat's cheese and ricotta until smooth. Finely chop 2 slices prosciutto, discarding any fat, and mix with the cheeses. Season with salt and ground black pepper. Stuff into the tomatoes, using your fingers, and refrigerate until required.

PROSCIUTTO WITH MELON

Cut a melon (rockmelon or honeydew) into thin wedges and remove the seeds. Wrap a slice of prosciutto around each piece of fruit, drizzle with a little extra virgin olive oil and grind some black pepper over each.

From left: Carpaccio; Pasta Frittata; Stuffed Cherry Tomatoes; Prosciutto with Melon; Marinated Eggplant

MARINATED EGGPLANT

Cut 750 g (1 lb 10 oz) slender eggplant (aubergine) into thick diagonal slices. Put in a colander and sprinkle well with salt. After 30 minutes, rinse and pat dry. Mix 3 tablespoons olive oil, 2 tablespoons balsamic vinegar, 2 crushed garlic cloves and 1 finely chopped anchovy fillet; whisk until smooth and season to taste. Heat a little oil in a large non-stick frying pan and brown the eggplant. Place in a bowl, add the dressing and 2 tablespoons chopped parsley and toss. Marinate for 4 hours and serve at room temperature.

MARINATED YOGHURT CHEESE BALLS

Preparation time: 35 minutes + 3 days
    draining + 3 hours refrigeration
Total cooking time: Nil
Makes 18 balls

1.5 kg (3 lb 5 oz) plain
    yoghurt
2 clean 50 x 50 cm (20 x
    20 inch) muslin (cheesecloth)
    squares
2 fresh bay leaves
3 sprigs fresh thyme
2 sprigs fresh oregano

500 ml (17 fl oz/2 cups)
    good-quality olive oil

1 Place the yoghurt in a bowl with 2 teaspoons salt and mix well. Put the muslin squares one on top of the other and place the yoghurt mixture in the centre. Gather up the corners and tie securely with string; suspend over a bowl. Refrigerate and leave to drain for 3 days.
2 Once drained, the yoghurt will become the texture and consistency of ricotta cheese. Remove from the cloth, and place in a bowl.
3 Roll a tablespoon of the mixture into a ball and place on a large tray.

Repeat with the remaining mixture to make 18 balls. Cover and refrigerate for 3 hours, or until quite firm.
4 Place the balls in a clean, dry 1 litre (4 cup) glass jar with the bay leaves, thyme and oregano sprigs. Fill the jar with the olive oil. Seal and refrigerate for up to 1 week. Return to room temperature for serving.

COOK'S FILE

Note: This dish is traditionally served at breakfast or as an appetizer.
Hint: Leave the bay leaves, thyme and oregano out of the fridge for 24 hours before use to remove excess moisture.

Place the yoghurt mixture in the muslin, gather up the corners and tie securely.

Roll the yoghurt mixture into balls and place on a large tray.

Place the labneh in the jar with the herbs and pour in the olive oil.

HUMMUS

Preparation time: 20 minutes +
  overnight soaking
Total cooking time: 1 hour 15 minutes
Makes 3 cups

220 g (7¾ oz/1 cup) dried
  chickpeas
2 tablespoons tahini

4 garlic cloves, crushed
2 teaspoons ground cumin
4 tablespoons lemon juice
3 tablespoons olive oil
large pinch cayenne
  pepper
extra lemon juice, optional
extra olive oil, to garnish
paprika, to garnish
chopped fresh parsley, to
  garnish

1 Soak the chickpeas in 1 litre (4 cups) water overnight. Drain and place in a large saucepan with 2 litres (8 cups) fresh water (enough to cover the chickpeas by 5 cm/2 inches). Bring to the boil, then reduce the heat and simmer for 1 hour 15 minutes, or until the chickpeas are very tender. Skim any scum from the surface. Drain well, reserve cooking liquid and leave until cool enough to handle. Pick over for any loose skins and discard.

2 Process the chickpeas, tahini, garlic, cumin, lemon juice, olive oil, cayenne pepper and 1½ teaspoons salt in a food processor until thick and smooth. With the motor still running, gradually add enough reserved cooking liquid to form a smooth creamy purée. Season with salt or extra lemon juice.

3 Spread onto a flat bowl or plate, drizzle with oil, sprinkle with paprika and scatter the parsley over the top. Serve with pitta bread or pide.

Pick through the cooled chickpeas to remove any loose skins.

Process the chickpea mixture with the reserved cooking liquid until creamy.

OLIVE TAPENADE

Preparation time: 10 minutes
Total cooking time: Nil
Makes 1½ cups

400 g (14 oz) Kalamata olives,
   pitted
2 garlic cloves, crushed
2 anchovy fillets in oil, drained
2 tablespoons capers in brine,
   rinsed, squeezed dry
2 teaspoons chopped fresh
   thyme
2 teaspoons Dijon mustard
1 tablespoon lemon juice
3 tablespoons olive oil
1 tablespoon brandy, optional

1 Place the Kalamata olives, crushed garlic, anchovies, capers, chopped thyme, Dijon mustard, lemon juice, olive oil and brandy in a food processor and process until smooth. Season to taste with salt and freshly ground black pepper. Spoon into a clean, warm jar, cover with a layer of olive oil, seal and refrigerate for up to 1 week. Serve on bruschetta or with a meze plate.

COOK'S FILE

Note: When refrigerated, the olive oil may solidify, making it an opaque white colour. This is a property of olive oil and will not affect the flavour of the dish. Simply bring the dish to room temperature before serving and the olive oil with return to a liquid state. The word 'tapenade' comes from the French word tapéno, meaning capers. Tapenade is the famous olive, anchovy and caper spread, originating from Provence.

Hint: To make sure your storage jar is very clean, preheat the oven to 120°C (250°F/Gas ½). Wash the jar and lid thoroughly in hot soapy water (or preferably in a dishwasher) and rinse well with hot water. Put the jar on a baking tray and place in the oven for 20 minutes, or until fully dry and you are ready to use it. Do not dry the jar or lid with a tea towel.

Use an olive pitter or small sharp knife to remove the stones from the olives.

Process all the ingredients in a food processor until smooth.

PESTO

Preparation time: 10 minutes
Total cooking time: 2 minutes
Makes 1 cup

4 tablespoons pine nuts
50 g (1¾ oz/1 cup) small fresh
    basil leaves
2 garlic cloves, crushed

½ teaspoon sea salt
125 ml (4 fl oz/½ cup) olive oil
4 tablespoons finely grated
    Parmesan cheese
20 g (¾ oz/½ cup) pecorino
    cheese, finely grated

1 Preheat the oven to 180°C (350°F/ Gas 4). Spread the pine nuts on a baking tray and bake for 2 minutes, or until lightly golden. Allow to cool.

2 Place the pine nuts, basil, garlic, salt and oil in a food processor and process until smooth. Transfer to a bowl and stir in the cheeses. Serve with a meze plate, pasta, meat or soup.

COOK'S FILE

Note: Pesto is a famous Italian sauce, served with dishes such as chicken, fish and pizza.

Bake the pine nuts in a moderate oven until lightly golden.

Process the pine nuts, basil, garlic, sea salt and oil until smooth.

Stir the Parmesan and pecorino into the basil mixture.

SKORDALIA

Preparation time: 15 minutes
Total cooking time: 10 minutes
Makes 2 cups

500 g (1 lb 2 oz) floury potatoes,
    peeled and cut into 2 cm
    (¾ inch) cubes (see Notes)
5 garlic cloves, crushed
ground white pepper
185 ml (6 fl oz/¾ cup) olive oil
2 tablespoons white vinegar

1 Bring a saucepan of water to the boil, add the potato and cook for 10 minutes, or until very soft.
2 Drain the potato and mash until quite smooth. Stir in the garlic, 1 teaspoon salt and a pinch of white pepper. Gradually pour in the oil, mixing well with a wooden spoon. Add the vinegar and season, if needed. Serve with crusty bread or crackers, or with grilled meat, fish or chicken.

COOK'S FILE

Notes: Use King Edward, russet or pontiac potatoes.
Do not make skordalia with a food processor—the processing will turn the potato into a gluey mess.
Storage: Skordalia will keep in an airtight container for up to 2–3 days in the fridge. The potato will absorb the salt so check the seasoning before serving.

Boil the potato in a large saucepan of lightly salted water until very soft.

Drain the potato and then mash with a potato masher until smooth.

Gradually add the oil to the potato mixture, mixing well.

TZATZIKI

Preparation time: 10 minutes +
  15 minutes standing
Total cooking time: Nil
Makes 2 cups

2 Lebanese (short) cucumbers
  (about 300 g/10½ oz)
400 g (14 oz) Greek-style plain
  yoghurt
4 garlic cloves, crushed
3 tablespoons finely chopped
  fresh mint, plus extra to
  garnish
1 tablespoon lemon juice

1 Cut the cucumbers in half lengthways, scoop out the seeds and discard. Leave the skin on and coarsely grate the cucumber into a small colander. Sprinkle with salt and leave over a large bowl for 15 minutes to drain off any bitter juices.
2 Meanwhile, place the Greek-style yoghurt, crushed garlic, mint and lemon juice in a bowl, and stir until well combined.
3 Rinse the cucumber under cold water then, taking small handfuls, squeeze out any excess moisture.
4 Combine the grated cucumber with the yoghurt mixture, then season to taste with salt and freshly ground

black pepper. Serve immediately or refrigerate until ready to serve, garnished with the extra mint.

COOK'S FILE

Note: Tzatziki is often served as a dip with flatbread or Turkish pide but is also suitable to serve as a sauce to accompany seafood and meat.
Storage: Tzatziki will keep in an airtight container in the refrigerator for 2–3 days.

Cut the cucumbers in half and scoop out the seeds with a teaspoon.

Mix the yoghurt, garlic, mint and lemon juice together

Squeeze the grated cucumber to remove any excess moisture.

MARINATED FETA

Preparation time : 10 minutes +
  24 hours soaking + 1 week maturing
Total cooking time : Nil
Fills a 750 ml (26 fl oz/3 cup) jar

4 garlic cloves, peeled
125 ml (4 fl oz/½ cup) lemon
  juice
400 g (14 oz) good-quality soft
  feta
6 fresh thyme sprigs
2 fresh bay leaves, lightly
  crushed
½ teaspoon black peppercorns
up to 375 ml (13 fl oz/1½ cups)
  good-quality olive oil

1 Soak the garlic cloves in the lemon juice for 24 hours. Drain and pat dry with paper towel. Drain the feta and cut into 2 cm (¾ inch) cubes. Layer the feta, thyme, garlic, bay leaves and peppercorns in a 750 ml (26 fl oz/3 cup) jar with a tight-fitting lid.
2 Fill the jar with oil to completely cover. Seal the jar and refrigerate for 1 week before using. Refrigerate for up to 3 weeks after opening.

COOK'S FILE

Storage: The oil may solidify in the fridge. Bring to room temperature for serving. Chill after opening; use within 2 weeks.

Drain the soft feta well and cut into 2 cm (¾ inch) cubes.

Fill the jar with good-quality olive oil to cover the contents.

TARAMOSALATA

Preparation time: 10 minutes +
    10 minutes soaking
Total cooking time: Nil
Makes 1½ cups

5 slices white bread, crusts
    removed
4 tablespoons milk
100 g (3½ oz) tinned tarama
    (mullet roe)

1 egg yolk
½ small onion, grated
1 garlic clove, crushed
2 tablespoons lemon
    juice
4 tablespoons olive oil
pinch ground white pepper

1 Soak the bread in the milk for 10 minutes. Press in a strainer to extract any excess milk, then place in a food processor with the tarama, egg yolk, onion and garlic. Process for

30 seconds, or until smooth, then add 1 tablespoon lemon juice.
2 With the motor running, slowly pour in the olive oil. The mixture should be smooth and of a dipping consistency. Add the remaining lemon juice and a pinch of white pepper. If the dip tastes too salty, add another piece of bread.

COOK'S FILE

Variation: Try smoked cod's roe instead of the mullet roe.

Using a cheese grater grate half a small onion.

Press the soaked bread pieces in a strainer to extract any excess milk.

Process the bread, tarama, egg yolk, onion and garlic until smooth.

BABA GHANNOUJ

Preparation time: 20 minutes +
   30 minutes cooling
Total cooking time: 50 minutes
Makes 1¾ cups

2 eggplants (aubergines)
   (1 kg/1 lb 2 oz)
3 garlic cloves, crushed
½ teaspoon ground cumin
4 tablespoons lemon juice
2 tablespoons tahini
pinch cayenne pepper
1½ tablespoons olive oil
1 tablespoon finely chopped
   fresh flat-leaf (Italian)
   parsley
black olives, to garnish

1 Preheat the oven to 200°C (400°F/
Gas 6). Pierce the eggplants several
times with a fork, then cook over an
open flame for about 5 minutes, or
until the skin is black and blistering,
then place in a roasting tin and bake
for 40–45 minutes, or until the
eggplants are very soft and wrinkled.
Place in a colander over a bowl to
drain off any bitter juices and leave to
stand for 30 minutes, or until cool.
2 Carefully peel the skin from the
eggplant, chop the flesh and place in a
food processor with the garlic, cumin,
lemon, tahini, cayenne and olive oil.
Process until smooth and creamy.
Alternatively, use a potato masher or
fork. Season to taste with salt and stir
in the parsley. Spread onto a flat bowl
or plate and garnish with the olives.
Serve with flatbread or pide.

COOK'S FILE

Note: If you prefer, you can simply
roast the eggplant in a roasting tin in
a 200°C (400°F/Gas 6) oven for 1 hour,
or until very soft and wrinkled.
The name baba ghannouj is roughly
translated as 'poor man's caviar'.

*Carefully peel the skin away from the baked
eggplant.*

*Process the eggplant, garlic, cumin, lemon,
tahini, cayenne and olive oil.*

BOREK

Preparation time: 1 hour
Total cooking time: 20 minutes
Makes 24

400 g (14 oz) soft feta
2 eggs, lightly beaten
25 g (1 oz/¾ cup) chopped fresh
    flat-leaf (Italian) parsley
375 g (13 oz) filo pastry
4 tablespoons good-quality
    olive oil

1 Preheat the oven to 180°C (350°F/ Gas 4). Lightly grease a baking tray.
2 Crumble the feta into a large bowl using a fork or your fingers. Mix in the eggs and parsley, and season with black pepper.
3 Lightly brush 4 sheets of pastry with olive oil and place the sheets on top of each other. Cut the pastry into four 7 cm (2¾ inch) strips.
4 Place 2 rounded teaspoons of the feta mixture in one corner of each strip and fold diagonally, creating a triangle pillow effect. Place on the

baking tray, seam-side-down, and brush the top with olive oil. Repeat with the remaining pastry and filling to make 24 boreks. Discard any leftover pastry. Bake for 20 minutes, or until golden. Serve as part of a large meze plate.

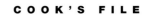
COOK'S FILE

Note: Keep the filo pastry covered with a damp tea (dish) towel when you are not using it so it doesn't dry out.

Cut the lightly oiled filo pastry layers into four strips.

Place some feta mixture in the corner of each pastry strip.

Fold the pastry diagonally, creating a triangle pillow effect.

Bruschetta

To make basic bruschetta, cut a crusty Italian loaf into twelve 1.5 cm (¾ inch) diagonal slices. Toast or grill (broil) the slices until golden. Bruise 2 garlic cloves with the flat of a knife, peel and rub the cloves over both sides of the hot bread. Drizzle the tops with a little extra virgin olive oil and finish with one of these delicious toppings.

ANCHOVY, TOMATO AND OREGANO

Deseed and roughly chop 3 vine-ripened tomatoes and mix with 1 small chopped red onion, a 90 g (3¾ oz) jar drained, minced anchovy fillets and 2 tablespoons olive oil. Spoon some of the mixture onto each bruschetta. Drizzle with extra virgin olive oil, and garnish with chopped fresh oregano and freshly ground black pepper.

BLACK OLIVE PATE, ROCKET AND FETA

Place 100 g (3½ oz) trimmed baby rocket leaves, 75 g (2½ oz) crumbled Greek feta and 2 tablespoons olive oil in a bowl, and mix together well. Spread 2 teaspoons of black olive pâté onto each bruschetta slice and top with the feta mixture. Drizzle with extra virgin olive oil and season with sea salt and freshly ground black pepper.

SEMI-DRIED TOMATO PESTO, ARTICHOKE AND BOCCONCINI

Spread 1 teaspoon of good-quality semi-dried (sun-blushed) tomato pesto onto each slice of bruschetta. Slice 12 (360 g/12¼ oz) bocconcini and place on top of the pesto. Chop 55 g (2 oz) drained marinated artichoke hearts in oil and place over the bocconcini slices. Sprinkle with finely chopped fresh flat-leaf (Italian) parsley.

PESTO, RED CAPSICUM AND PARMESAN

Cut 3 red capsicums (peppers) into large flattish pieces and remove the seeds and membrane. Cook the capsicum pieces, skin-side-up, under a hot grill (broiler) until the skin blackens and blisters. Place in a plastic bag and leave to cool. When cool enough to handle, peel away the skin and discard. Cut the flesh into 1 cm (½ inch) strips. Spread 2 teaspoons good-quality basil pesto onto each slice of the bruschetta. Top with the capsicum strips and 50 g (1¾ oz/½ cup) fresh Parmesan shards. Drizzle with extra virgin olive oil and season with sea salt and ground black pepper.

MUSHROOM AND GOAT'S CHEESE

Preheat the oven to 180°C (350°F/ Gas 4). Mix 125 ml (4 fl oz/½ cup) olive oil with 3 chopped garlic cloves, 2 tablespoons chopped flat-leaf (Italian) parsley and 1 tablespoon dry sherry. Place 6 large field mushrooms on a foil-lined baking tray and spoon on all but 2 tablespoons of mixture. Bake for 20 minutes, or until soft. Mix 150 g (5½ oz) goat's cheese with 1 teaspoon chopped fresh thyme, then spread over the bruschetta. Warm the remaining oil mixture. Cut the mushrooms in half and place one half on each bruschetta. Drizzle with the remaining oil. Season with sea salt and ground black pepper.

PAN CON TOMATE

Place 4 deseeded and roughly chopped large vine-ripened tomatoes, 15 g (½ oz/½ cup) roughly torn basil leaves, 2 tablespoons olive oil and ½ teaspoon caster (superfine) sugar in a bowl and mix together well. Season with plenty of sea salt and freshly ground black pepper and set the mixture aside for 10–15 minutes so the flavours have time to infuse and develop. Cut a ripe vine-ripened tomato in half and rub it on the oiled side of the slices of bruschetta, squeezing the tomato to extract as much of the liquid as possible. Carefully spoon 2 tablespoons of the tomato mixture onto each slice of bruschetta and serve immediately.

Left to right: Anchovy, tomato and oregano bruschetta; Black olive pâté, rocket and feta bruschetta; Semi-dried tomato pesto, artichoke and bocconcini bruschetta; Pesto, red capsicum and Parmesan bruschetta; Mushroom and goat's cheese bruschetta; Pan con tomate.

FRIED HALOUMI CHEESE

Preparation time: 5 minutes
Total cooking time: 2 minutes
Serves 6

400 g (14 oz) haloumi cheese
4 tablespoons olive oil
2 tablespoons lemon juice

1 Pat the haloumi dry with paper towel; cut into 1 cm (½ inch) slices.
2 Pour the oil into a large frying pan to a depth of 5 mm (¼ inch) and heat over medium-high heat. Cook the cheese in a single layer for 1 minute each side, or until golden. Remove from the heat and pour on the lemon juice. Season with pepper and serve immediately as part of a meze spread. Serve with crusty bread.

COOK'S FILE

Note: Saganaki means a two-handled frying pan. This dish is traditionally served in the saganaki at the table. It is served with bread that has been dipped into the leftover lemon-flavoured oil in the pan.

Cook the haloumi slices in olive oil until golden on both sides.

Remove the pan from the heat and pour on the lemon juice.

PATATAS BRAVAS

Preparation time: 15 minutes
Total cooking time: 1 hour
Serves 6

1 kg (2 lb 4 oz) desiree potatoes
olive oil, for deep-frying
500 g (1 lb 2 oz) ripe Roma
　　(plum) tomatoes
2 tablespoons olive oil, extra
¼ red onion, finely chopped
2 garlic cloves, crushed
3 teaspoons paprika
¼ teaspoon cayenne pepper
1 bay leaf
1 teaspoon sugar
1 tablespoon chopped fresh
　　flat-leaf (Italian) parsley

1 Peel the potatoes and cut into 2 cm (¾ inch) cubes. Rinse then drain well and pat completely dry. Fill a deep fryer or large heavy-based saucepan one third full of oil and heat to 180°C (350°F), or until a cube of bread dropped in the oil browns in 15 seconds. Cook the potato in batches for 10 minutes, or until golden. Drain on crumpled paper towels. Do not discard the oil.

2 Score a cross in the base of each tomato. Place in a bowl of boiling water for 1 minute, then plunge into cold water and peel the skin away from the cross. Chop the flesh.

3 Heat the extra oil in a saucepan and cook the onion over medium heat for 3 minutes, or until soft and light gold. Add the garlic and spices and cook for 1–2 minutes, or until fragrant.

4 Add the tomato, bay leaf, sugar and 100 ml (3½ fl oz) water. Cook, stirring occasionally, for 20 minutes, or until thick and pulpy. Cool slightly and

remove the bay leaf. Place the sauce in a food processor and process until smooth, adding a little water if necessary. Prior to serving, return the sauce to the pan and simmer over low heat for 2 minutes, or until heated through. Season well.

5 Reheat the oil to 180°C (350°F), or until a cube of bread dropped in the

oil browns in 15 seconds. Recook the potato in batches for 2 minutes, or until very crisp and golden. Drain on paper towels. This second frying makes the potato extra crispy and stops the sauce soaking in at once. Serve on a platter and pour the sauce over the top. Garnish with parsley.

Deep-fry the potato cubes in olive oil until golden.

Cook the tomato mixture for 20 minutes, or until thick and pulpy.

Deep-fry the potato cubes again, until very crispy and golden.

GRILLED CALAMARI WITH SALSA VERDE

Preparation time: 30 minutes +
30 minutes marinating
Total cooking time: 15 minutes
Serves 4

1 kg (2 lb 4 oz) calamari (squid)
250 ml (9 fl oz/1 cup) olive oil
2 tablespoons lemon juice
2 garlic cloves, crushed
2 tablespoons chopped fresh
    oregano
2 tablespoons chopped fresh
    flat-leaf (Italian) parsley
6 lemon wedges

Salsa verde
2 anchovy fillets, drained
1 tablespoon capers
1 garlic clove, crushed
2 tablespoons chopped fresh
    flat-leaf (Italian) parsley
2 tablespoons olive oil

1 To clean the calamari, hold onto the hood and gently pull the tentacles away from the head. Cut out the beak and discard with any intestines still attached to the tentacles. Rinse the tentacles in cold running water, pat dry and cut into 5 cm (2 inch) lengths. Place in a bowl. Clean out the hood cavity and remove the transparent backbone. Under cold running water, pull away the skin, rinse and dry well. Cut into 1 cm (½ inch) rings and place in the bowl with the tentacles. Add the oil, lemon juice, garlic and oregano and toss to coat the calamari. Refrigerate for 30 minutes.

2 To make the salsa verde, crush the anchovy fillets in a mortar and pestle or in a bowl with a wooden spoon.

Rinse the capers and dry with paper towels. Chop the capers very finely and add to the anchovies. Add the garlic and parsley, then slowly stir in the olive oil. Season with black pepper and salt, if necessary (the anchovies may be very salty). Mix well.

3 Drain the calamari and cook on a barbecue hotplate in 4 batches for 1–2 minutes each side, basting with the marinade. To serve, sprinkle with salt, pepper and fresh parsley, and serve with the salsa verde and lemon wedges.

Hold the calamari and gently pull the tentacles away from the head.

Combine the anchovies, capers, garlic and parsley.

Cook the calamari in batches on a hot barbecue or grill.

PICKLED CALAMARI

Preparation time: 25 minutes + 1 week
  maturing
Total cooking time: 5 minutes
Serves 4

1 kg (2 lb 4 oz) small calamari
  (squid)
4 fresh bay leaves
4 sprigs fresh oregano
10 whole black peppercorns
2 teaspoons coriander seeds
1 small red chilli, halved,
  deseeded
625 ml (21½ fl oz/2½ cups)
  good-quality white wine
  vinegar
2–3 tablespoons olive oil

1 Grasp the calamari body in one hand and the head and tentacles in the other and pull apart to separate. Cut the tentacles from the head by cutting below the eyes. Discard the head. Push out the beak and discard. Pull the quill from inside the body and discard. Pull away the skin under cold running water. The flaps can be used. Cut the hood into 7 mm (⅜ inch) rings.
2 Place 2 litres (8 cups) water and 1 bay leaf in a large saucepan. Bring to the boil and add the calamari and 1 teaspoon salt. Reduce the heat and simmer for 5 minutes. Drain and dry well.
3 Pack the calamari into a very clean, dry 500 ml (17 fl oz/2 cup) jar with a sealing lid. Add the oregano, peppercorns, coriander seeds, chilli and remaining bay leaves. Cover completely with the vinegar then gently pour in enough olive oil to cover by 2 cm (¾ inch). Seal and refrigerate for 1 week before opening.

COOK'S FILE

Note: To make sure your storage jar is very clean, wash it, and the lid, in hot soapy water, or in a dishwasher, rinse well in hot water and then dry in a 120°C (250°F/Gas ½) oven for 20 minutes, or until you are ready to use them. Don't dry with a tea (dish) towel.

Push the beak up and out of the body, and then discard it.

Remove the transparent quill from the body of the calamari.

Gently simmer the calamari rings for 5 minutes, then drain.

Pour enough oil into the jar to cover all the ingredients by 2 cm (¾ inch).

AIOLI WITH CRUDITES

Preparation time: 15 minutes
Total cooking time: 1 minute
Serves 4

4 garlic cloves, crushed
2 egg yolks
300 ml (10½ fl oz) light olive or
    vegetable oil
1 tablespoon lemon juice
pinch ground white pepper
12 asparagus spears,
    trimmed
26 radishes, trimmed
½ telegraph (long) cucumber,
    deseeded, halved and cut
    into batons
1 witlof head (Belgian endive),
    leaves separated

1 Place the garlic, egg yolks and a pinch of salt in the bowl of a food processor. Process for 10 seconds.
2 With the motor running, add the oil in a thin, slow stream. The mixture will start to thicken. When this happens, add the oil a little faster. Process until all the oil is incorporated and the mayonnaise is thick and creamy Transfer to a bowl, stir in the lemon juice and pepper.
3 Bring a saucepan of water to the boil, add the asparagus and cook for 1 minute, then plunge into a bowl of iced water. Arrange asparagus, radish, cucumber and witlof on a platter around the bowl of aïoli. Aïoli can also be used as a sandwich spread or as a sauce for chicken or fish.

COOK'S FILE

Note: Should the mayonnaise start to curdle, beat in 1–2 teaspoons boiling water. If this fails, put another egg yolk in a clean bowl and very slowly whisk in the curdled mixture, one drop at a time, then continue as above.

Hint: For best results, make sure all the ingredients are at room temperature when making this recipe.

Seed the cucumbers, then halve widthways and cut into batons.

Stir the lemon juice into the thick and creamy mayonnaise.

Refresh the asparagus spears by plunging into a bowl of iced water.

FALAFEL

Preparation time: 35 minutes +
48 hours soaking + 50 minutes
standing
Total cooking time: 10 minutes
Makes 30

150 g (5½ oz/1 cup) dried split
    broad (fava) beans (see Note)
220 g (7¾ oz/1 cup) dried
    chickpeas
1 onion, roughly chopped
6 garlic cloves, roughly chopped
2 teaspoons ground coriander
1 tablespoon ground cumin
15 g (½ oz/½ cup) chopped fresh
    flat-leaf (Italian) parsley
¼ teaspoon chilli powder
½ teaspoon bicarbonate of soda
    (baking soda)
3 tablespoons chopped fresh
    coriander (cilantro) leaves
light oil, for deep-frying

1 Place broad beans in a large bowl, cover with 750 ml (26 fl oz/3 cups) water and leave to soak for 48 hours. (Drain the beans, rinse and cover with fresh water once or twice.)
2 Place the chickpeas in a large bowl, cover with 750 ml (26 fl oz/3 cups) water and soak for 12 hours.
3 Drain the beans and chickpeas and pat dry with paper towel. Process in a food processor with the onion and garlic until smooth.
4 Add the ground coriander, cumin, parsley, chilli powder, bicarbonate of soda and fresh coriander. Season with salt and freshly ground black pepper, and mix until well combined. Transfer to a large bowl, knead and leave for 30 minutes.
5 Shape tablespoons of the mixture into balls, flatten slightly, place on a tray and leave for 20 minutes.
6 Fill a deep, heavy-based saucepan one-third full of oil and heat to 180°C (350°F), or until a cube of bread browns in 15 seconds. Cook the falafel

in batches for 1–2 minutes, or until golden. Drain on paper towel. Serve hot or cold with hummus, baba ghannouj and pitta bread.

COOK'S FILE

Note: Split broad beans are available from specialist food stores. It is best to get the split broad beans as they are already skinned. If whole broad beans are used they will need to be skinned after soaking. To do this, firmly squeeze each bean to allow the skin to pop off, or slice the skin with your fingernail and then peel it off.

Process the soaked and drained broad beans and chickpeas until very smooth.

Shape the mixture into balls, then flatten slightly into rounds.

Marinating Olives

Cracking the olives means to cut a slit around the olives using a sharp knife to allow flavours to infuse into the olives. To sterilize the storage jar, rinse with boiling water then place in a warm oven to dry. Olive oil solidifies with refrigeration, so take the olives out of the fridge 30 minutes before serving.

MIXED OLIVES WITH HERBS

Place 200 g (7 oz) small black olives (Riverina or Ligurian), 200 g (7 oz) cracked green olives, 200 g (7 oz) cracked Kalamata olives, 3 sprigs thyme, 1 tablespoon fresh oregano leaves, 1 teaspoon paprika, 2 bay leaves and 2 teaspoons lemon zest in a bowl and toss well. Spoon into a 1 litre (4 cup) sterilized wide-necked jar and add 450 ml (16 fl oz) olive oil. Marinate for 1–2 weeks in the fridge. Keeps for 1 month in the fridge.

CHILLI OLIVES

Soak 3 thinly sliced garlic cloves in vinegar or lemon juice for 24 hours. Drain and mix in a bowl with 500 g (1 lb 2 oz) cured (wrinkled) black olives, 3 tablespoons chopped fresh flat-leaf (Italian) parsley, 1 tablespoon dried chilli flakes, 3 teaspoons crushed coriander seeds and 2 teaspoons crushed cumin seeds. Spoon into a 1 litre (4 cup) sterilized wide-necked jar and add 500 ml (2 cups) olive oil. Marinate for 1–2 weeks in the fridge. Keeps for 1 month in the fridge.

ANCHOVY-STUFFED GREEN OLIVES WITH PRESERVED LEMON

Toss 500 g (1 lb 2 oz) anchovy-stuffed green olives in a bowl with ½ preserved lemon, pith and flesh removed, rind washed and thinly sliced, 2 tablespoons of liquid from the lemons and 1 tablespoon coriander seeds. Spoon into a 1 litre (4 cup) sterilized wide-necked jar and add 500 ml (2 cups) olive oil. Marinate for 1–2 weeks in the fridge. Will keep for 1 month in the fridge.

LEMON, THYME AND ROSEMARY OLIVES

Soak 2 thinly sliced garlic cloves in vinegar or lemon juice for 24 hours. Drain and place in a bowl with 500 g (1 lb 2 oz) cracked Kalamata olives, 2 crushed bay leaves, 4 slices lemon, cut into quarters, 3 sprigs fresh thyme, 1 sprig of fresh rosemary, ½ teaspoon black peppercorns and 3 tablespoons lemon juice, and toss to combine. Spoon into a 1 litre (4 cup) sterilized wide-necked jar and pour in 500 ml (17 fl oz/2 cups) olive oil. Marinate for 1–2 weeks in the fridge. Will keep for 1 month in the fridge.

CORIANDER AND ORANGE OLIVES

Place 500 g (1 lb 2 oz) jumbo green olives in a large bowl and add 2 teaspoons crushed coriander seeds, 3 teaspoons orange zest, 3 tablespoons orange juice, ¼ teaspoon cayenne pepper, 3 tablespoons chopped fresh coriander (cilantro) leaves and toss to combine thoroughly Carefully spoon into a 1 litre (4 cup), sterilized wide-necked jar and pour in 500 ml (17 fl oz/2 cups) olive oil or enough to completely cover. Leave to marinate for 1–2 weeks in the fridge. Will keep for 1 month in the fridge.

FENNEL, ORANGE AND DILL OLIVES

Soak 2 thinly sliced garlic cloves in vinegar or lemon juice for 24 hours. Drain and place the garlic in a large bowl with 500 g (1 lb 2 oz) cracked black olives, 4 thin slices orange, cut into quarters, 2 teaspoons crushed fennel seeds and 2 tablespoons chopped fresh dill and toss to combine well. Spoon into a 1 litre (4 cup) sterilized wide necked jar and pour in 500 ml (17 fl oz/2 cups) olive oil or enough to completely cover. Marinate for 1–2 weeks in the fridge. Will keep for 1 month in the fridge.

Left to right: Mixed olives with herbs; Chilli olives; Anchovy-stuffed green olives with preserved lemon; Lemon, thyme and rosemary olives; Coriander and orange olives; Fennel, orange and dill olives.

SALT COD FRITTERS

Preparation time: 15 minutes +
  24 hours soaking
Total cooking time: 50 minutes
Makes 35

500 g (1 lb 2 oz) salt cod
1 large potato (200 g/7 oz),
  unpeeled
2 tablespoons milk
olive oil, for deep-frying
1 small onion, finely chopped
2 garlic cloves, crushed
3 tablespoons self-raising flour
2 eggs, separated
1 tablespoon finely chopped
  fresh flat-leaf (Italian)
  parsley

1 Soak the cod in water for 24 hours, changing the water regularly. Bring a saucepan of water to the boil, add the potato and cook for 20 minutes, or until soft. When cool enough to handle, peel and mash with the milk and 2 tablespoons of the olive oil.

2 Drain the cod, cut into large pieces and place in a saucepan. Cover with water, bring to the boil over high heat, then reduce the heat to medium and cook for 10 minutes, or until soft and a froth forms on the surface. Drain. When cool enough to handle, remove the skin and any bones, then mash with a fork until flaky. (You should have about 200 g/7 oz).

3 Meanwhile, heat 1 tablespoon olive oil in a frying pan, add the onion and cook over medium heat for 5 minutes, or until softened and starting to brown. Add the garlic and cook for 1 minute. Remove from the heat.

4 Combine the potato, cod, onion mixture, flour, egg yolks and parsley in a bowl and season. Whisk the egg whites until stiff then fold into the mixture. Fill a large heavy-based saucepan one-third full with olive oil and heat to 190°C (375°F), or until a cube of bread dropped in the oil browns in 10 seconds. Drop heaped tablespoons of the mixture into the oil and cook for 2 minutes, or until puffed and golden. Drain on paper towel and serve immediately.

Remove the skin and any bones from the cooked salt cod.

Fold the whisked egg whites into the potato and cod mixture.

Deep-fry the fritters in hot oil until puffed and golden.

STUFFED SARDINES

Preparation time: 30 minutes
Total cooking time: 30 minutes
Serves 6

750 g (1 lb 10 oz) small fresh
    sardines
2 teaspoons olive oil
100 g (3½ oz) ling fillet or other
    white firm-fleshed fish
600 g (1 lb 5 oz) cooked medium
    prawns (shrimp), peeled,
    deveined
3 tablespoons cooked arborio or
    other medium-grain rice
3 garlic cloves, crushed
1 tablespoon finely chopped
    fresh mint
1 tablespoon finely chopped
    fresh basil
1 tablespoon finely chopped
    fresh chives
2 tablespoons grated Parmesan
    cheese
2 teaspoons lemon juice
1 egg, lightly beaten
3 tablespoons fresh
    breadcrumbs
2 tablespoons olive oil
olive oil, extra, to serve
lemon juice, extra, to serve

1 Preheat the oven to 180°C (350°F/
Gas 4). Grease a shallow 30 x 25 cm
(12 x 10 inch) ovenproof dish.
2 Remove the heads, tails and fins
from the sardines. Make a slit along
the underside, and remove the
intestines and backbone. Rinse
and pat dry. Trim the edges of
24 sardines and lay them out flat on
a work surface, skin-side-down.
Finely chop the remainder and place in
a bowl.

3 Heat the oil in a frying pan and
cook the ling over medium heat for
4–5 minutes each side, or until cooked.
Do not overbrown. Flake and add to
the chopped sardines. Finely chop the
prawns and add to the bowl along
with the rice, garlic, mint, basil, chives,
Parmesan and lemon juice. Mix, then
season and stir in the egg.
4 Place 12 butterflied sardines in the
prepared dish, skin-side-down and
side-by-side. Divide the filling among
them, covering each fillet and pressing
firmly onto it. Cover with the
remaining sardines, skin-side-up.

Scatter the breadcrumbs over the top
and drizzle with the olive oil. Bake for
20–25 minutes, or until golden. Drizzle
with oil and lemon juice and serve.

COOK'S FILE

Note: If only large sardines are
available, trim those butterflied to 8 x
4 cm (3 x 1 ½ inch) and use 120 g (4 oz)
chopped for the filling. If buying
butterflied sardines, you will need
400 g (14 oz). Cod is traditional for this
recipe, but ling or any firm, white fish
works well.

*Make a slit along the underside of the
sardines with a very sharp knife.*

*Remove the intestines and then the
backbones, and rinse under cold water*

*Place the remaining sardines over the
mixture, skin-side-up.*

MELITZANOSALATA

Preparation time: 20 minutes +
  3 hours refrigeration
Total cooking time: 1 hour
Serves 6

2 large eggplants (aubergines)
2 garlic cloves, roughly
  chopped
4 tablespoons chopped fresh
  flat-leaf (Italian) parsley
1 small onion, grated
½ red capsicum (pepper),
  deseeded and chopped
1 large ripe tomato, finely
  chopped

2 small red chillies, deseeded
60 g (2¼ oz/¾ cup) soft white
  breadcrumbs
4 tablespoons lemon juice
125 ml (4 fl oz/½ cup) good-
  quality olive oil
1–2 tablespoons olive oil, extra
7 black olives

1 Preheat the oven to 180°C (350°F/
Gas 4). Prick the eggplants with a fork
a few times, place on a large baking
tray and bake for 1 hour.
2 Remove the skin from the eggplant
and discard. Roughly chop the flesh
and place in a sieve to drain. Press the
flesh against the sieve with the back
of a knife.

3 Place the eggplant, garlic, parsley,
onion, capsicum, tomato, chilli and
breadcrumbs in a food processor,
season and process until combined but
a little coarse.
4 While the motor is running, add the
lemon juice and oil alternately, in a
steady stream. The mixture will
thicken.
5 Transfer to a large bowl, cover and
refrigerate for 3 hours to firm the
mixture and infuse the flavours. To
serve, spread on a large shallow
serving platter, drizzle with the extra
oil and garnish with black olives.

*Wear gloves when handling chillies to
protect your hands.*

*Remove the skin from the eggplant and
roughly chop the flesh.*

*Process the ingredients until they are
combined, but still a little coarse.*

DOLMADES

Preparation time: 40 minutes +
   15 minutes soaking
Total cooking time: 45 minutes
Makes 24

200 g (7 oz) packet vine leaves
   in brine
250 g (9 oz/1 cup) medium-grain
   rice
1 small onion, finely chopped
1 tablespoon olive oil
50 g (1¾ oz) pine nuts, toasted
2 tablespoons currants
2 tablespoons chopped fresh
   dill
1 tablespoon finely chopped
   fresh mint
1 tablespoon finely chopped
   fresh flat-leaf (Italian)
   parsley
4 tablespoons olive oil, extra
2 tablespoons lemon juice
500 ml (17 fl oz/2 cups) chicken
   stock or vegetable stock

1 Place the vine leaves in a bowl, cover with hot water and soak for 15 minutes. Remove and pat dry. Cut off any stems. Reserve some leaves to line the saucepan and discard any that have holes. Meanwhile, soak the rice in boiling water for 10 minutes to soften, then drain.
2 Place the rice, onion, oil, pine nuts, currants, herbs and salt and pepper in a large bowl, and mix well.
3 Lay some leaves vein-side-down on a flat surface. Place 1 tablespoon of the filling in the middle of each leaf; fold the stalk end over the filling, then the left and right sides into the middle, and finally roll firmly towards the tip. The dolmade should resemble a small cigar. Repeat with the remaining filling and leaves.
4 Using the reserved vine leaves, line the bottom of a large heavy-based pan. Drizzle with 1 tablespoon of oil. Place the dolmades in the pan, packing tightly in one layer. Pour the remaining lemon juice and oil on top.
5 Pour the stock over the dolmades and cover with an inverted plate to stop them moving around while cooking. Bring to the boil, then reduce the heat and simmer, covered, for 45 minutes. Remove with a slotted spoon. Serve warm or cold.

COOK'S FILE

Note: Any unused leaves can be stored in brine in an airtight container in the refrigerator for up to 1 week.

Fold the sides of the vine leaf into the middle and roll up towards the tip.

Pack the dolmades tightly into the pan and pour on the oil and lemon juice.

Remove the cooked dolmades from the pan with a slotted spoon.

41

PRESERVED LEMONS

Preparation time: 1 hour + 6 weeks
  standing
Total cooking time: Nil
Fills a 2 litre (8 cup) jar

8–12 small thin-skinned lemons
315 g (11 oz/1 cup) rock salt
500 ml (17 fl oz/2 cups) lemon
    juice (8–10 lemons)
½ teaspoon black peppercorns
1 bay leaf
1 tablespoon olive oil

1 Scrub the lemons under warm running water with a soft bristle brush to remove the wax coating. Cut into quarters, leaving the base attached at the stem end. Gently open each lemon, remove any visible pips and pack 1 tablespoon of the salt against the cut edges of each lemon. Push the lemons back into shape and pack tightly into a 2 litre (8 cup) jar with a clip or tight-fitting lid. (Depending on the size of the lemons, you may not need all 12. They should be firmly packed and fill the jar.)

2 Add 250 ml (9 fl oz/1 cup) of the lemon juice, peppercorns, bay leaf and remaining rock salt to the jar. Fill the jar to the top with the remaining lemon juice. Seal and shake to combine all the ingredients. Leave in a cool, dark place for 6 weeks, inverting each week. (In warm weather, store in the refrigerator.) The liquid will be cloudy initially, but will clear by the fourth week.

3 To test if the lemons are preserved, cut through the centre of one of the lemon quarters. If the pith is still white, the lemons are not ready. Re-seal and leave for a week before testing again. The lemons should be soft-skinned and the pith should be the same colour as the skin.

4 Once the lemons are preserved, cover the brine with a layer of olive oil. Replace the oil each time you remove some of the lemon pieces.

COOK'S FILE

Storage time: Preserved lemons can be stored for up to 6 months in a cool, dark place.

Hint: Serve preserved lemons with Moroccan-flavoured dishes such as grilled (broiled) meats or use to flavour couscous, stuffings, tagines and casseroles. Only the rind is used in cooking. Discard the flesh and bitter pith, rinse and finely slice or chop the rind before adding it to the dish.

Cut the lemons into quarters, without cutting all the way through the base.

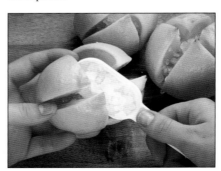

Pack the rock salt against the cut edges of each lemon.

Fill the jar to the top with the remaining lemon juice.

ROLLED CAPSICUMS

Preparation time: 20 minutes +
30 minutes marinating
Total cooking time: 10 minutes
Serves 6

2 red capsicums (peppers)
2 yellow capsicums (peppers)
2 green capsicums (peppers)
3 tablespoons olive oil
1 teaspoon lemon juice
2 cloves garlic, crushed

185 g (6 oz) flaked tuna, drained
100 g (3⅓ oz) anchovies,
drained and chopped
4 tablespoons black olives,
pitted and chopped
2 tablespoons capers, drained
1 tablespoon chopped parsley

1 Cut the capsicums into quarters lengthways, remove the seeds and membrane and brush with a little of the oil. Cook until a hot grill (broiler), skin-side-up, until skins are black and blistered. Cover with a tea (dish) towel

and leave to cool. Peel away the skin.
2 Combine the remaining oil, lemon juice, garlic and a little salt. Marinate the capsicums in this for 30 minutes. In another bowl, mix together the tuna, anchovies, olives and capers.
3 Drain the capsicums, reserving the marinade, and place 2 teaspoons of tuna filling on each piece. Roll up and arrange on a serving dish. Drizzle with the reserved marinade and then garnish with chopped parsley and cracked black pepper.

Remove the seeds and membrane from the capsicums.

Leave the capsicum in the marinade for 30 minutes.

Place 2 teaspoonsful of filling on each piece of capsicum and roll up.

Seafood antipasto

CHAR-GRILLED OCTOPUS

Combine 170 ml (5½ fl oz/⅔ cup) olive oil, 4 tablespoons chopped fresh oregano, 4 tablespoons chopped fresh parsley, 3 finely chopped small red chillies and 3 cloves of crushed garlic in a large bowl. Wash 1 kg (2 lb) baby octopus and dry well. Slit the head open and remove the gut. Grasp the body firmly and push the beak out with your index finger. Add the octopus to the oil mixture and marinate for 3–4 hours or overnight. Drain, reserving the marinade. Cook on a very hot barbecue or in a very hot pan for 3–5 minutes, or until the flesh turns white. Turn frequently and brush with the marinade during cooking.

SCALLOP FRITTERS

Combine 6 lightly beaten eggs with 3 tablespoons grated Parmesan, 3 cloves crushed garlic, 125 g (4½ oz/1 cup) plain (all-purpose) flour and 2 tablespoons each chopped fresh thyme and oregano. Mix well with a wooden spoon until smooth. Fold in 250 g (8 oz) cleaned and chopped scallops. Heat oil for shallow-frying until moderately hot. Pour quarter-cupfuls of batter into the hot oil and cook in batches for 4–5 minutes over moderate heat, until golden brown. Drain on paper towels and serve with mayonnaise.

SARDINES IN VINE LEAVES

Place 12 fresh vine leaves in a large heatproof bowl and cover with boiling water. Leave for 2–3 minutes, rinse with cold water, drain and pat dry. If using vine leaves in brine, soak in cold water for 30 minutes, drain and pat dry. Preheat the oven to 180°C (350°F/Gas 4). Heat 1 tablespoon olive oil in a frying pan and add 1 crushed garlic clove, 1 finely chopped spring onion (scallion) and 2 tablespoons pine nuts. Cook, stirring, until the pine nuts just begin to turn brown. Combine in a bowl with 3 tablespoons chopped parsley, 2 teaspoons finely grated lemon zest and 3 tablespoons fresh white breadcrumbs. Season with salt and freshly ground black pepper. Fill 12 sardine fillets with the breadcrumb mixture and wrap each in a vine leaf. Place in a single layer in a well greased baking dish. Drizzle with 2 tablespoons olive oil and bake for 30 minutes. Serve at room temperature, with mayonnaise flavoured with crushed garlic.

From left: Char-grilled Octopus; Scallop Fritters; Sardines in Vine Leaves; Marinated Seafood; Smoked Cod Frittata with Rocket; Mussels with Crispy Prosciutto

MUSSELS WITH CRISPY PROSCIUTTO

Heat 1 tablespoon oil in a small frying pan. Add 1 finely chopped onion, 6 thin slices prosciutto, chopped, and 4 crushed garlic cloves. Cook until the prosciutto is crispy and onion softened, then set aside. Add 1.5 kg (3 lb) cleaned mussels to a large pot of boiling water and cook for 5 minutes, discarding any that don't open. Remove the mussels from their shells, keeping half of each shell. Place two mussels on each half-shell and top with the prosciutto mixture. Combine 50 g (1¾ oz/½ cup) grated Parmesan and 60 g (2¼ oz/½ cup) grated Cheddar cheese and sprinkle over the prosciutto. Cook under a preheated grill (broiler) until the cheese has melted and the mussels are warmed through.

SMOKED COD FRITTATA WITH ROCKET

Place 500 g (1 lb) smoked cod in a pan with enough milk and water to cover. Bring to the boil, then reduce the heat and simmer for 3–4 minutes. Remove with a slotted spoon and flake the flesh. Whisk 8 eggs in a bowl. Add 50 g (1¾ oz/ ½ cup) grated Parmesan and 60 g (2¼ oz/½ cup) grated Cheddar cheese, 2 tablespoons chopped fresh thyme, 30 g (1 oz/½ cup) torn basil leaves and the fish. Mix to combine. Heat 2 tablespoons olive oil in a large heavy-based frying pan. Pour in the mixture and cook over medium heat for 5 minutes, or until nearly cooked. Place under a hot grill (broiler) for 3–4 minutes, or until just set and lightly golden. Transfer to a large serving platter and pile 40 g (1½ oz/ 2 cups) torn rocket (arugula) leaves in the centre.

MARINATED SEAFOOD

Slice 500 g (1 lb) small squid hoods into rings. Shell and devein 500 g (1 lb) raw prawns (shrimp). Scrub and remove the beards from 500 g (1 lb) mussels, discarding any which are already open. Put 750 ml (26 fl oz/3 cups) water, 125 ml (4 fl oz/½ cup) white wine vinegar, ½ teaspoon of salt and 3 bay leaves in a large pan and bring to the boil. Add the squid and 500 g (1 lb) scallops, then reduce the heat to low and simmer for 2–3 minutes, or until the seafood has turned white. Remove the squid and scallops with a slotted spoon and place in a bowl. Repeat the process with the prawns, cooking until just pink. Return the liquid to the boil and add the mussels; cover, reduce the heat and simmer for about 3 minutes, until all the shells are open. Discard any mussels that haven't opened. Cool the mussels, remove the meat and add to the bowl. Whisk together 2 crushed garlic cloves, 125 ml (4 fl oz/½ cup) extra virgin olive oil, 3 tablespoons lemon juice, 1 tablespoon white wine vinegar, 1 teaspoon Dijon mustard and 1 tablespoon chopped parsley. Pour over the seafood and toss well. Refrigerate for 1–2 hours and then serve on a bed of lettuce leaves.

Note: Any seafood can be used for this dish—the most important thing to remember is that seafood should never be overcooked or it will become tough. To make this dish more economical, substitute white fish fillets for most of the prawns and scallops. Poach the fish in the cooking liquid for a few minutes, drain immediately and cut into chunks. Toss carefully with the rest of the seafood in the dressing and garnish with a few cooked prawns and scallops.

WHITEBAIT FRITTERS

Preparation time: 20 minutes + resting
Total cooking time: 15 minutes
Makes 10

3 tablespoons self-raising flour
3 tablespoons plain (all-purpose)
    flour
½ teaspoon bicarbonate of soda
    (baking soda)
1 teaspoon salt
freshly ground black pepper

1 egg, lightly beaten
3 tablespoons dry white wine
2 teaspoons chopped fresh
    flat-leaf (Italian) parsley
1 garlic clove, crushed
½ small onion, grated
200 g (6½ oz) Chinese or
    New Zealand whitebait
olive oil, for shallow frying

1 Sift the flours, bicarbonate of soda, salt and pepper into a bowl. Stir through the egg and wine, whisk until smooth, then add the parsley, garlic, onion and whitebait. Cover and leave for 20 minutes.

2 Heat the oil in a frying pan and then drop in tablespoons of batter. When the batter is puffed and bubbles appear on the surface, carefully turn to cook the other side.

3 Drain on paper towels and serve immediately with lemon wedges.

COOK'S FILE

Note: The Chinese or New Zealand whitebait is very small and fine and can be bought fresh or frozen.

Add the parsley, garlic, onion and whitebait, cover and leave for 20 minutes.

Heat the oil in a frying pan, then drop in tablespoons of batter.

Cook both sides of the fritters, then lift out of the pan and drain on paper towels.

ITALIAN OMELETTE

Preparation time: 20 minutes
Total cooking time: 15 minutes
Serves 4

2 tablespoons olive oil
1 onion, finely chopped
125 g (4½ oz) ham, sliced
6 eggs
3 tablespoons milk
350 g (12 oz/2 cups) cooked
    spiral pasta (150 g/
    5½ oz uncooked)

3 tablespoons freshly grated
    Parmesan cheese
2 tablespoons chopped fresh
    parsley
1 tablespoon
chopped fresh basil
60 g (2¼ oz/½ cup) freshly
    grated Cheddar cheese

1 Heat half the oil in a pan. Add onion and stir over low heat until tender. Add ham to the pan and stir for 1 minute, then transfer to a plate.
2 In a bowl, whisk the eggs and milk together, then season with salt and pepper. Stir in the pasta, Parmesan, herbs and onion mixture.
3 Heat the remaining oil in the same pan, then pour in the egg mixture. Sprinkle with the cheese. Cook over medium heat until mixture begins to set around the edges. Place under a hot grill (broiler) to complete the cooking. Cut into wedges to serve.

COOK'S FILE

Hint: Serve with a crisp green or mixed salad, if desired.

Soups and starters

PAPPA AL POMADORO

Preparation time: 20 minutes
  + 5 minutes standing
Total cooking time: 25 minutes
Serves 4

750 g (1 lb 10 oz) vine-ripened
    tomatoes
1 loaf (450 g/1 lb) day-old
    crusty Italian bread
1 tablespoon olive oil
3 garlic cloves, crushed
1 tablespoon tomato paste
    (concentrated purée)
1.25 litres (5 cups) hot vegetable
    stock
4 tablespoons torn fresh basil
    leaves
2–3 tablespoons extra virgin
    olive oil
extra virgin olive oil, extra,
    to serve

1 Score a cross in the base of each tomato. Place in a bowl of boiling water for 1 minute, remove, then plunge into cold water and peel the skin away from the cross. Cut the tomatoes in half and scoop out the seeds with a teaspoon. Roughly chop the tomato flesh.
2 Remove most of the crust from the bread and discard. Cut the bread into 3 cm (1¼ inch) pieces.
3 Heat the oil in a large saucepan. Add the garlic, tomato and tomato paste, then reduce the heat and simmer, stirring occasionally, for 10–15 minutes, or until reduced and thickened. Add the stock and bring to the boil, stirring for 2–3 minutes. Reduce the heat to medium, add the bread pieces and cook, stirring, for 5 minutes, or until the bread softens and absorbs most of the liquid. Add more stock or water if necessary.
4 Stir in the torn basil leaves and extra virgin olive oil, and leave for 5 minutes so the flavours have time to develop. Drizzle with a little extra virgin olive oil and serve.

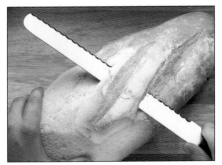

Remove most of the crust from the loaf of bread and discard.

Reduce the heat and simmer for 15 minutes, or until reduced.

Add the bread pieces to the tomato mixture and cook, stirring.

RED GAZPACHO

Preparation time: 40 minutes
+ 5 minutes soaking + 2 hours
refrigeration
Total cooking time: Nil
Serves 4

1 kg (2 lb 4 oz) vine-ripened
   tomatoes
2 slices day-old white Italian
   bread, crust removed, broken
   into pieces
1 red capsicum (pepper),
   deseeded and roughly
   chopped
2 garlic cloves, chopped
1 small green chilli, chopped,
   optional
1 teaspoon sugar
2 tablespoons red wine
   vinegar
2 tablespoons extra virgin
   olive oil
8 ice cubes

Garnish
½ Lebanese (short) cucumber,
   deseeded and finely diced
½ red capsicum (pepper),
   deseeded and finely diced
½ green capsicum (pepper),
   deseeded and finely diced
½ red onion, finely diced
½ tomato, diced

1 Score a cross in the base of each tomato. Place in a bowl of boiling water for 1 minute, remove, then plunge into cold water and peel away the skin from the cross. Cut the tomatoes in half, scoop out the seeds and roughly chop the flesh.
2 Soak the bread in cold water for 5 minutes, then squeeze out any excess liquid. Place the bread in a food processor with the tomato, capsicum, garlic, chilli, sugar and vinegar, and process until smooth.
3 With the motor running, add the oil to make a smooth mixture. Season with salt and ground black pepper.

Refrigerate for at least 2 hours. Add a little extra vinegar, if desired.
4 To make the garnish, place all the ingredients in a bowl and mix well. Serve the soup in bowls with 2 ice cubes in each bowl. Spoon the garnish into separate bowls.

Soak the bread in water; then squeeze out any excess liquid.

Process the bread, tomato, capsicum, garlic, chilli, sugar and vinegar

Place the garnish ingredients in a bowl and mix together well.

CHICKPEA SOUP

Preparation time: 15 minutes
  + overnight soaking
Total cooking time: 1 hour 30 minutes
Serves 4

330 g (11½ oz/1½ cups) dried
    chickpeas
½ brown onion
1 bay leaf
½ head (8 cloves) garlic,
    unpeeled
2 tablespoons olive oil
1 celery stalk, chopped
1 large onion, extra, finely
    chopped
3 garlic cloves, extra, chopped

1 teaspoon ground cumin
1 teaspoon paprika
¼ teaspoon dried chilli
    powder
3 teaspoons chopped fresh
    oregano
1 litre (4 cups) vegetable stock
2 tablespoons lemon juice
olive oil, extra to drizzle

1 Place the chickpeas in a bowl and cover with water. Soak overnight, then drain. Transfer the chickpeas to a saucepan. Add the onion, bay leaf, garlic and 1.5 litres (6 cups) water. Bring to the boil, then reduce the heat and simmer for 55–60 minutes, or until the chickpeas are tender. Drain, reserving 500 ml (17 fl oz/2 cups)

cooking liquid. Discard the onion, bay leaf and garlic.
2 Heat the oil in the same saucepan, add the celery and extra onion, and cook over medium heat for 5 minutes, or until golden. Add the extra garlic and cook for a further 1 minute. Add the cumin, paprika, chilli powder and 2 teaspoons of the oregano, and cook, stirring, for 1 minute. Return the chickpeas to the pan and stir to coat with the spices.
3 Pour in the vegetable stock and reserved cooking liquid, bring to the boil, then reduce the heat and simmer for 20 minutes. Stir in the lemon juice and remaining oregano and serve drizzled with olive oil.

Cook the chickpeas, onion, bay leaf and garlic until the chickpeas are tender.

Add the cooked chickpeas to the pan and stir to coat with the spices.

Stir in the lemon juice and remaining fresh oregano.

AJO BLANCO

Preparation time: 20 minutes +
  5 minutes soaking + refrigeration
Total cooking time: 3 minutes
Serves 4–6

1 loaf (200 g/7 oz) day-old white
  Italian bread, crust removed
155 g (5½ oz/1 cup) whole
  blanched almonds
3–4 garlic cloves, chopped
125 ml (4 fl oz/½ cup) extra
  virgin olive oil
4 tablespoons sherry vinegar or
  white wine vinegar
315–375 ml (11–13 fl oz/1¼-
1½ cups) vegetable stock
  or water
2 tablespoons olive oil, extra
75 g (2½ oz) day-old white
  Italian bread, extra, crust
  removed and cut into 1 cm
  (½ inch) cubes
200 g (7 oz) small seedless
  green grapes

1 Soak the bread in a bowl of cold water for 5 minutes, then squeeze to remove any excess moisture. Place the almonds and garlic in a food processor and process until well ground. Add the bread and process to a smooth paste.
2 With the motor running, add the oil in a slow steady stream until the mixture is the consistency of thick mayonnaise. Slowly add the sherry vinegar and 315 ml (11 fl oz/1¼ cups) of the stock, or water, until the mixture has reached the desired consistency. Blend for 1 minute. Season with salt, then refrigerate for at least 2 hours. The soup thickens on refrigeration so add more stock or water to reach the desired consistency.
3 Heat the extra olive oil in a large frying pan. Add the bread cubes and toss over medium heat for 2–3 minutes, or until evenly golden brown. Drain on crumpled paper towels. Serve the soup very cold garnished with the grapes and the bread cubes.

Process the bread, almonds and garlic to a smooth paste.

Add the oil to the bread mixture until it resembles thick mayonnaise.

Pan-fry the bread cubes until they are evenly golden brown.

BOUILLABAISSE WITH ROUILLE

Preparation time: 30 minutes
  + 5 minutes soaking
Total cooking time: 1 hour 15 minutes
Serves 6

500 g (1 lb 2 oz) ripe tomatoes
3 tablespoons olive oil
1 large onion, chopped
2 leeks, sliced
4 garlic cloves, crushed
1–2 tablespoons tomato paste
  (concentrated purée)
6 sprigs fresh flat-leaf (Italian)
  parsley
2 bay leaves
2 sprigs fresh thyme
1 sprig fresh fennel
¼ teaspoon saffron threads
2 kg (2 lb 4 oz) seafood
  trimmings, e.g. fish heads,
  bones, shellfish remains
1 tablespoon Pernod or Ricard
4 potatoes, cut into 1.5 cm
  (⅝ inch) slices
1.5 kg (3 lb 5 oz) fish fillets
  and steaks, such as snapper,
  red fish, blue-eye and bream,
  cut into large chunks
  (see Note)
2 tablespoons chopped fresh
  flat -leaf (Italian) parsley

Toasts
½ baguette, cut into twelve
  1.5 cm (⅝ inch) slices
2 large garlic cloves, halved

Rouille
3 slices day-old Italian white
  bread, crusts removed
1 red capsicum (pepper),
  deseeded, quartered
1 small red chilli, deseeded,
  chopped
3 garlic cloves, crushed
1 tablespoon chopped fresh basil
4 tablespoons olive oil

1 Score a cross in the base of each tomato. Place the tomatoes in a bowl of boiling water for 1 minute, remove, then plunge into cold water and peel the skin away from the cross. Roughly chop the tomatoes.
2 Heat the oil in a large saucepan over low heat, add the onion and leek and cook for 5 minutes without browning. Add the garlic, tomato and 1 tablespoon tomato paste, and simmer for 5 minutes. Stir in 2 litres (8 cups) cold water, then add the parsley, bay leaves, thyme, fennel, saffron and seafood trimmings. Bring to the boil, then reduce the heat and simmer for 30–40 minutes.
3 Strain into a large saucepan, pressing the juices out of the ingredients. Set aside 3 tablespoons stock. Add the Pernod to the pan and stir in extra tomato paste if needed to enrich the colour. Season. Bring to the boil, add the potato, then reduce the heat and simmer for 5 minutes.
4 Add the blue-eye and bream and cook for 2–3 minutes, then add the red fish and snapper, and cook for 5–6 minutes, or until cooked.
5 To make the toasts, toast the bread until golden on both sides. While still warm, rub with the garlic.
6 To make the rouille, soak the bread, in enough cold water to cover, for 5 minutes. Cook the capsicum, skin-side-up, under a hot grill (broiler) until the skin blackens and blisters. Place in a plastic bag and leave to cool, then peel away the skin. Roughly chop the flesh. Squeeze the bread dry and place in a food processor with the capsicum, chilli, garlic and basil. Process to a smooth paste. With the motor running, gradually add the oil until the consistency resembles mayonnaise. Thin the sauce with 1–2 tablespoons of the reserved fish stock. Season with salt and ground black pepper.
7 To serve, place 2 pieces of toast in the base of six soup bowls. Spoon in the soup and fish pieces and scatter some parsley over the top. Serve with the rouille.

COOK'S FILE

Note: It is important to try to use at least four different varieties of fish, choosing a range of textures and flavours.
Rascasse, where available, is traditional, but cod, bass, John dory, halibut, monkfish, turbot, hake and red mullet are also used. Shellfish such as lobster, scallops or mussels can be used.

Simmer the onion, leek, garlic, tomato and tomato paste for 5 minutes.

Cook the firmer-fleshed fish pieces slightly longer than the delicate pieces.

Rub the halved garlic cloves over the toasted bread.

Process the rouille to the consistency of mayonnaise.

55

AVGOLEMONO WITH CHICKEN

Preparation time: 30 minutes
Total cooking time: 30 minutes
Serves 4

1 onion, halved
2 cloves
1 carrot, cut into chunks
1 bay leaf
500 g (1 lb 2 oz) chicken breast
  fillets
4 tablespoons short-grain rice
3 eggs, separated
3 tablespoons lemon juice
2 tablespoons chopped fresh
  flat-leaf (Italian) parsley
4 thin lemon slices, to garnish

1 Stud the onion halves with the cloves and place in a large saucepan with 1.5 litres (6 cups) water. Add the carrot, bay leaf and chicken. Season with salt and pepper. Slowly bring to the boil, then reduce the heat and simmer for 10 minutes, or until the chicken is cooked.

2 Strain the stock into a clean saucepan, reserving the chicken and discarding the vegetables. Add the rice to the stock, bring to the boil, then reduce the heat and simmer for 15 minutes, or until tender. Tear the chicken into shreds.

3 Whisk the egg whites until stiff peaks form, then beat in the yolks. Slowly beat in the lemon juice. Gently stir in 150 ml (5 fl oz) of the hot (not boiling) soup and beat thoroughly. Add the egg mixture to the soup and stir gently over low heat until thickened slightly. It should still be quite thin. Do not let it boil or the eggs may scramble. Add the shredded chicken and season.

4 Set aside for 3–4 minutes to allow the flavours to develop, then sprinkle the parsley over the top. Garnish with the lemon slices and serve.

COOK'S FILE

Note: Avgolemono is a Greek soup made with egg and lemon. Serve immediately as it doesn't keep well.

Simmer the chicken breast fillets for 10 minutes, or until cooked.

Simmer the rice in the strained stock until tender

Gently stir some of the hot soup into the egg mixture and beat thoroughly.

Add the shredded chicken breast fillets to the soup.

LENTIL AND SILVERBEET SOUP

Preparation time: 20 minutes
+ overnight refrigeration
Total cooking time: 3 hours
20 minutes
Serves 6

Chicken stock
1 kg (2 lb 4 oz) chicken
    trimmings (necks, ribs,
    wings), fat removed
1 small onion, roughly chopped
1 bay leaf
3–4 sprigs fresh flat-leaf
    (Italian) parsley
1–2 sprigs fresh oregano or
    thyme

280 g (10 oz/1½ cups) brown
    lentils, washed
850 g (1 lb 14 oz) silverbeet
    (Swiss chard)
3 tablespoons olive oil
1 large onion, finely chopped
4 garlic cloves, crushed
25 g (1 oz/½ cup) finely chopped
    fresh coriander (cilantro)
    leaves
4 tablespoons lemon juice
lemon wedges, to serve

1 To make the stock, place all the ingredients in a large saucepan, add 3 litres (12 cups) water and bring to the boil. Skim scum from the surface. Reduce the heat, simmer for 2 hours. Strain the stock, discarding the trimmings, onion and herbs. Chill overnight. You need 1 litre (4 cups).

2 Skim any fat from the stock. Place the lentils in a large saucepan, add the stock and 1 litre (4 cups) water. Bring to the boil, then reduce the heat and simmer, covered, for 1 hour.

3 Meanwhile, remove the stems from the silverbeet and shred the leaves. Heat the oil in a saucepan over medium heat and cook the onion for 2–3 minutes, or until transparent. Add the garlic and cook for 1 minute. Add the silverbeet and toss for 2–3 minutes, or until wilted. Stir into the lentils. Add coriander and lemon juice, season, simmer, covered, for 15–20 minutes. Serve with the lemon wedges.

Skim any fat from the surface of the stock before adding the lentils.

Stir the silverbeet into the onion mixture and cook until wilted.

Add the coriander and lemon juice to the silverbeet and lentil mixture.

PASTA AND BEAN SOUP

Preparation time: 15 minutes +
overnight soaking + 10 minutes
resting
Total cooking time: 1 hour 45 minutes
Serves 4

200 g (7 oz) dried borlotti
(cranberry) beans
3 tablespoons olive oil
90 g (3¼ oz) piece pancetta,
finely diced
1 onion, finely chopped
2 garlic cloves, crushed
1 celery stalk, thinly sliced
1 carrot, diced
1 bay leaf
1 sprig fresh rosemary
1 sprig fresh flat-leaf (Italian)
parsley
400 g (14 oz) tinned diced
tomatoes, drained
1.5 litres (6 cups) vegetable
stock
2 tablespoons finely chopped
fresh flat-leaf (Italian)
parsley
150 g (5½ oz) ditalini or other
small dried pasta
extra virgin olive oil, to drizzle
freshly grated Parmesan cheese,
to serve

1 Place the beans in a large bowl, cover with cold water and leave to soak overnight. Drain and rinse.
2 Heat the oil in a large saucepan, add the pancetta, onion, garlic, celery and carrot, and cook over medium heat for 5 minutes, or until golden. Season with pepper. Add the bay leaf, rosemary, parsley, tomato, stock and beans, and bring to the boil. Reduce the heat and simmer for 1½ hours, or

until the beans are tender. Add more boiling water if necessary to maintain the liquid level.
3 Discard the bay leaf, rosemary and parsley sprigs. Scoop out 1 cup of the bean mixture and purée in a food processor or blender. Return to the

pan, season with salt and ground black pepper, and add the parsley and pasta. Simmer for 6 minutes, or until the pasta is al dente. Remove from the heat and set aside for 10 minutes. Serve drizzled with extra virgin olive oil and garnished with Parmesan.

Cook the pancetta, onion, garlic, celery and carrot for 5 minutes.

Purée 1 cup of the bean mixture in a food processor.

Add the pasta to the soup and cook until al dente.

MINESTRONE WITH PESTO

Preparation time: 25 minutes
  + overnight soaking
Total cooking time: 2 hours
Serves 6

125 g (4½ oz) dried borlotti
  (cranberry) beans
1 large onion, coarsely chopped
2 garlic cloves
3 tablespoons coarsely chopped
  fresh flat-leaf (Italian)
  parsley
60 g (2¼ oz) pancetta, chopped
3 tablespoons olive oil
1 celery stalk, halved
  lengthways, then cut into
  1 cm (½ inch) slices
1 carrot, halved lengthways,
  then cut into 1 cm (½ inch)
  slices
1 potato, diced
2 teaspoons tomato paste
  (concentrated purée)
400 g (14 oz) tinned Italian
  diced tomatoes
6 fresh basil leaves, roughly
  torn
2 litres (8 cups) chicken or
  vegetable stock
2 thin zucchini (courgettes), cut
  into 1.5 cm (⅝ inch) slices
115 g (4 oz/¾ cup) shelled peas
60 g (2¼ oz) green beans, cut
  into 4 cm (1½ inch) lengths
80 g (2¾ oz) silverbeet (Swiss
  chard) leaves, shredded
75 g (2½ oz) ditalini or other
  small pasta

Pesto
30 g (1 oz/1 cup) fresh basil
  leaves

20 g (½ oz) pine nuts, lightly
  toasted
2 garlic cloves
100 ml (3½ fl oz) olive oil
3 tablespoons freshly grated
  Parmesan cheese

1 Put the beans in a large bowl, cover with water and soak overnight. Drain and rinse under cold water.
2 Process the onion, garlic, parsley and pancetta in a food processor until fine. Heat the oil in a saucepan and cook the pancetta mix over low heat, stirring occasionally, for 8–10 minutes.
3 Add the celery, carrot and potato, and cook for 5 minutes, then stir in the tomato paste, tomato, basil and borlotti beans. Season. Add the stock and bring to the boil. Cover and simmer, stirring occasionally, for 1 hour 30 minutes.
4 Season and add the zucchini, peas, green beans, silverbeet and pasta. Simmer for 8–10 minutes, or until the vegetables and pasta are al dente.
5 To make the pesto, process the basil, pine nuts and garlic with a pinch of salt in a food processor until finely chopped. With the motor running, slowly add the oil. Transfer to a bowl and stir in the Parmesan and pepper. Serve the soup with pesto on top.

Cook the processed onion, garlic, parsley and pancetta mixture.

Simmer until the pasta and vegetables are al dente.

Stir the Parmesan into the finely chopped basil mixture.

SEAFOOD SOUP

Preparation time: 40 minutes
Total cooking time: 1 hour 40 minutes
Serves 6

800 g (1 lb 10 oz) baby octopus
155 g (5 oz) small cleaned
   calamari tubes
500 g (1 lb) firm fish fillets
12 small mussels in shells
1 tablespoon olive oil
2 small onions, sliced
1 anchovy fillet, finely chopped
3 large ripe tomatoes, skinned
   and finely chopped
3 fresh mint leaves, torn
2 bay leaves
125 ml (4 fl oz/½ cup) dry white
   wine
315 g (10 oz) frozen peas
12 raw king prawns (shrimp),
   shelled and deveined with
   tails intact
2 tablespoons lemon juice

Garlic bread
6 slices crusty Italian bread
1 clove garlic, halved

Parsley pesto
20 g (¾ oz/1 cup) firmly packed
   flat-leaf (Italian) parsley
   leaves
2 cloves garlic, chopped
2 tablespoons lemon juice
2 tablespoons olive oil

1 Remove the heads and beaks from the octopus and cut the tentacles into smaller portions. Cut the calamari tubes into rings. Put the octopus in a large pan of boiling water, partially cover the pan and leave to simmer for 30 minutes. Add the calamari rings and simmer for 15–20 minutes, or until tender. Drain thoroughly.
2 Cut the fish fillets into bite-sized portions. Scrub the mussel shells and remove their beards. Refrigerate all the seafood on separate plates.
3 Heat the oil in a large pan and cook the onion over moderate heat until starting to colour. Stir in the anchovy, tomatoes, mint and bay leaves, wine, 1.5 litres (6 cups) water, and salt and pepper, to taste. Bring to the boil, lower the heat and simmer for 20 minutes.
4 To make garlic bread, preheat the oven to 160°C (315°F/Gas 2–3). Put the bread on a baking tray in a single layer. Bake for 20 minutes, or until crisp, turning once. Rub each slice of bread with the cut garlic.
5 To make parsley pesto, put the parsley, garlic, lemon juice and olive oil in a food processor. Process into a fine paste and season to taste with salt and pepper. Cover and refrigerate until ready to serve.
6 Just before serving, bring the soup back to the boil and add the peas, mussels and fish. Reduce the heat to simmer, uncovered, for 3 minutes or until the mussels start to open. Add the prawns, octopus and calamari. Bring back to the boil, then reduce the heat and simmer for 2–3 minutes, or until all the seafood is tender. Stir in the lemon juice and discard any unopened mussels. Place a slice of garlic bread in each serving bowl and ladle seafood soup over the top. Serve the parsley pesto separately.

COOK'S FILE

Note: To remove the beak from the octopus, turn the head inside out and push the beak (the dark hard bit) up firmly—it will pop out.

Remove the heads and beaks from the octopus and cut the tentacles into pieces.

Cut the fish fillets into bite-sized pieces. Choose skinless fillets.

Add the tomatoes, mint leaves, bay leaves, water, wine and seasoning.

Bake the bread in a single layer, turning over after 10 minutes.

Put the parsley, garlic, lemon juice, oil and salt and pepper in a food processor.

Bring the soup to the boil, then simmer until the mussels begin to open.

BROCCOLI AND PINE NUT SOUP

Preparation time: 10 minutes
Total cooking time: 30 minutes
Serves 6

30 g (1 oz) butter
1 onion, finely chopped
1.5 litres (6 cups) chicken stock
750 g (1½ lb) fresh broccoli

4 tablespoons pine nuts
extra pine nuts, to serve

1 Melt the butter in a large pan and cook the onion over moderate heat until soft but not browned. Add the stock and bring to the boil.
2 Remove the florets from the broccoli and set aside. Chop the broccoli stalks and add to the pan. Reduce the heat, cover and simmer for 15 minutes. Add the florets and simmer, uncovered, for 10 minutes, or until the florets are tender. Allow to cool completely.
3 Add the pine nuts and blend until smooth in a food processor (you may need to blend in batches, depending on the size of your processor). Season to taste with salt and pepper, then gently reheat. Sprinkle with extra pine nuts to serve. Delicious with toasted foccacia, drizzled with extra virgin olive oil.

Cook the onion until soft and then add the chicken stock.

Remove the florets from the broccoli and chop the stalks into even-sized pieces.

Let the soup cool, to prevent burns, then process with the pine nuts.

Add the polenta to the stock and water and stir constantly until very thick.

Use the back of a spoon to spread the polenta in the tin.

Build up the layers of sliced polenta, butter and cheese.

BAKED POLENTA WITH THREE CHEESES

Preparation time: 20 minutes
+ 2 hours chilling
Total cooking time: 45 minutes
Serves 4

Polenta
**600 ml (20 fl oz/2½ cups)
chicken stock**
**300 g (10½ oz/2 cups) polenta
(cornmeal)**
**50 g (1¾ oz/½ cup) freshly
grated Parmesan**

Cheese Filling
**100 g (3⅓ oz) havarti cheese,
sliced**
100 g (3⅓ oz) mascarpone
**100 g (3⅓ oz) blue cheese,
crumbled**
**100 g (3⅓ oz) butter, sliced
thinly**
**50 g (1¾ oz/½ cup) freshly
grated Parmesan**

1 To make polenta, brush a 1.75 litre (7 cup) loaf (bar) tin with oil. Put the stock and 500 ml (17 fl oz/2 cups) water in a large pan and bring to the boil. Add the polenta and stir for 10 minutes until very thick.
2 Remove from the heat and stir in the Parmesan. Spread into the tin and smooth the surface. Refrigerate for 2 hours, then cut into about 30 thin slices. Preheat the oven to 180°C (350°F/Gas 4).
3 Brush a large ovenproof dish with oil. Place a layer of polenta slices on the base. Top with a layer of half the combined havarti, mascarpone and blue cheeses and half the butter. Add another layer of polenta and top with the remainder of the three cheeses and butter. Add a final layer of polenta and sprinkle the Parmesan on top. Bake for 30 minutes, or until a golden crust forms. Serve immediately.

COOK'S FILE

Note: Havarti is actually a Danish cheese with a full flavour.

Add the final layer of sliced polenta and then sprinkle with Parmesan cheese.

FRITTO MISTO DI MARE

Preparation time: 20 minutes
Total cooking time: 10 minutes
Serves 4

200 g (7 oz) cuttlefish
800 g (1 lb 12 oz) red mullet
   fillets
½ teaspoon paprika
75 g (2½ oz) plain (all-purpose)
   flour
12 raw medium prawns (shrimp),
   peeled, deveined, tails intact
good-quality olive oil, for
   deep-frying
lemon wedges, to serve

1 Preheat the oven to 150°C (300°F/ Gas 2). Line a large baking tray with baking paper.
2 Place the cuttlefish bone-side-down on a board and, using a sharp knife, gently cut lengthways through the body. Open out, remove the cuttlebone and then gently remove the insides. Cut the flesh in half. Under cold running water, pull the skin away. Cut the cuttlefish and mullet into even-size pieces. Pat dry with paper towel. Season with salt and freshly ground black pepper. Mix the paprika and flour together in a bowl, add the seafood and toss to coat. Shake off any excess flour.
3 Fill a deep heavy-based saucepan

one third full of oil and heat to 190°C (375°F), or until a cube of bread dropped in the oil browns in 10 seconds. Add the seafood in batches and cook for 1 minute, or until golden and cooked through. Drain on crumpled paper towels. Keep warm on the baking tray in the oven while you cook the rest.
4 Place all the seafood on a serving platter. Sprinkle with extra salt and serve with lemon wedges.

Using a sharp knife, gently cut lengthways through the cuttlefish body.

Remove the cuttlebone and the insides from the cuttlefish.

Add the seafood to the flour and paprika mixture and toss to coat.

LENTIL AND BURGHUL FRITTERS WITH YOGHURT SAUCE

Preparation time: 20 minutes + 1 hour
30 minutes standing
Total cooking time: 1 hour 10 minutes
Makes 35

140 g (5 oz/¾ cup) brown lentils,
    rinsed
90 g (3¼ oz/½ cup) burghul
    (bulgur)
4 tablespoons olive oil
1 onion, finely chopped
2 garlic cloves, finely chopped
3 teaspoons ground cumin
2 teaspoons ground coriander
3 tablespoons finely chopped
    fresh mint leaves
4 eggs, lightly beaten
60 g (2¼ oz/½ cup) plain
    (all-purpose) flour
1 teaspoon sea salt

Yoghurt sauce
1 small Lebanese (short)
    cucumber, peeled
250 g (9 oz/1 cup) Greek-style
    plain yoghurt
1–2 garlic cloves, finely
    chopped

1 Place the lentils in a saucepan with 625 ml (21½ fl oz/2½ cups) water. Bring to the boil, then reduce the heat and simmer for 30 minutes, or until the lentils are tender.
2 Remove from the heat and add water to just cover the lentils. Pour in the burghul, cover and stand for 1½ hours, or until the burghul has expanded. Transfer to a bowl.
3 To make the yoghurt sauce, halve the cucumber, scoop out the seeds and discard. Grate the flesh and place in a bowl with the yoghurt and garlic, and mix together well.
4 Heat half the oil in a frying pan over medium heat. Cook the onion and garlic for 5 minutes, or until soft. Add the cumin and coriander.
5 Add this mixture, mint, eggs, flour and sea salt to the lentil mixture, and mix together well. The mixture should be thick enough to drop spoonfuls into the pan. If the mixture is too wet, add a little extra flour.
6 Heat the remaining oil in the cleaned frying pan over medium heat. Working in batches, drop heaped tablespoons of mixture into the pan. Cook for 3 minutes each side, or until browned. Drain, season with salt and serve with the yoghurt sauce.

Add the burghul to the lentils and leave to stand for 1 hour 30 minutes.

Combine the lentil mixture, onion mixture, mint, eggs, flour and sea salt.

Cook the fritters in a frying pan until browned on both sides.

ARTICHOKE AND PROVOLONE QUICHES

Preparation time: 40 minutes
+ 30 minutes refrigeration
Total cooking time: 35 minutes
Serves 6

250 g (9 oz/2 cups) plain
    (all-purpose) flour
125 g (4 oz) cold butter, chopped
1 egg yolk

Filling
1 small eggplant (aubergine),
    sliced

6 eggs, lightly beaten
3 teaspoons wholegrain mustard
150 g (5 oz) provolone cheese,
    grated
200 g (6½ oz) marinated
    artichokes, sliced
125 g (4 oz) semi-dried
    (sun-blushed) tomatoes

1 Process the flour and butter in a processor for about 15 seconds until crumbly. Add the egg yolk and 3 tablespoons of water. Process in short bursts until the mixture comes together. Add a little extra water if needed. Turn out onto a floured surface and gather into a ball. Cover

with plastic wrap and refrigerate for at least 30 minutes.

2 Preheat the oven to 190°C (375°F/Gas 5) and grease six 11 cm (4½ inch) oval pie tins.

3 To make the filling, brush the sliced eggplant with olive oil and place under a grill until golden. Combine the eggs, mustard and cheese in a jug.

4 Roll out the pastry and line the tins. Trim the excess pastry and decorate the edges. Place one eggplant slice, the artichokes and tomatoes in the tins, pour the egg mixture over and bake for 25 minutes, or until golden.

Gather the pastry into a ball and cover with plastic wrap.

Brush each slice of eggplant with a little olive oil.

Place one slice of eggplant in the bottom of each lined pie tin.

ITALIAN SUMMER TART

Preparation time: 40 minutes +
  50 minutes refrigeration
Total cooking time: 1 hour
Serves 4–6

185 g (6½ oz/1½ cups) plain
  (all-purpose) flour
90 g (3 oz) cold butter, chopped
1 egg yolk

Filling
1 tablespoon olive oil
2 small red onions, sliced
1 tablespoon balsamic vinegar
1 teaspoon soft brown sugar
1 tablespoon thyme leaves
170 g (5½ oz) jar marinated
  quartered artichokes, drained
2 slices prosciutto, cut into strips
12 black olives
thyme leaves, to garnish

1 Place the flour and butter in a food processor and process for 15 seconds, or until the mixture resembles fine breadcrumbs. Add the egg yolk and 2–3 tablespoons of water. Process in short bursts until the mixture just comes together, adding a little extra water if necessary. Turn out onto a floured surface and gather into a ball. Cover with plastic wrap and refrigerate for at least 30 minutes.

2 Roll the pastry between 2 sheets of baking paper until it is large enough to fit and overlap a 35 x 10 cm (14 x 4 inch) rectangular loose-based flan (tart) tin. Carefully lift the pastry into the tin and press it well into the sides. Trim off any excess pastry using a sharp knife or by rolling the rolling pin across the top of the tin. Cover and refrigerate for a further 20 minutes. Preheat the oven to 190°C (375°F/Gas 5). Cover the pastry shell with baking paper and fill evenly with baking beads, rice or beans. Bake for 15 minutes. Remove the paper and beads and bake for a further 15 minutes, or until the pastry is golden and cooked. Allow to cool on a wire rack.

3 Heat the oil in a pan, add onion and cook, stirring occasionally, for 15 minutes. Add the balsamic vinegar and brown sugar and cook for a further 15 minutes. Remove from the heat, stir through the thyme leaves and set aside to cool.

4 Spread the onion evenly over the base of the cooked pastry. Arrange the quartered artichoke pieces on top of the onion, then fill the spaces in-between with the rolled-up pieces of prosciutto and the black olives. Sprinkle with the extra thyme leaves and freshly ground black pepper. Serve at room temperature.

Once the mixture resembles fine crumbs, add the egg yolk and a little water.

Fill the spaces in between with rolled-up pieces of prosciutto and black olives.

BAKED RICOTTA

Preparation time: 15 minutes
  + overnight chilling
Total cooking time: 20 minutes
Serves 8

1 egg white
750 g (1½ lb) fresh ricotta
    cheese, well drained
60 g (2 oz) semi-dried (sun-
    blushed) tomatoes in oil,
    drained and chopped
cracked black pepper
2 tablespoons chopped flat-leaf
    (Italian) parsley
½ teaspoon finely grated
    lemon zest
1 clove garlic, crushed
1 tablespoon extra virgin
    olive oil

1 Preheat the oven to 180°C (350°F/ Gas 4). Line the base of a 20 cm (8 inch) round shallow cake tin with foil and brush well with olive oil.
2 Beat the egg white with a fork until frothy. Add ricotta and mix thoroughly. Put half the mixture in the tin and spread evenly over the base. Scatter with the tomato and cracked pepper, spoon the remainder of the ricotta over the top and smooth the surface.
3 Put the parsley, lemon zest and garlic in a bowl and mix well. Sprinkle over the ricotta, top with extra cracked pepper and then drizzle with oil. Brush a circle of foil with oil and place, oil-side-down, over the ricotta. Bake for 20 minutes, or until lightly set. Remove the foil.
4 Leave to cool in the tin, then cover with foil and refrigerate overnight. Carefully turn out onto a tray, remove the foil and then cover with a plate and

invert so that the parsley is on top. Serve in wedges at room temperature as an entrée, garnished with rocket leaves and black olives, or as part of an antipasto.

COOK'S FILE

Hint: The best way to thoroughly drain ricotta is to leave it in a colander overnight, weighed down with a tin or plate. Put a large bowl underneath to catch the liquid.
Variation: Try semi-dried capsicum instead of tomatoes. Drizzle the oil from the tomatoes or capsicum on top, instead of virgin olive oil.

To drain ricotta, leave it in a colander over a bowl and weigh down with a tin.

Scatter the chopped tomatoes and cracked pepper over the ricotta.

Lightly oil a circle of foil and place it, oil-side-down, over the ricotta.

PARMESAN PEARS

Preparation time: 15 minutes
Total cooking time: 10 minutes
Serves 6

3 firm ripe pears
40 g (1⅓ oz) butter
6 thin slices pancetta, finely
    chopped
2 spring onions (scallions),
    finely sliced

60 g (2¼ oz/¾ cup) fresh white
    breadcrumbs
4 tablespoons grated
    Parmesan

1 Cut the pears in half and remove the cores with a melon baller or teaspoon.
2 Melt butter in a frying pan. Brush the pears with a little melted butter and place, cut-side-up, on an oven tray. Put under a preheated grill (broiler) for 4 minutes, or until heated through.

3 Add the pancetta and onions to the remaining butter in the pan. Cook until the onions are soft but not brown. Add the breadcrumbs and black pepper.
4 Scatter the pancetta mixture over the pears, sprinkle with Parmesan and grill (broil) until golden brown. Serve warm as an entrée, or with roast chicken.

A melon baller is ideal for cutting out the cores of the pears.

Cook the pancetta and spring onions until soft. Add the breadcrumbs and pepper.

Sprinkle the Parmesan over the pears and grill until golden brown.

69

ROASTED TOMATO AND ZUCCHINI TARTLETS

Preparation time: 45 minutes
Total cooking time: 1 hour 20 minutes
Serves 6

3 Roma (plum) tomatoes, halved
    lengthways
1 teaspoon balsamic vinegar
1 teaspoon olive oil
3 small zucchini (courgettes),
    sliced
375 g (12 oz) block puff pastry
1 egg yolk, beaten, to glaze
12 small black olives
24 capers, rinsed and drained

Pistachio mint pesto
75 g (2½ oz/½ cup) unsalted
    shelled pistachio nuts
40 g (1½ oz/2 cups) firmly
    packed mint leaves
2 cloves garlic, crushed
4 tablespoons olive oil
50 g (1¾ oz/½ cup) freshly
    grated Parmesan

1 Preheat the oven to 150°C (300°F/ Gas 2). Place the tomatoes, cut-side-up, on a baking tray. Roast for 30 minutes, brush with the combined vinegar and oil and roast for a further 30 minutes. Increase the oven to 210°C (415°F/ Gas 6–7).
2 To make the pesto, place the pistachios, mint and garlic in a processor and process for 15 seconds. With the motor running, slowly pour in the olive oil. Add the Parmesan and process briefly.
3 Preheat the grill (broiler) and line with foil. Place the zucchini in a single layer on the foil and brush with the remaining balsamic vinegar and oil.

Grill (broil) for about 5 minutes, turning once.
4 Roll the pastry out to 25 x 40 cm (10 x 16 inches) and cut out six 12 cm (4¾ inch) circles. Put on a greased baking tray and brush with egg yolk.

Spread a tablespoon of pesto on each, leaving a 2 cm (¾ inch) border. Divide the zucchini among the pastries and top with tomato halves. Bake for 15 minutes, or until golden. Top with olives, capers and black pepper.

Roast the tomatoes for 30 minutes, then brush with the vinegar and oil.

Add the grated Parmesan to the pesto and process briefly until well mixed.

Arrange a few grilled zucchini slices over the pesto, leaving a clear border.

SEMOLINA GNOCCHI

Preparation time: 15 minutes
+ 1 hour refrigeration
Total cooking time: 40 minutes
Serves 4

750 ml (26 fl oz/3 cups) milk
¼ teaspoon ground nutmeg
85 g (3 oz/⅔ cup) semolina
1 egg, beaten
150 g (5½ oz/1½ cups) freshly
    grated Parmesan cheese
60 g (2¼ oz) butter or
    margarine, melted

125 ml (4 fl oz/½ cup) cream
75 g (2½ oz/½ cup) freshly
    grated mozzarella cheese
¼ teaspoon ground nutmeg,
    extra

1 Line a deep 29 x 19 x 3 cm (11½ x 7½ x 1¼ inch) swiss roll tin with baking paper.
2 Place milk and nutmeg in a medium pan. Season. Bring to the boil. Reduce heat and gradually stir in semolina. Cook, stirring occasionally, for 5–10 minutes, or until semolina is very stiff. Remove from heat. Add egg and 100 g (3½ oz/1 cup) Parmesan cheese to semolina mixture and stir to combine. Spread mixture in prepared tin. Refrigerate for 1 hour, or until firm.
3 Preheat oven to 180°C (350°F/Gas 4). Cut semolina into rounds using a floured 4 cm (1½ inch) cutter. Arrange in a greased shallow casserole dish.
4 Pour butter over top, followed by cream. Sprinkle with combined remaining Parmesan and mozzarella cheese. Sprinkle with extra nutmeg. Bake 20–25 minutes, or until golden.

1

2

3

Vegetable
dishes

STUFFED ZUCCHINI BLOSSOMS

Preparation time: 25 minutes
Total cooking time: 20 minutes
Serves 4

125 g (4½ oz/½ cup) ricotta cheese
60 g (2¼ oz/½ cup) finely grated Cheddar or mozzarella cheese
2 tablespoons chopped chives
12 zucchini (courgette) blossoms
4 tablespoons plain (all-purpose) flour

Batter
125 g (4½ oz/1 cup) plain (all-purpose) flour
1 egg, lightly beaten
185 ml (6 fl oz/¾ cup) iced water
oil for deep frying

Tomato sauce
1 tablespoon olive oil, extra
1 small onion, finely chopped
1 garlic clove, crushed
425 g (15 oz) tinned tomatoes
½ teaspoon dried oregano

1 Combine ricotta, Cheddar or mozzarella, and chives in a small mixing bowl. Gently open out zucchini blossoms, remove stamens and spoon in cheese mixture. Close up blossoms and twist ends to seal. Dust lightly with flour and shake off excess.
2 To make batter, place flour in a medium bowl, make a well in centre. Add the egg and water and beat until all liquid is incorporated and batter is free of lumps. Heat oil in a large pan until moderately hot. Using tongs, dip each blossom into batter then lower into oil. Fry blossoms until just golden; drain on paper towel. Serve immediately with tomato sauce.
3 To make tomato sauce, heat oil in a small pan, add the onion. Cook over medium heat for 3 minutes, until onion is soft. Add the garlic and cook for another minute. Add the undrained, crushed tomatoes and oregano and stir to combine. Bring mixture to boil, reduce heat and simmer gently for 10 minutes. Serve sauce hot.

COOK'S FILE

Note: Small zucchini blossoms often have a baby zucchini still attached to them; larger blossoms are sometimes available without the zucchini.

1

2

3

MUSHROOM CAPS WITH GARLIC AND THYME

Preparation time: 20 minutes
Total cooking time: 25 minutes
Serves 6

6 large flat or field mushrooms
   (about 80 g/2¾ oz each)
2 tablespoons oil
1 small onion, finely chopped
3 rashers bacon, finely chopped
2 garlic cloves, crushed
4 slices white bread
1 tablespoon fresh thyme leaves

1 Preheat oven to 180°C (350°F/ Gas 4). Line a large baking tray with foil, brush with oil or melted butter. Using your fingers, peel the skin from the mushrooms. Remove the stems and finely chop. Heat oil in a heavy-based frying pan. Add the onion and bacon and cook over medium heat until golden. Add chopped mushroom stems and garlic, cook for 3 minutes over medium heat until soft, stirring occasionally. Transfer to a medium mixing bowl to cool.
2 Remove crusts from bread, tear into pieces and place in the bowl of the food processor. Using pulse action, process for 20 seconds, or until fluffy crumbs form.
3 Add the breadcrumbs and the thyme to the bowl and stir until well combined. Place the mushrooms on the prepared tray and top with the breadcrumb mixture. Grind pepper over. Bake for 20 minutes, or until the mushrooms are tender and bread-crumbs are golden. Serve at once.

COOK'S FILE

Storage time: Topping may be prepared up to four hours in advance. Cook mushrooms just before serving.

1

2

3

WARM CHICKPEA AND SILVERBEET SALAD WITH SUMAC

Preparation time: 30 minutes
  + overnight soaking
Total cooking time: 2 hours
Serves 4

250 g (9 oz) dried chickpeas
125 ml (4 fl oz/½ cup) olive oil
1 onion, cut into thin wedges
2 tomatoes
1 teaspoon sugar
¼ teaspoon ground cinnamon
2 garlic cloves, chopped

1.5 kg (3 lb 5 oz) silverbeet
  (Swiss chard)
3 tablespoons chopped fresh
  mint
2–3 tablespoons lemon juice
1½ tablespoons ground sumac
  (see Note)

1 Place the chickpeas in a large bowl, cover with water and leave to soak overnight. Drain and place in a large saucepan. Cover with water and bring to the boil, then simmer for 1¾ hours, or until tender. Drain.

2 Heat the oil in a frying pan, add the onion and cook over low heat for 3–4 minutes, or until soft and just starting to brown. Cut the tomatoes in half, remove the seeds and dice the flesh. Add to the pan with the sugar, cinnamon and garlic, and cook for 2–3 minutes, or until softened.

3 Wash the silverbeet and dry with paper towel. Trim the stems and shred the leaves. Add to the tomato mix with the chickpeas; cook for 3–4 minutes, or until the silverbeet wilts. Add the mint, lemon juice and sumac; season, and cook for 1 minute. Serve at once.

COOK'S FILE

Note: Sumac is available from Middle Eastern speciality shops.

Scoop the seeds out of the halved tomatoes with a teaspoon.

Add the tomato, sugar, cinnamon and garlic to the pan and cook until soft.

Add the silverbeet and chickpeas and cook until the spinach is wilted.

GREEK SALAD

Preparation time: 20 minutes
Total cooking time: Nil
Serves 4

4 tomatoes, cut into
  wedges
1 telegraph (long) cucumber,
  peeled, halved, deseeded and
  cut into small cubes
2 green capsicums (peppers),
deseeded, halved lengthways
  and cut into strips
1 red onion, finely sliced
16 Kalamata olives
250 g (9 oz) good-quality firm
  feta, cut into cubes
3 tablespoons fresh flat-leaf
  (Italian) parsley leaves
12 whole fresh mint leaves
125 ml (4 fl oz/½ cup)
  good-quality olive oil
2 tablespoons lemon juice
1 garlic clove, crushed

1 Place the tomato, cucumber, capsicum, onion, olives, feta and half the parsley and mint leaves in a large salad bowl, and gently mix together.
2 Place the oil, lemon juice and garlic in a screw-top jar, season and shake until combined. Pour over the salad and lightly toss. Garnish with the remaining parsley and mint.

Peel, halve and seed the cucumber, then cut into small cubes.

Cut the good-quality firm feta into even-sized cubes.

Gently mix the salad ingredients together without breaking up the feta.

LENTIL SALAD

Preparation time: 15 minutes
+ 30 minutes standing
Total cooking time: 30 minutes
Serves 4–6

½ brown onion
2 cloves
300 g (10½ oz/1½ cups) puy
   lentils (see Note)
1 strip lemon zest
2 garlic cloves, peeled
1 fresh bay leaf

2 teaspoons ground cumin
2 tablespoons red wine vinegar
3 tablespoons olive oil
1 tablespoon lemon juice
2 tablespoon fresh mint leaves,
   finely chopped
3 spring onions (scallions),
   finely chopped

1 Stud the onion with the cloves and place in a saucepan with the lentils, zest, garlic, bay leaf, 1 teaspoon cumin and 875 ml (30 fl oz/3½ cups) water. Bring to the boil and cook over medium heat for 25–30 minutes, or until the water absorbs. Discard the onion, rind and bay leaf. Reserve the garlic; finely chop.
2 Whisk together the vinegar, oil, juice, garlic and remaining cumin. Stir through the lentils with the mint and spring onion. Season well. Leave for 30 minutes to let the flavours absorb. Serve at room temperature.

COOK'S FILE

Note: Puy lentils are small, green lentils from France. They are available dried from gourmet food stores.

Stud the brown onion half with the cloves.

Cook the lentils, then discard the onion, lemon rind and bay leaf.

Whisk together the vinegar, oil, lemon juice, garlic and cumin.

ITALIAN BAKED EGGPLANT WITH TOMATO AND MOZZARELLA

Preparation time: 20 minutes
Total cooking time: 40 minutes
Serves 6

6 large slender eggplants
    (aubergines) (700 g/1 lb 9 oz)
4 tablespoons olive oil
1 tablespoon olive oil, extra
2 onions, finely chopped
2 garlic cloves, crushed
400 g (14 oz) tinned diced
    tomatoes
1 tablespoon tomato paste
    (concentrated purée)
3 tablespoons chopped fresh
    flat-leaf (Italian) parsley
1 tablespoon chopped fresh
    oregano
1 teaspoon sugar
125 g (4½ oz) mozzarella, grated

1 Preheat the oven to 180°C (350°F/ Gas 4). Cut the eggplants in half lengthways, keeping the stems attached. Score the flesh by cutting a criss-cross pattern with a sharp knife, being careful not to cut through the skin. Heat half the oil in a large frying pan, add half the eggplant and cook for 2–3 minutes each side, or until the flesh is soft. Remove. Repeat with the remaining oil and eggplant. Cool slightly. Scoop out the flesh, leaving a 2 mm (⅛ inch) border. Finely chop the flesh and reserve the shells.

2 In the same pan, heat the extra oil and cook the onion over medium heat for 5 minutes. Add the garlic and cook for 30 seconds, then add the tomato, tomato paste, herbs, sugar and eggplant flesh, and cook, stirring occasionally, over low heat for 8–10 minutes, or until the sauce is thick and pulpy. Season.

3 Arrange the eggplant shells in a lightly greased baking dish and spoon in the tomato filling. Sprinkle with the mozzarella and bake for 5–10 minutes, or until the cheese has melted.

Score the eggplant in a criss-cross pattern without cutting the skin.

Scoop the flesh out of the cooked eggplant, leaving a narrow border.

Spoon the tomato filling into the eggplant shells.

POLENTA SQUARES WITH MUSHROOM RAGU

Preparation time: 25 minutes +
  20 minutes refrigeration +
  10 minutes standing
Total cooking time: 40 minutes
Serves 4

500 ml (17 fl oz/2 cups)
  vegetable stock
150 g (5½ oz/1 cup) medium-
  grain polenta
20 g (½ oz) butter
75 g (2½ oz/¾ cup) grated
  Parmesan cheese
5 g (⅛ oz) dried porcini
  mushrooms
200 g (7 oz) Swiss brown
  mushrooms
300 g (10½ oz) field
  mushrooms
125 ml (4 fl oz/½ cup) olive oil
1 onion, chopped
3 garlic cloves, finely chopped
1 fresh bay leaf
2 teaspoons chopped fresh
  thyme
2 teaspoons chopped fresh
  oregano
15 g (½ oz/½ cup) finely
  chopped fresh flat-leaf
  (Italian) parsley
1 tablespoon balsamic vinegar
3 tablespoons grated Parmesan
  cheese, extra

1 Place the stock and a pinch of salt in a large saucepan and bring to the boil. Add the polenta in a steady stream, stirring constantly. Reduce the heat and simmer, stirring occasionally, for 15–20 minutes. Remove from the heat and stir in the butter and Parmesan.

2 Grease a 20 cm (8 inch) square shallow cake tin, spread the mixture into the tin. Refrigerate for 20 minutes.
3 Soak the porcini mushrooms in 125 ml (4 fl oz/½ cup) boiling water for 10 minutes, or until softened. Drain, reserving 4 tablespoons liquid. Wipe the mushrooms with a damp cloth to remove any dirt. Thickly slice the Swiss brown mushrooms, and coarsely chop the field mushrooms.
4 Heat 4 tablespoons olive oil in a large frying pan, add the mushrooms and cook for 4–5 minutes. Remove from the pan. Heat the remaining oil in the pan, add the onion and cook over medium heat for 2–3 minutes, or until transparent.

5 Add the reserved soaking liquid, garlic, bay leaf, thyme and oregano, season and cook for 1 minute. Return the mushrooms to the pan and add the parsley and balsamic vinegar, and cook over medium heat for 1 minute. Remove the bay leaf.
6 Sprinkle the extra Parmesan over the polenta. Place under a medium grill (broiler) for 10 minutes, or until lightly brown and the cheese melts. Cut into four 10 cm (4 inch) squares.
7 Place a polenta square in the centre of each serving plate and top with the mushrooms. Season with pepper.

Spread the polenta mixture into the prepared cake tin.

Add the chopped parsley and balsamic vinegar to the mushroom mixture.

Sprinkle Parmesan over the polenta and grill (broil) until the cheese has melted.

PUMPKIN RISOTTO

Preparation time: 25 minutes
Total cooking time: 1 hour
Serves 4–6

600 g (1 lb 5 oz) pumpkin, cut
 into 1 cm (½ inch) cubes
3 tablespoons olive oil
500 ml (17 fl oz/2 cups)
 vegetable stock
1 onion, finely chopped
2 garlic cloves, finely chopped
1 tablespoon chopped fresh
 rosemary
440 g (15½ oz/2 cups) arborio
 rice
125 ml (4 fl oz/½ cup) white
 wine
30 g (1 oz) butter
4 tablespoons grated Parmesan
 cheese
3 tablespoons finely chopped
 fresh flat-leaf (Italian)
 parsley

1 Preheat the oven to 200°C (400°F/ Gas 6). Toss the pieces of pumpkin in 2 tablespoons of the oil, place in a baking dish and roast for 30 minutes, or until tender and golden. Turn the pumpkin pieces halfway through the cooking time.

2 Heat stock and 750 ml (26 fl oz/ 3 cups) water in a saucepan, cover and keep at a low simmer.

3 Heat the remaining oil in a large saucepan, and cook the onion, garlic and rosemary, stirring, over low heat for 5 minutes, or until the onion is cooked but not browned. Add the rice and stir to coat. Stir in the wine for 2–3 minutes, or until absorbed.

4 Add 125 ml (4 fl oz/½ cup) stock, stirring constantly over medium heat until all liquid is absorbed. Continue adding stock 125 ml (4 fl oz/½ cup) at a time, stirring constantly for 20 minutes, or until all the stock is absorbed and the rice is tender and creamy. Season to taste with salt and freshly ground black pepper and stir in the pumpkin, butter, Parmesan and parsley. Serve immediately.

Add the wine to the rice and stir until absorbed.

Gradually add the stock to the rice until it is all absorbed and the rice is tender.

Stir the pumpkin, butter, Parmesan and parsley through the rice.

RATATOUILLE

Preparation time: 30 minutes
Total cooking time: 40 minutes
Serves 4–6

6 vine-ripened tomatoes
5 tablespoons olive oil
500 g (1 lb 2 oz) eggplant
   (aubergine), cut into 2 cm
   (¾ inch) cubes
375 g (13 oz) zucchini
   (courgettes), cut into 2 cm
   (¾ inch) slices
1 green capsicum (pepper),
   seeded, cut into 2 cm
   de(¾ inch) cubes
1 red onion, cut into wedges
3 garlic cloves, finely chopped
2 teaspoons chopped fresh
   thyme
¼ teaspoon cayenne pepper
2 bay leaves
1 tablespoon red wine vinegar
1 teaspoon caster (superfine)
   sugar
3 tablespoons shredded fresh
   basil

1 Score a cross in the base of each tomato. Place in a bowl of boiling water for 1 minute, remove, then plunge into cold water and peel skin away from the cross. Roughly chop.
2 Heat 2 tablespoons oil in a large saucepan and cook the eggplant over medium heat for 4–5 minutes, or until soft but not browned. Remove. Add 2 tablespoons oil to the pan and cook the zucchini for 3–4 minutes, or until softened. Remove from the pan. Add the capsicum to the pan, cook for 2 minutes, then remove.
3 Heat the remaining oil, add the onion and cook for 2–3 minutes, or

until softened. Add the garlic, thyme, cayenne and bay leaves. Cook, stirring, for 1 minute. Return all the vegetables to the pan. Add the tomato, vinegar and sugar. Simmer for 20 minutes, stirring occasionally. Stir in the basil. Season. Serve hot or cold.

Note: Ratatouille takes quite a long time to prepare and so is traditionally made in large quantities. It is then eaten over several days as an hors d'oeuvre, side dish or main meal.

Peel the skin away from the cross cut in the base of the tomato.

Cook the eggplant until softened but not browned, then remove.

Simmer the mixture for 20 minutes, stirring occasionally.

INSALATA CAPRESE

Preparation time: 10 minutes
Total cooking time: Nil
Serves 4

3 large vine-ripened tomatoes
250 g (9 oz) bocconcini (see Note)
12 fresh basil leaves
3 tablespoons extra virgin
    olive oil
4 basil leaves, roughly torn,
    extra, optional

1 Slice the tomatoes into 1 cm (½ inch) slices, making twelve slices altogether. Slice the bocconcini in to twenty-four 1 cm (½ inch) slices.
2 Arrange tomato slices on a serving plate, alternating them with 2 slices of bocconcini. Place the basil leaves between the bocconcini slices.
3 Drizzle with the oil, sprinkle with the basil, if desired, and season well with salt and ground black pepper.

Slice the bocconcini into twenty-four 1 cm (½ inch) thick slices.

COOK'S FILE

Note: This popular summer salad is most successful with very fresh buffalo mozzarella if you can find it. We've used bocconcini in this recipe as it can be difficult to find very fresh mozzarella.

Arrange the tomato slices on a serving plate, alternating with the bocconcini.

SPAGHETTI SIRACUSANI

Preparation time: 15 minutes
Total cooking time: 1 hour
Serves 4–6

1 large green capsicum (pepper)
2 tablespoons olive oil
2 garlic cloves, crushed
2 x 425 g (15 oz) tinned tomatoes, crushed
2 zucchini (courgettes), chopped
2 anchovy fillets, chopped
1 tablespoon capers, chopped

3 tablespoons black olives, pitted and halved
2 tablespoons chopped fresh basil leaves
500 g (1 lb 2 oz) spaghetti or linguine
50 g (1¾ oz/½ cup) freshly grated Parmesan cheese, to serve

1 Remove membrane and seeds from the capsicum. Slice into thin strips. Heat the oil in a large deep pan. Add the garlic and stir for 30 seconds over low heat.

2 Add the capsicum strips, tomatoes, zucchini, anchovies, capers, olives and 125 ml (4 fl oz/½ cup) water to the pan. Cook for 20 minutes, stirring occasionally.

3 Stir in the basil, then season with salt and pepper. Meanwhile, add the pasta to a large saucepan of rapidly boiling water and cook until the pasta is just tender. Drain thoroughly. Divide pasta among warmed serving bowls and top with the sauce. Sprinkle with Parmesan and serve immediately.

BUCATINI WITH FARMHOUSE SAUCE

Preparation time: 20 minutes
Total cooking time: 25 minutes
Serves 4–6

2 tablespoons olive oil
250 g (9 oz) mushrooms
1 eggplant (aubergine)
2 garlic cloves, crushed
825 g (1 lb 13 oz) tinned
  tomatoes, crushed

500 g (1 lb 2 oz) bucatini or
  spaghetti
3 tablespoons chopped fresh
  parsley

1 Heat oil in a medium heavy-based pan. Wipe the mushrooms with paper towel, then cut into slices. Chop the eggplant into small cubes.
2 Add the mushrooms, eggplant and garlic to the pan and cook, stirring, for 4 minutes. Add the tomatoes, then cover and simmer for 15 minutes. Meanwhile, add the pasta to a large saucepan of rapidly boiling water and cook until just tender. Drain and return to the pan.
3 Season the sauce with salt and ground black pepper, then stir in the parsley. Add the sauce to the pasta and toss well. Serve immediately in warmed pasta bowls.

COOK'S FILE

Hint: If the pasta is cooked before you are ready to serve, toss a little olive oil through it after draining.

STUFFED CAPSICUM

Preparation time: 20 minutes
Total cooking time: 40 minutes
Serves 4

4 tablespoons olive oil
125 g (4½ oz/⅔ cup) couscous
15 g (½ oz) butter
4 large red or yellow capsicums
  (peppers)
3 tablespoons pine nuts
1 onion, finely chopped
2 teaspoons ground cumin
1 teaspoon ground coriander
75 g (2½ oz) raisins
3 tablespoons chopped fresh
  mint
2 tablespoons chopped fresh
  coriander (cilantro) leaves

Yoghurt dressing
250 g (9 oz/1 cup) Greek-style
  plain yoghurt
2 tablespoons chopped fresh
  mint

1 Place 250 ml (9 fl oz/1 cup) water in a saucepan and bring to the boil. Add 1 tablespoon of the oil, a pinch of salt and the couscous. Remove from the heat and leave for 2 minutes, or until the couscous is tender and has absorbed all the liquid. Stir in the butter with a fork and cook over low heat for 3 minutes.

2 Preheat the oven to 190°C (375°F/Gas 5). Grease a baking tray. Slice the tops off the capsicums and remove the seeds and membrane, reserving the tops. Plunge the capsicums into a saucepan of boiling water for 2 minutes; drain on paper towel.

3 Heat a frying pan over high heat. Add the pine nuts and dry-fry for 2–3 minutes, or until golden brown. Remove the pine nuts from the pan. Heat 1 tablespoon of the olive oil in the pan, add the onion and cook over medium heat for 5 minutes, or until softened. Add the cumin and coriander, and cook for 1 minute. Remove from the heat and stir into the couscous with the pine nuts, raisins and herbs, and season well.

4 Fill each capsicum with some of the couscous stuffing and place on the tray. Drizzle the remaining olive oil over the capsicums and replace the

lids. Bake for 20–25 minutes, or until tender. Meanwhile, combine the yoghurt and mint, and place in a

serving dish. Serve the capsicums with the dressing and a salad.

Add the butter to the couscous and cook for 3 minutes.

Spoon the couscous mixture into the capsicum shells.

OKRA IN TOMATO SAUCE AND CORIANDER

Preparation time: 5 minutes
Total cooking time: 15 minutes
Serves 4–6

3 tablespoons olive oil
1 onion, chopped
2 garlic cloves, crushed
500 g (1 lb 2 oz) fresh okra
　(see Note)

425 g (15 oz) tinned chopped
　tomatoes
2 teaspoons sugar
3 tablespoons lemon juice
55 g (2 oz/1¾ cups) fresh
　coriander (cilantro) leaves,
　finely chopped

1 Heat the oil in a large frying pan, add the onion and cook over medium heat for 4 minutes, or until transparent and golden. Add the garlic and cook for a further minute.

2 Add the okra and cook, stirring, for 4–5 minutes. Add the tomatoes, sugar and juice, and simmer, stirring occasionally, for 3–4 minutes, or until softened. Stir in the coriander, remove from the heat and serve.

COOK'S FILE

Note: If fresh okra is not available, use tinned (800 g/1 lb 12 oz). Rinse and drain before adding with the coriander.

Add the garlic to the onion and cook for a further minute.

Stir the okra into the onion mixture and simmer for a few minutes.

Stir in the tomato, sugar and lemon juice and simmer until softened.

STUFFED ZUCCHINI

Preparation time: 20 minutes
Total cooking time: 45 minutes
Serves 4

8 zucchini (courgettes)
35 g (1¼ oz) white bread, crusts
    removed
milk, for soaking
125 g (4 oz) ricotta cheese
3 tablespoons grated Cheddar
    cheese
4 tablespoons grated Parmesan

2 teaspoons chopped fresh
    oregano
2 teaspoons chopped fresh
    thyme
1 garlic clove, crushed
1 egg yolk

1 Preheat the oven to 190°C (375°F/ Gas 5). Cook the zucchini in boiling salted water for 5 minutes, then drain. Meanwhile, soak the bread in milk until soft, then squeeze dry. Cut the zucchini in half and scoop out the flesh with a teaspoon.

2 Chop the zucchini flesh finely. Place

in a bowl, add the bread, cheeses, herbs, garlic, egg yolk and season with salt and pepper. Mix together, adding a little milk to make it bind together if necessary.

3 Fill the zucchini shells with the stuffing. Brush an ovenproof baking dish with oil and arrange the zucchini close together. Bake in the oven for 35–40 minutes, until golden on top. Serve immediately.

Cut the zucchini in half and scoop out the flesh with a teaspoon.

Combine the zucchini, cheeses, herbs, garlic and egg yolk in a bowl.

Arrange the stuffed zucchini close together in the oiled baking dish.

SPINACH AND PANCETTA PIE

Preparation time: 30 minutes
Total cooking time: 55 minutes
Serves 4–6

45 g (1½ oz) butter
2 tablespoons olive oil
1 large onion, finely chopped
2 garlic cloves, finely chopped
125 g (4 oz) finely sliced
    pancetta, chopped
220 g (7¾ oz/1 cup) arborio rice
750 ml(26 fl oz/3 cups) beef
    stock
800 g (1 lb 10 oz) English
    spinach, coarsely chopped
4 eggs, lightly beaten
50 g (1¾ oz/½ cup) freshly
    grated Parmesan
1 teaspoon coarsely cracked
    black pepper
4 tablespoons dry breadcrumbs

1 Heat the butter and 1 tablespoon oil in a large frying pan and cook the onion for 3–4 minutes. Add the garlic and pancetta and cook for 1 minute.

2 Add the rice and stir to coat. Pour in half the stock, reduce the heat, cover and simmer for 8 minutes, adding the remaining stock gradually as it is absorbed. Continue cooking the rice until all the stock has been absorbed. Preheat the oven to 180°C (350°F/Gas 4).

3 Fold the spinach into the rice, cover and simmer for a further 2 minutes, or until just wilted. Transfer to a bowl and leave to cool a little. Stir in the eggs, Parmesan and cracked pepper.

4 Sprinkle a greased 23 cm (9 inch) springform tin with 3 tablespoons of the breadcrumbs. Spoon in the filling, drizzle with the remaining oil and sprinkle the remaining breadcrumbs over the top. Bake for 40–45 minutes, then cool in the tin. Cut into wedges and serve at room temperature.

Fry the onion in the butter and then add the garlic and pancetta.

Add a little stock from time to time as the liquid is absorbed.

When cooled a little, stir through the eggs, Parmesan and pepper.

Lightly grease a springform tin and then sprinkle with dry breadcrumbs.

COOK'S FILE

Note: Ready-made stock in a tetra pack is very good but can be salty: use half stock, half water.

RICOTTA LASAGNE

Preparation time: 1 hour
Total cooking time: 1 hour 30 minutes
Serves 8

500 g (1 lb) fresh spinach
    lasagne sheets
30 g (1 oz/½ cup) fresh basil
    leaves, coarsely chopped
2 tablespoons fresh
    breadcrumbs
3 tablespoons pine nuts
2 teaspoons paprika
1 tablespoon grated
    Parmesan

Ricotta filling
750 g (1½ lb) fresh ricotta
50 g (1¾ oz/½ cup) grated
    Parmesan
freshly ground black pepper
pinch of nutmeg

Tomato sauce
1 tablespoon olive oil
2 onions, chopped
2 garlic cloves, crushed
800 g (1 lb 10 oz) tinned
    tomatoes, crushed
1 tablespoon tomato paste
    (concentrated purée)

Béchamel sauce
60 g (2 oz) butter
60 g (2¼ oz/½ cup) plain
    (all-purpose) flour
500 ml (17 fl oz/2 cups) milk
2 eggs, lightly beaten
4 tablespoons grated Parmesan

1 Lightly grease a 25 x 32 cm (10 x 13 inch) baking dish. Cut the pasta sheets into large pieces and cook, 2–3 at a time, in boiling water for 3 minutes. Drain and spread on damp tea (dish) towels until needed.

2 To make ricotta filling, put the ricotta and Parmesan cheeses, pepper and nutmeg in a bowl and mix together. Set aside.

3 To make tomato sauce, heat the oil in a frying pan, add the onion and cook for about 10 minutes, stirring occasionally, until very soft. Add the garlic and cook for 1 more minute. Add the tomato and tomato paste and stir until well combined. Stir until the mixture comes to the boil. Reduce the heat and simmer uncovered for 15 minutes, or until thickened, stirring occasionally.

4 To make béchamel sauce, heat the butter in a small pan. When starting to foam, add the flour and stir for 3 minutes, or until just coloured. Remove from the heat; add the milk gradually, stirring after each addition, then return to the heat and stir until sauce boils and thickens. Remove from the heat and stir in the eggs. Return to moderate heat and stir until almost boiling, but do not boil. Add the cheese and season to taste. Put plastic wrap onto the surface to prevent a skin forming. Preheat the oven to 200°C (400°F/Gas 6).

5 Put a layer of lasagne sheets in the dish. Spread with a third of the ricotta filling, sprinkle with basil, then top with a third of the tomato sauce. Repeat layers, finishing with pasta.

6 Pour over the béchamel sauce, spread until smooth, then sprinkle with the combined breadcrumbs, pine nuts, paprika and Parmesan. Bake for 45 minutes, or until browned. Leave for 10 minutes before serving.

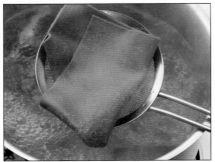

Cook the lasagne in a large pan of boiling water, 2–3 sheets at a time.

Simmer the tomato sauce, uncovered, for 15 minutes until it has thickened.

Stir the béchamel sauce until it boils and thickens.

Placing plastic wrap onto the surface of the sauce will stop a skin forming.

Use the back of a spoon to spread a layer of tomato sauce over the ricotta filling.

Sprinkle the pine nut and breadcrumb mixture over the béchamel sauce.

ITALIAN PEAR SALAD

Preparation time: 20 minutes
Total cooking time: Nil
Serves 4

4 ripe green or red pears
250 g (8 oz) bocconcini, sliced
4 thin slices prosciutto, cut into
   bite-sized pieces
4 fresh figs, quartered
3 tablespoons walnut pieces

Dressing
3 tablespoons extra virgin
   olive oil
¼ teaspoon finely grated
   lemon zest
1 tablespoon lemon juice
1 tablespoon chopped chives

1 Cut the pears into quarters and use a melon baller or teaspoon to remove the cores. Arrange the pears in a serving dish and scatter with the sliced bocconcini, prosciutto, figs and walnut pieces.

2 To make the dressing, put the oil, lemon zest and juice, and chives in a small bowl and whisk to combine. Season with salt and pepper, to taste. Drizzle the dressing over the salad and serve immediately.

COOK'S FILE

Note: If fresh figs are unavailable or out of season, use dried figs.

Using a large sharp knife, cut each bocconcini into about 4 slices.

Using a sharp knife, cut the fresh figs into quarters.

Cut the pears into quarters and use a melon bailer to remove the cores.

MEDITERRANEAN SALAD

Preparation time: 25 minutes
Total cooking time: 5 minutes
Serves 4–6

oil, for cooking
4 chorizo sausages, thickly
   sliced
150 g (5 oz) rocket
   (arugula)
2 red capsicums (peppers), cut
   into pieces
2 green capsicums (peppers), cut
   into pieces

1 fennel bulb, thinly sliced
4 Roma (plum) tomatoes, cut
   into wedges
2 Lebanese (short) cucumbers,
   sliced
300 g (10 oz) marinated
   artichokes, quartered
2 tablespoons chopped dill
250 g (8 oz) feta cheese, broken
   into large pieces

Dressing
1 teaspoon finely grated
   orange zest
3 tablespoons orange juice
2 teaspoons red wine vinegar

1 garlic clove, crushed
3 tablespoons olive oil

1 Heat a little oil in a non-stick frying pan. Fry the chorizo slices in batches until browned. Drain on paper towel.
2 Trim the coarse stems from the rocket and combine with the fried chorizo slices, capsicum, fennel, tomato, cucumber, artichokes, dill and feta in a bowl.
3 To make the dressing, put the orange zest and juice, vinegar, garlic and oil in a bowl, and whisk to combine. Pour over the salad and toss gently to coat.

Thickly slice the chorizo sausages, and cut the capsicums into large pieces.

Use your fingers to break the feta cheese into large pieces.

Fry the chorizo in a little oil, then drain on paper towels.

CAPSICUM FRITTATA

Preparation time: 15 minutes
Total cooking time: 40 minutes
Serves 4

660 g (1 lb 7 oz) jar pimiento pieces
4 rashers bacon, optional
1 tablespoon olive oil
2 medium red onions, finely chopped
6 eggs, lightly beaten
60 g (2¼ oz/½ cup) grated Cheddar cheese
50 g (1¾ oz/½ cup) grated Parmesan cheese

1 tablespoon plain (all-purpose) flour
3 tablespoons chopped fresh parsley

1 Preheat oven to 180°C (350°F/ Gas 4). Grease a 23 cm (9 inch) ovenproof pie plate. Rinse pimiento pieces, drain. Pat with paper towel. Cut into thin strips. Trim fat from bacon; place bacon on a cold grill (broiler) tray. Cook under medium-high heat until crisp. Drain on paper towels. Cut into small pieces.

2 Heat oil in medium pan. Add onions, cook over medium heat for 2 minutes. Remove and drain on paper towel.

3 Combine eggs, pimiento, bacon and onions. Add combined cheeses, flour and parsley. Season with salt and ½ teaspoon ground black pepper. Mix well. Spoon into prepared pie plate. Bake for 25–30 minutes, or until set and firm to touch. Serve hot or cold with a green salad and crusty bread.

COOK'S FILE

Hint: Pimiento is bottled red capsicum (pepper). Substitute 2 fresh red capsicum, grilled (broiled), if desired.

1

2

3

FILO VEGETABLE STRUDEL

Preparation time: 30 minutes
+ 30 minutes standing
Total cooking time: 1 hour 10 minutes
Serves 6–8

1 large eggplant (aubergine),
    sliced
1 red capsicum (pepper)
3 zucchini (courgettes), sliced
    lengthways
2 tablespoons olive oil
6 sheets filo pastry
50 g (1¾ oz) baby English
    spinach leaves
60 g (2 oz) feta cheese, sliced

1 Preheat the oven to 190°C (375°F/ Gas 5). Sprinkle the eggplant slices with a little salt and leave to drain in a colander for 30 minutes. Pat dry with paper towel.
2 Cut the capsicum into quarters and remove the seeds. Place, skin-side-up, under a medium grill (broil) for 10 minutes, or until soft and lightly browned, and then peel the skins away. Brush the eggplant and zucchini slices with olive oil and grill (broiler) for 5–10 minutes, or until golden brown. Set aside to cool.
3 Brush one sheet of filo pastry at a time with olive oil, then lay them on top of each other. Place half the eggplant slices lengthways down the centre of the filo, top with a layer of

zucchini, capsicum, spinach and feta cheese. Repeat the layers until the vegetables and cheese are used up. Tuck in the ends of the pastry, then roll up like a parcel; brush lightly with oil and place on a baking tray seam-side-down. Bake for 35 minutes, or until golden brown.

COOK'S FILE

Note: Unopened filo can be stored in the refrigerator for up to a month. Once opened, use within 2–3 days.

Cut a large eggplant into thin slices with a sharp knife.

Build up layers of eggplant, zucchini, capsicum, spinach and feta cheese.

Tuck in the ends of the pastry, then roll up like a parcel to make a strudel.

PEPPERONATA TART

Preparation time: 30 minutes + chilling
Total cooking time: 1 hour
Serves 4–6

310 g (11 oz/2½ cups) plain
    (all-purpose) flour
pinch of cayenne pepper
125 g (4 oz) butter, cubed
90 g (3 oz) cream cheese, cubed
1 egg yolk, beaten
1 tablespoon lemon juice

Filling
1 large red capsicum (pepper)
1 large green capsicum (pepper)
2 large yellow capsicums
    (pepper)
2 tablespoons olive oil
3 large onions, sliced into rings
400 g (12⅔ oz) tinned tomatoes,
    chopped
fresh thyme leaves, to garnish

1 Sift the flour, a pinch of salt and cayenne pepper into a food processor. Add the butter, cream cheese, combined egg yolk and lemon juice and process in short bursts, adding 2–3 tablespoons water, until the mixture forms a firm dough when pressed together. Turn onto a lightly floured surface and gather together into a ball. Wrap in plastic wrap and chill for 30 minutes. Roll out to fit a 25 cm (10 inch) greased spring-form tin, to cover the base and halfway up the side. Refrigerate for 30 minutes.
2 Preheat the oven to 200°C (400°F/ Gas 6). Put baking paper over the pastry and fill with rice or dried beans. Bake for 15 minutes, then reduce the oven to 180°C (350°F/Gas 4), remove the beans and paper and cook for 15–20 minutes, or until golden brown. Allow to cool.
3 To make filling, cut capsicums into large pieces and deseed. Place, skin-side-up, under a hot grill (broiler) until black. Cool under a tea (dish) towel. Remove the skins and chop the flesh.
4 Heat the oil and fry the onions for 3–4 minutes, or until soft. Add the tomatoes, capsicum and seasoning to taste. Cook over low heat for 10 minutes until the liquid has reduced. Cool, then spoon into the pastry case and sprinkle with thyme.

Process until the mixture forms a firm dough when pressed together.

Cooling the capsicum under a tea towel makes the skin easier to peel away.

Use uncooked rice, chickpeas or beans for blind baking pastry.

Spoon the capsicum and tomato filling into the pastry base.

FENNEL WITH PECORINO CHEESE

Preparation time: 15 minutes
Total cooking time: 25 minutes
Serves 4

4 fennel bulbs
1 garlic clove, crushed
½ lemon, sliced
2 tablespoons olive oil
1 teaspoon salt
3 tablespoons butter, melted
2 tablespoons grated pecorino
  cheese

1 Cut the top shoots and base off the fennel and remove the tough outer layers. Cut into segments and place in a pan with the garlic, lemon, oil and salt. Cover with water and bring to the boil. Reduce the heat and simmer for 20 minutes, or until just tender.

2 Drain well and place in a heatproof dish. Drizzle with the butter. Sprinkle with the cheese and season with salt and pepper to taste.
3 Place under a preheated grill (broiler) until the cheese has browned. Best served immediately.

COOK'S FILE

Note: If pecorino (a hard sheep's milk cheese) is not available, then use Parmesan instead.

Trim the tops and bases from the fennel and remove the tough outer layers.

Place the fennel, garlic, lemon, oil and salt in a pan.

Sprinkle grated pecorino cheese over the fennel and brown under a grill.

BAKED MUSHROOMS

Preparation time: 15 minutes
Total cooking time: 15 minutes
Serves 4

250 g (8 oz) button mushrooms
200 g (6½ oz) oyster mushrooms
200 g (6½ oz) shiitake
  mushrooms
100 g (3⅓ oz) Swiss brown
  mushrooms

Topping
80 g (2¾ oz/1 cup) fresh
  breadcrumbs

3 tablespoons freshly grated
  Parmesan
2 tablespoons chopped fresh
  flat-leaf (Italian) parsley
1 tablespoon chopped fresh
  thyme
2 garlic cloves, crushed
1 teaspoon cracked pepper
2 tablespoons extra virgin olive
  oil

1 Preheat the oven to 180°C (350°F/
Gas 4). Wipe the mushrooms with a
damp paper towel. Trim away the hard
tips and discard. Cut any large
mushrooms in half lengthways.
2 Sprinkle the base of a large baking

dish with a little water. Place the
mushrooms in a single layer in the
dish, stems upwards.
3 To make topping, mix together the
breadcrumbs, Parmesan, herbs, garlic
and pepper, sprinkle over the
mushrooms and drizzle with oil. Bake
for 12–15 minutes and serve warm.

COOK'S FILE

Note: Use day-old bread which is
slightly stale to make breadcrumbs.
Simply remove the crusts and chop in
a food processor until crumbs form.
Hint: Always wipe mushrooms clean
with a damp paper towel—washing
will make them soggy.

*Trim the hard tips from the stalks and cut
any large mushrooms in half.*

*Place the mushrooms, stems upwards, in
one layer in a baking dish.*

*Mix together the breadcrumbs, cheese,
herbs, garlic and pepper.*

Put the spinach, cheese, pepper and nutmeg in a bowl and mix well.

Cook until both sides of the pancake are golden, then remove with a spatula.

Remove from the heat and add salt and pepper, to taste, and grated cheese.

Divide the filling among the pancakes and roll up.

CHEESE AND SPINACH PANCAKES

Preparation time: 40 minutes
Total cooking time: 50 minutes
Serves 4

250 g (8 oz) cooked, drained
  English spinach, chopped
125 g (4½ oz/½ cup) ricotta
  cheese
3 tablespoons grated Cheddar
  cheese
ground black pepper
freshly grated nutmeg
3 tablespoons grated Parmesan
  cheese
½ teaspoon paprika
40 g (1½ oz/½ cup) fresh
  breadcrumbs

Batter
125 g (4½ oz/1 cup) plain
  (all-purpose) flour
310 ml (10¾ fl oz/1¼ cups) milk
1 egg
butter, for cooking

Cheese sauce
2 tablespoons butter
3 tablespoons plain (all-purpose)
  flour
440 ml (15¼ fl oz/1¾ cups) milk
125 g (4½ oz/1 cup) grated
  Cheddar cheese

1 Put the spinach, cheeses, pepper and nutmeg in a bowl and mix well.
2 To make batter, sift the flour and a pinch of salt into a bowl. Add half the milk and the egg. Whisk until smooth; add the remaining milk. Heat a teaspoon of butter in a frying pan and pour in a thin layer of batter. Cook the base until golden, then flip. The batter should make 8 pancakes.
3 To make cheese sauce, melt butter over low heat, add flour and cook for 1 minute. Remove from heat and slowly stir in milk. Return to heat and bring to the boil, stirring constantly. Remove from the heat and add the salt and pepper and the grated cheese.
4 Preheat the oven to 180°C (350°F/ Gas 4). Divide the filling among the pancakes, roll up and put in a greased ovenproof dish. Pour cheese sauce

over the pancakes. Mix the Parmesan, paprika and breadcrumbs together and sprinkle over the sauce. Bake for 30 minutes, or until golden brown.

VEGETABLE TAGINE WITH COUSCOUS

Preparation time: 25 minutes
Total cooking time: 45 minutes
Serves 6

¼ teaspoon saffron threads
2 tablespoons olive oil
2 onions, thinly sliced
3 garlic cloves, crushed
2 thin carrots, cut into 5 mm
    (¼ inch) slices
1 cinnamon stick
2 teaspoons ground cumin
1 teaspoon ground ginger
½ teaspoon ground turmeric
½ teaspoon cayenne pepper
300 g (10½ oz) pumpkin, cut
    into 2 cm (¾ inch) cubes
4 ripe tomatoes, peeled,
    deseeded and quartered
400 g (14 oz) tinned chickpeas,
    drained and rinsed
500 ml (17 fl oz/2 cups)
    vegetable stock
1 zucchini (courgette), halved
    lengthways then cut into 1 cm
    (½ inch) slices
4 tablespoons raisins
50 g (1¾ oz/1 cup) roughly
    chopped coriander (cilantro)
    leaves
2 tablespoons flaked almonds,
    toasted

Couscous
500 ml (17 fl oz/2 cups)
    vegetable stock
500 g (1 lb 2 oz) instant couscous
1 tablespoon olive oil
2 teaspoons low-fat margarine

1 Dry-fry the saffron threads in a small frying pan over low heat for

1 minute, or until darkened. Remove from the heat and cool.

2 Heat the oil in a large flameproof casserole dish. Add the onion, garlic, carrot, cinnamon stick, ground cumin, ground ginger, ground turmeric, cayenne and saffron. Cook over medium–low heat, stirring often, for 10 minutes. Add the pumpkin, tomato and chickpeas. Stir to coat. Add the stock, then bring to the boil. Cover and simmer for 10 minutes. Stir in the zucchini, raisins and half the coriander. Cover and simmer for a further 20 minutes.

3 To make the couscous, bring the stock to the boil in a large saucepan. Place the couscous in a large heatproof bowl and add the oil and the hot stock. Cover and leave for 5 minutes, then fluff the grains with a fork. Stir in the margarine and season.

4 Spoon the couscous onto a large serving platter. Spoon the vegetables and sauce on top and sprinkle with the almonds and the remaining coriander. Serve at once.

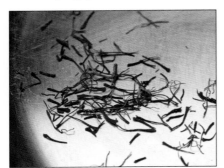

Fry the saffron threads in a dry frying pan until darkened.

Stir in the pumpkin cubes, tomato and chickpeas until they are well coated.

Stir the margarine into the couscous with a fork.

Roll the dough into long even-sized ropes, then cut it into pieces.

Place a piece of dough in your palm and press gently with the tines of a fork.

RICOTTA AND HERB GNOCCHI WITH FRESH TOMATO SAUCE

Preparation time: 40 minutes + 1 hour chilling
Total cooking time: 30 minutes
Serves 4

Gnocchi
450 g (1 lb) reduced-fat ricotta
   cheese
4 tablespoons grated fresh
   Parmesan cheese
20 g (¾ oz/½ cup) chopped
   mixed fresh herbs (parsley,
   basil, chives, thyme,
   oregano)
pinch of nutmeg
120 g(4¼ oz/1½ cups) fresh
   white breadcrumbs
2 small eggs, beaten
plain (all-purpose) flour,
   for rolling

Tomato Sauce
1 tablespoon olive oil
1 onion, finely chopped
2 garlic cloves, crushed
125 ml (4 fl oz/½ cup) dry
   white wine

800 g (1 lb/12 oz) ripe tomatoes,
   peeled, deseeded and diced
1 tablespoon shredded basil

1 To make the gnocchi, combine the ricotta, Parmesan, herbs, nutmeg, breadcrumbs and egg in a bowl. Season well. Cover and chill for at least 1 hour.

2 To make the tomato sauce, heat the oil in a large frying pan. Add the onion and garlic and gently cook over low heat without browning for 6–7 minutes, or until softened. Add the wine, increase the heat and cook until it has almost evaporated. Add the tomatoes, reduce the heat to medium and simmer for 5–8 minutes, or until the sauce has reduced and thickened a little. Season well with salt and pepper, then stir in the basil. Keep warm.

3 Remove the gnocchi mixture from the refrigerator and transfer to a lightly floured work surface. Knead gently, working in a little flour if you find it is sticking to your hands–the dough should be light and soft, a little damp to touch, but not sticky. Take about one-fifth of the dough and roll it with your hands on the lightly floured work surface to form a long, even rope the thickness of your ring finger. Cut into 2 cm (¾ inch) pieces. Place a piece in the palm of your hand and, using the tines of a fork, press gently with your fingers, flipping the gnocchi as you do so–it will be rounded into a concave shell shape, ridged on the outer surface. Place on a tray lined with baking paper and continue with the remaining dough.

4 Cook the gnocchi in a large saucepan of boiling salted water in batches. The gnocchi are cooked when they all rise to the surface after 2–3 minutes. Remove with a slotted spoon and drain well. Keep warm while cooking the remainder.

5 Place the gnocchi in a serving bowl, spoon on the sauce. Garnish with extra grated Parmesan, if desired.

MUSHROOMS IN TOMATO SAUCE

Preparation time: 15 minutes
Total cooking time: 20 minutes
Serves 4 as a side dish

2 tablespoons olive oil
2 garlic cloves, sliced
600 g (1¼ lb) large button

mushrooms, halved
2 tablespoons tomato paste
  (concentrated purée)
2 tablespoons chopped fresh
  marjoram
250 g (8 oz) cherry tomatoes,
  halved
freshly ground black
  pepper
1 tablespoon chopped fresh
  oregano leaves

1 Heat the oil in a pan, add the garlic and stir over moderate heat for 1 minute; do not brown.
2 Add the mushrooms and cook, stirring, for 5 minutes, until combined and beginning to soften.
3 Stir through the tomato paste, marjoram and cherry tomatoes and cook over low heat until the mushrooms are soft. Serve sprinkled with pepper and oregano leaves.

Stir the garlic over medium heat until fragrant but not browned.

Add the mushrooms to the pan and stir until they begin to soften.

Cook over low heat until the mushrooms are soft.

Cook the leek until soft, then add the stock, thyme and potato.

Lift out half the potato with tongs and put into an ovenproof dish.

Spoon the leek and stock mixture around the side, trying to keep the top dry.

Bake, uncovered, until the potatoes on top are golden brown.

OVEN-BAKED POTATO, LEEK AND OLIVES

Preparation time: 20 minutes
Total cooking time: 1 hour
Serves 4–6

2 tablespoons extra virgin
   olive oil
1 leek, finely sliced
375 ml (13 fl oz/1½ cups)
   chicken stock
2 teaspoons chopped fresh
   thyme
1 kg (2 lb) potatoes, unpeeled,
   cut into thin slices
6–8 pitted black olives, sliced
50 g (1¾ oz/½ cup) freshly
   grated Parmesan cheese
30 g (1 oz) butter, chopped

1 Preheat the oven to 180°C (350°F/ Gas 4). Brush a shallow 1.25 litre (5 cup) ovenproof dish with a little olive oil. Heat the remaining oil in a large pan and cook the leek over moderate heat until soft. Add the stock, thyme and potato. Cover and leave to simmer for 5 minutes.

2 Using tongs, lift out half the potato and put in the ovenproof dish. Sprinkle with olives and Parmesan and season with salt and pepper.

3 Layer with the remaining potato, then spoon the leek and stock mixture in at the side of the dish, keeping the top dry.

4 Scatter chopped butter over the potato and then bake, uncovered, for 50 minutes, or until cooked and golden brown. Leave in a warm place for about 10 minutes before serving.

COOK'S FILE

Note: Keeping the top layer of potato dry as you pour in the stock mixture will give it a crisp finish.

CARAWAY POLENTA WITH BRAISED LEEKS

Preparation time: 10 minutes
Total cooking time: 30 minutes
Serves 4

1.5 litres (6 cups) chicken stock
225 g (8 oz/1½ cups) polenta
 (cornmeal)
2 teaspoons caraway seeds
45 g (1½ oz) butter

2 large leeks, cut into thin strips
250 g (9 oz) Italian Fontina
 cheese, cut into cubes

1 Place the stock in a large heavy-based pan and bring to the boil. Pour in the polenta in a fine stream, stirring continuously. Add the caraway seeds and then reduce the heat and simmer for about 20–25 minutes, or until the polenta is very soft.
2 Melt the butter in a frying pan over moderate heat and add the leeks.

Cover and cook gently, stirring occasionally, until wilted. Add the Fontina cubes, stir a couple of times and remove from the heat.
3 Pour the polenta onto individual plates in nest shapes and spoon the leeks and cheese into the centre.

COOK'S FILE

Hint: Ready-made stock can be quite salty, so use half stock, half water.

Use a sharp knife to cut the leeks into very thin, long strips.

Bring the stock to the boil, then pour in the polenta, stirring continuously.

Cook the leeks in the butter until wilted, then stir in the cheese.

When the pancetta starts to curl at the edges, add the peas and half the wine.

Put the stock and water in a separate pan and keep at simmering point.

Fry the onion in the butter and then add the rice and stir until well combined.

Once the rice is cooked, stir in the pea mixture and Parmesan cheese.

PEA AND PANCETTA RISOTTO

Preparation time: 25 minutes
Total cooking time: 45 minutes
Serves 4

1 tablespoon olive oil
1 celery stalk, chopped
2 tablespoons chopped fresh
  flat-leaf (Italian) parsley
freshly ground black pepper
75 g (2½ oz) sliced pancetta,
  coarsely chopped
250 g (8 oz) peas (fresh or
  frozen)
125 ml (4 fl oz/½ cup) dry white
  wine
750 ml (26 fl oz/3 cups) chicken
  stock
60 g (2 oz) butter
1 onion, chopped
440 g (15½ oz/2 cups) arborio
  rice
4 tablespoons freshly grated
  Parmesan cheese

1 Heat the oil in a frying pan, add the celery, parsley and black pepper and cook over medium heat for a few minutes to soften the celery. Add the pancetta and stir until it just begins to curl. Add the peas and half the wine, bring to the boil, then reduce the heat and simmer uncovered until almost all the liquid has evaporated. Set aside.
2 Put stock and 750 ml (26 fl oz/ 3 cups) water in a separate pan and keep at simmering point.
3 Heat the butter in a large heavy-based saucepan. Add the onion and stir until softened. Add the rice and stir well. Pour in the remaining wine; allow it to bubble and evaporate. Add 125 ml (4 fl oz/½ cup) hot stock to the rice mixture. Stir constantly over low heat, with a wooden spoon, until all the stock has been absorbed. Repeat the process until all the stock has been added and the rice is creamy and tender (about 25–30 minutes).
4 Add the pea mixture and Parmesan and serve immediately. Serve with Parmesan shavings and black pepper.

FATTOUSH

Preparation time: 15 minutes
Total cooking time: 10 minutes
Serves 6

2 pitta bread rounds (17 cm/
   7 inch)
6 cos (romaine) lettuce leaves,
   shredded
1 large Lebanese (short)
   cucumber, cubed
4 tomatoes, cut into 1 cm
   (½ inch) cubes
8 spring onions (scallions),
   chopped

4 tablespoons finely chopped
   fresh flat-leaf (Italian)
   parsley
1 tablespoon finely chopped
   fresh mint
2 tablespoons finely chopped
   fresh coriander (cilantro)

Dressing
2 garlic cloves, crushed
100 ml (3½ fl oz) extra virgin
   olive oil
100 ml (3½ fl oz) lemon juice

1 Preheat the oven to 180°C (350°F/
Gas 4). Split the bread in half through
the centre and bake on a baking tray

for 8–10 minutes, or until golden and
crisp, turning halfway through. Break
into pieces.
2 To make the dressing, whisk all the
ingredients together until combined.
3 Place the bread and remaining
salad ingredients in a serving bowl
and toss to combine. Pour on the
dressing and toss well. Season. Serve
immediately.

COOK'S FILE

Note: This is a popular Middle
Eastern peasant salad which is served
as an appetizer or to accompany a
light meal.

*Split the pitta bread rounds in two through
the centre.*

*Once the bread is golden and crisp, break it
into small pieces.*

*Place the bread pieces and salad ingredients
in a bowl and toss well.*

ROASTED FENNEL AND ORANGE SALAD

Preparation time: 30 minutes
Total cooking time: 1 hour
Serves 4

8 baby fennel bulbs
100 ml (3½ fl oz) olive oil
1 teaspoon sea salt
2 oranges
1 tablespoon lemon juice
1 red onion, halved and thinly
    sliced
100 g (3½ oz) Kalamata olives
2 tablespoons chopped fresh
    mint
1 tablespoon roughly chopped
    fresh flat-leaf (Italian)
    parsley

1 Preheat the oven to 200°C (400°F/ Gas 6). Trim and reserve the fennel fronds. Remove the stalks and cut a 5 mm (¼ inch) slice off the base of each fennel bulb. Slice each fennel into 6 wedges. Place in a baking dish and drizzle with 3 tablespoons of the oil. Add the salt and plenty of pepper. Bake for 40–60 minutes, or until the fennel is tender and slightly caramelized. Cool.

2 Cut a slice off the top and bottom of each orange. Using a small sharp knife, slice off the skin and pith, following the curves of the orange. Remove as much pith as possible. Slice down the side of a segment between the flesh and the membrane. Repeat with the other side and lift the segment out. Do this over a bowl to catch the segments and juices. Repeat with all the segments. Squeeze any juice from the membrane. Drain and reserve the juice.

3 Whisk the remaining olive oil into the orange juice and the lemon juice until emulsified. Season well. Combine the orange segments, onion and olives in a bowl, pour on half the dressing and add half the mint. Mix well. Transfer to a serving dish. Top with the roasted fennel, drizzle with the remaining dressing, and scatter with the parsley and the remaining mint. Roughly chop the reserved fronds and scatter over the salad.

Use a sharp knife to slice each of the baby fennels into wedges.

Bake the fennel until tender and slightly caramelized.

Remove the orange skin and pith with a small sharp knife.

Cut the orange between the flesh and the membrane to remove the segments.

SPANOKOPITA

Preparation time: 25 minutes
+ cooling
Total cooking time: 1 hour
Serves 4–6

1.5 kg (3 lb 5 oz) silverbeet
   (Swiss chard)
3 tablespoons olive oil
1 white onion, finely chopped
10 spring onions (scallions),
   chopped (include some green)
1½ tablespoons chopped fresh
   dill
200 g (7 oz) Greek feta,
   crumbled
125 g (4½ oz) cottage cheese
3 tablespoons finely grated
   kefalotyri cheese (see Note)
¼ teaspoon ground nutmeg
4 eggs, lightly beaten
10 sheets filo pastry
80 g (2¾ oz) butter, melted, for
   brushing

1 Rinse and drain the silverbeet thoroughly. Discard the stems and shred the leaves. Heat the olive oil in a large frying pan, add the onion and cook, stirring, over medium heat for 5 minutes, or until softened. Add the spring onion and silverbeet and cook, covered, over medium heat for 5 minutes. Add the dill and cook, uncovered, for 3–4 minutes, or until most of the liquid has evaporated. Remove from the heat and cool to room temperature.

2 Preheat the oven to 180°C (350°F/ Gas 4) and grease a 20 x 25 cm (8 x 10 inch) 2.5 litre (10 cups) baking dish. Place the cheeses in a bowl, stir in the silverbeet mixture; add the nutmeg. Gradually add the egg; beat after each addition. Season.

3 Line the base and sides of the baking dish with a sheet of filo pastry. Brush with butter and cover with another sheet. Repeat using five sheets. Spoon in the filling and level the surface. Fold any exposed pastry up and over to cover the filling. Cover with a sheet of filo, brush with butter and continue until all the sheets are used. Roughly trim the pastry with kitchen scissors then tuck the excess inside the wall of the dish.

4 Brush the top with butter. Using a sharp knife, score the surface into diamonds. Sprinkle a few drops of cold water on top to discourage the pastry from curling. Bake for 45 minutes, or until the pastry is puffed and golden. Leave to rest at room temperature for 10 minutes before serving.

COOK'S FILE

Note: Use pecorino cheese if kefalotyri is unavailable.

Spoon the spinach and cheese mixture into the filo-lined dish.

Cover with the remaining filo pastry sheets, then tuck in the excess pastry.

GREEN BEANS WITH TOMATO AND OLIVE OIL

Preparation time: 10 minutes
Total cooking time: 25 minutes
Serves 4

4 tablespoons olive oil
1 large onion, chopped
3 garlic cloves, finely
   chopped

400 g (14 oz) tinned tomatoes,
   diced
½ teaspoon sugar
750 g (1 lb 10 oz) green beans,
   trimmed
3 tablespoons chopped fresh
   flat- leaf (Italian) parsley

1 Heat the olive oil in a large frying pan, add the onion and cook over medium heat for 4–5 minutes, or until softened. Add the garlic and cook for a further 30 seconds.
2 Add 125 ml (4 fl oz/½ cup) water, the tomatoes and sugar. Season. Bring to the boil. Reduce the heat and simmer for 10 minutes, or until reduced slightly.
3 Add the beans and parsley and simmer for a further 10 minutes, or until the beans are tender and the tomato mixture is pulpy. Season with salt and black pepper, and serve immediately as a side dish.

Using a sharp knife, finely chop the garlic cloves.

Cook the chopped onion in the olive oil until softened.

Simmer the tomato mixture until reduced slightly.

SPAGHETTI PRIMAVERA

Preparation time: 15 minutes
Cooking time: 15 minutes
Serves 4

400 g (14 oz) spaghetti
4 tablespoons extra virgin
  olive oil
200 g (7 oz) fresh asparagus,
  trimmed and cut into 5 cm
  (2 inch) lengths
155 g (5½ oz/1 cup) frozen
  peas
155 g (5½ oz/1 cup) frozen
  broad (fava) beans
1 leek, thinly sliced

2 tablespoons finely chopped
  fresh flat-leaf (Italian)
  parsley
250 ml (9 fl oz/1 cup) thick
  (double/heavy) cream
4 tablespoons grated Parmesan
  cheese

1 Cook the pasta in a large saucepan of boiling water until al dente. Rinse and drain well, then return to the pan, toss with 2 tablespoons of the oil and keep warm.
2 Meanwhile, bring a saucepan of water to the boil and cook the asparagus and peas for 2 minutes, or until bright green and tender. Remove with a slotted spoon and plunge into

cold water. Return the pan to the boil and cook the broad beans for 2 minutes, or until tender. Drain, cool, then slip off their skins.
3 Heat the remaining oil in a frying pan and cook the leek over low heat for 2–3 minutes, or until soft but not brown. Add the blanched vegetables and cook for 1 minute, or until warmed through. Stir in the parsley and cream and simmer for 2–3 minutes. Toss the sauce and Parmesan through the pasta, season well and serve.

COOK'S FILE

Note: If fresh broad beans and peas are in season, use them and peel the pods before cooking.

1

2

3

ROASTED VEGETABLE AND FETA TARTS

Preparation time: 1 hour
Total cooking time: 1 hour
Serves 6

1 small red capsicum (pepper),
   cubed
1 small yellow capsicum
   (pepper), cubed
300 g (10 oz) eggplant
   (aubergine), cubed
2 zucchini (courgettes), sliced
125 g (4 oz) cherry tomatoes
3 garlic cloves, crushed
2 tablespoons olive oil
1 teaspoon cumin seeds
3–4 sheets ready-rolled
   shortcrust pastry
300 g (10 oz) feta cheese
300 g (10 oz) ricotta cheese
2 teaspoons balsamic vinegar
1 tablespoon chopped parsley

1 Preheat the oven to 200°C (400°F/ Gas 6). Place the capsicum, eggplant, zucchini and tomatoes in a baking dish lined with baking paper. Mix together the garlic, olive oil, cumin seeds and a pinch of salt. Drizzle over the vegetables. Roast for about 30 minutes, or until tender.
2 Line twelve 8 cm (3 inch) fluted loose-based flan (tart) tins with the pastry, pressing it well into the sides, and trim off any excess. Prick the bases with a fork and bake for 10 minutes, or until cooked and golden.
3 Mash together the feta and ricotta cheeses with a fork until smooth. Spoon into the tart shells and smooth with the back of a spoon dipped in hot water. Bake for 15–20 minutes, or until golden and warmed through.
4 Drizzle the balsamic vinegar over the roasted vegetables and mix well. Then spoon into each cooked tart and sprinkle with parsley.

COOK'S FILE

Hint: If you roll out all the trimmings from the pastry to line some of the tins you should only need to use 3 sheets of ready-rolled shortcrust (pie) pastry overall, otherwise use 4 sheets and keep the trimmings for another recipe.

Cut the vegetables into small cubes before roasting.

Drizzle the flavoured oil over the chopped vegetables and roast until tender.

Prick the pastry bases all over with a fork and bake until golden.

Smooth the cheese filling with the back of a spoon dipped in hot water.

ARTICHOKES WITH LEMON AND GARLIC

Preparation time: 40 minutes
Total cooking time: 50–60 minutes
Serves 2–4

4 small globe artichokes
1 tablespoon lemon juice

Dressing
1 lemon
3 tablespoons olive oil
2 tablespoons herbed or
    balsamic vinegar
2 teaspoons soft brown sugar
1 tablespoon fresh thyme leaves
salt and cracked black pepper
    to taste

155 g (5½ oz/1 cup) fresh or
    frozen broad (fava) beans
6–8 large garlic cloves
1 tablespoon olive oil
caper berries for garnish

1 Lightly trim stalks of artichokes. Trim outer points of leaves. Cut artichokes in half lengthways. Sprinkle cut surfaces with lemon juice. Steam artichokes for 30 minutes or until tender; top up pan with extra boiling water if necessary. Remove from heat and set aside to cool.
2 To make dressing, place lemon in microwave oven for 30 seconds on high. (If a microwave is unavailable, plunge lemon into a bowl of boiling water for 1 minute; drain.) Squeeze lemon all over to soften. Cut into 5 mm

(¼ inch) slices and place in a large screwtop jar. Add the oil, vinegar, sugar, thyme, and salt and pepper. Place lid on jar and shake vigorously to combine ingredients.
3 Steam, microwave or boil broad beans until they are just tender. Plunge into a bowl of iced water to retain colour; peel if desired. Drain.
Place garlic in a small baking dish, drizzle with oil. Bake in a preheated oven at a temperature of 180°C (350°F/ Gas 4) for 30–40 minutes. Arrange the artichokes and broad beans on a serving platter. Drizzle with dressing, placing lemon slices between artichokes. Scatter caper berries and roasted garlic over top of artichokes.

1

2

3

TABBOULEH

Preparation time: 20 minutes + 1 hour
  30 minutes soaking + 30 minutes
  drying
Total cooking time: Nil
Serves 6

130 g (4½ oz/¾ cup) burghul
  (bulgar)
3 ripe tomatoes (300 g/10½ oz)
1 telegraph (long) cucumber
4 spring onions (scallions),
  sliced
120 g (4¼ oz/4 cups) chopped
  fresh flat-leaf (Italian)
  parsley
10 g (¼ oz/½ cup) fresh mint,
  chopped

Dressing
4 tablespoons lemon juice
3 tablespoons olive oil
1 tablespoon extra virgin
  olive oil

1 Place the burghul in a bowl, cover with 500 ml (17 fl oz/2 cups) water and leave for 1 hour 30 minutes.
2 Cut the tomatoes in half, squeeze gently to remove any excess seeds and cut into 1 cm (½ inch) cubes. Cut the cucumber in half lengthways, remove the seeds with a teaspoon and cut the flesh into 1 cm (½ inch) cubes.
3 To make the dressing, whisk the lemon juice and 1½ teaspoons salt in a bowl until well combined. Season well with freshly ground black pepper and slowly whisk in the olive oil and extra virgin olive oil.
4 Drain the burghul and squeeze out any excess water. Spread the burghul on a clean tea (dish) towel or paper towel and leave to dry for 30 minutes.

Place the burghul in a large salad bowl, add the tomato, cucumber, spring onion and herbs, and toss to combine. Pour the dressing over the salad and toss until evenly coated. Delicious served with bread.

Whisk the olive oil and extra virgin olive oil into the lemon juice.

Drain the burghul and squeeze out any excess water.

Toss the salad ingredients together before adding the dressing.

ROAST TOMATO, EGG AND SALAMI SALAD

Preparation time: 15 minutes
Total cooking time: 30 minutes
Serves 6

12 Roma (plum) tomatoes, halved lengthways
1 bulb garlic, cloves separated
1 teaspoon fine sea salt flakes
8 eggs, hard-boiled and quartered

100 g (3¼ oz) marinated black olives
50 g (1¾ oz) spicy salami, sliced into thin strips
3 spring onions (scallions), sliced
2 tablespoons shredded basil leaves
2 tablespoons extra virgin olive oil
2 tablespoons balsamic vinegar

1 Preheat the oven to 200°C (400°F/Gas 6). Put the tomato halves and garlic on a baking tray, sprinkle with the sea salt and some cracked black pepper and bake for 30 minutes, or until tender.

2 Arrange the tomato halves on a serving platter, top with the garlic, hard-boiled eggs, olives, salami, spring onion and basil.

3 Drizzle the olive oil and balsamic vinegar over the salad. Serve the salad hot or cold.

Pull the bulb of garlic apart to separate the individual cloves.

Slice the spring onions, and shred the basil leaves.

Sprinkle the tomato halves and garlic cloves with the sea salt flakes.

MEDITERRANEAN PASTA SALAD WITH BLACK OLIVE DRESSING

Preparation time: 30 minutes
Total cooking time: 25 minutes
Serves 4

250 g (8 oz) fusilli pasta
1 red capsicum (pepper)
1 yellow or green capsicum
  (pepper)
1 tablespoon sunflower oil
2 tablespoons olive oil
2 garlic cloves, crushed
1 eggplant (aubergine), cubed
2 zucchini (courgettes), thickly
  sliced
2 large ripe tomatoes, peeled,
  deseeded and chopped
3 tablespoons chopped flat-leaf
  (Italian) parsley
1 teaspoon seasoned pepper
150 g (5 oz) feta cheese,
  crumbled

Black olive dressing
6 large marinated black olives,
  pitted
125 ml (4 fl oz/½ cup) olive oil
2 tablespoons balsamic vinegar

1 Add the fusilli pasta to a large pan of gently boiling water and cook for 10–12 minutes, or until al dente. Drain, spread in a single layer on a baking tray to dry, then refrigerate, uncovered, until chilled.
2 Cut the red and yellow capsicum in half lengthways, removing the seeds and white membrane, then cut into large pieces. Place, skin-side-up, under a hot grill (broiler) until the skin blackens and blisters. Leave under a tea (dish) towel or in a plastic bag to

cool, then peel away and discard the skin. Slice the flesh into thick strips.
3 Heat the sunflower and olive oil in a frying pan. Add the garlic and eggplant and fry quickly, tossing constantly, until lightly browned. Remove from the heat and place in a large bowl. Steam or microwave the zucchini for 1–2 minutes, or until just tender. Rinse under cold water, drain, and add to the eggplant.
4 To make the dressing, process the olives in a food processor until finely

chopped. Gradually add the olive oil, processing until thoroughly combined after each addition. Add the vinegar, season with salt and ground black pepper and process to combine.
5 Combine the pasta, capsicum, eggplant, zucchini, tomato, parsley and pepper in a large bowl. Spoon onto individual serving plates or a large salad platter, top with the feta cheese and drizzle with the dressing.

Drain the cooked pasta and spread on a tray to dry.

Remove the seeds and white membrane from the halved capsicums.

Fry the cubed eggplant quickly until it is lightly browned.

Dissolve the sugar in the water, add the yeast and leave until frothy.

Cook the onions in the oil until they are soft and golden.

Knead the dough on a floured surface for about 10 minutes, until smooth.

Spread the cooked onion over the pizza base and then scatter with olives.

OLIVE AND ONION TART

Preparation time: 25 minutes
Total cooking time: 35–40 minutes
Serves 4–6

1 teaspoon sugar
1½ teaspoons dried yeast
125 ml (4 fl oz/½ cup) olive oil
5 onions, thinly sliced
125 g (4½ oz/1 cup) self-raising
   flour
60 g (2¼ oz/½ cup) plain
   (all-purpose) flour
185 g (6½ oz/1 cup) black olives
2 tablespoons grated Parmesan
   cheese

1 Dissolve sugar in 125 ml (4 fl oz/ ½ cup) warm water. Sprinkle with yeast and leave for 10 minutes, or until frothy.
2 Heat 3 tablespoons oil in a frying pan and fry the onion for 10 minutes, or until soft. Leave to cool. Preheat the oven to 220°C (425°F/Gas 7).
3 Sift together the self-raising flour, plain flour and a good pinch of salt in a bowl. Make a well in the centre and pour in the yeast mixture and 2 tablespoons oil. Bring together to form a dough and knead on a lightly floured surface for 10 minutes, or until smooth. Extra flour may be necessary.
4 Roll out the dough to line a greased 30 cm (12 inch) pizza tray. Spread with

cooked onions then olives. Brush the crust with the remaining olive oil. Bake for 25–30 minutes. Serve hot or cold sprinkled with grated Parmesan.

MEDITERRANEAN QUICHE

Preparation time: 50 minutes +
  15 minutes refrigeration
Total cooking time: 1 hour 25 minutes
Serves 6–8

2 sheets ready-rolled shortcrust
  (pie) pastry
3 tablespoons olive oil
2 garlic cloves, crushed
1 medium onion, diced
1 small fresh chilli, deseeded
  and finely chopped
1 red capsicum (pepper),
  chopped into bite-sized pieces
1 yellow capsicum (pepper),
  chopped into bite-sized pieces
400 g (13 oz) tinned tomatoes,
  drained and chopped
2 tablespoons chopped oregano
4 eggs, lightly beaten
4 tablespoons freshly grated
  Parmesan cheese

1 Grease a loose-based fluted flan (tart) tin measuring 22.5 cm (8¾ inches) across the base. Place the 2 sheets of pastry so that they are slightly overlapping and roll out until large enough to fit the prepared tin. Press well into the sides and trim off any excess using a sharp knife. Cover and chill for 15 minutes. Preheat the oven to 190°C (375°F/Gas 5). Cover the pastry shell with baking paper and fill evenly with baking beads or rice. Bake for 10 minutes. Remove the paper and rice and bake for a further 10 minutes, or until golden. Cool on a wire rack.

2 Heat the oil and fry the garlic and onion until soft. Add the chilli, red and yellow capsicum and cook for 6 minutes. Stir in the tomatoes and oregano and simmer, covered, for 10 minutes. Remove the lid and cook until the liquid has evaporated. Remove from the heat and cool.

3 Stir the eggs and Parmesan into the tomato mixture and spoon into the pastry shell. Bake for 35–45 minutes, or until the filling has set.

Remove the baking paper and rice from the pastry shell.

Add the finely chopped chilli and cubed red and yellow capsicum.

Cook the vegetables until the liquid has evaporated.

Spoon the filling mixture evenly into the pastry case.

Bread and pizza

GREEK OLIVE BREAD

Preparation time: 30 minutes + 2 hour
  30 minutes rising
Total cooking time: 35 minutes
Makes 1 loaf

375 g (13 oz/3 cups) plain
  (all-purpose) flour
7 g (¼ oz) sachet dry yeast
2 teaspoons sugar
2 tablespoons olive oil
110 g (3¾ oz) Kalamata olives,
  pitted, halved
2 teaspoons plain (all-purpose)
  flour, extra
1 small sprig fresh oregano,
  leaves removed and torn into
  small pieces
olive oil, to glaze

1 Place a third of the flour in a large bowl and stir in 1 teaspoon salt. Place the yeast, sugar and 250 ml (9 fl oz/ 1 cup) warm water in a small bowl, and mix well. Add to the flour and stir to make a thin, lumpy paste. Cover with a tea (dish) towel. Leave in a warm place for 45 minutes, or until doubled in size.
2 Stir in the remaining flour, the oil and 125 ml (4 fl oz/ ½ cup) warm water. Mix with a wooden spoon until a rough dough forms. Transfer to a lightly floured work surface and knead for 10–12 minutes, incorporating as little extra flour as possible to keep the dough soft and moist, but not sticky. Form into a ball. Oil a clean large bowl and roll the dough around in it to lightly coat in the oil. Cut a cross on top, cover the bowl with a tea towel and set aside in a warm place for 1 hour, or until doubled in size.
3 Grease a baking tray and dust with

flour. Punch down the dough on a lightly floured surface. Roll out to a 30 x 25 x 1 cm (12 x 10 x ½ inch) rectangle. Squeeze any excess liquid from the olives and toss to coat in the extra flour. Scatter over the dough and top with the oregano. Roll up tightly, lengthways, pressing firmly to expel any air pockets. Press the ends together to form an oval loaf 25 cm (10 inch) long. Transfer to the tray,

seam-side-down. Slide the tray into a large plastic bag and leave in a warm place for 45 minutes, or until doubled.
4 Preheat the oven to 220°C (425°F/ Gas 7). Brush the top of the loaf with oil and bake for 30 minutes. Reduce the heat to 180°C (350°F/Gas 4) and bake for a further 5 minutes. Cool on a wire rack. Serve warm or cold.

Leave the yeast mixture in a warm place until doubled in size.

Scatter the olives and oregano over the dough and roll up lengthways.

When the dough has doubled, remove from the bag.

TURKISH FLATBREAD

Preparation time: 30 minutes
+ 2 hours 20 minutes rising
Total cooking time: 20 minutes
Makes 6

½ teaspoon sugar
2 x 7 g (¼ oz) sachets dry
    yeast
60 g (2¼ oz/½ cup) plain
    (all-purpose) flour
435 g (15½ oz/3½ cups) bread
    flour (see Note)
3 tablespoons olive oil
1 egg, lightly beaten with
    3 tablespoons water
nigella or sesame seeds, to
    sprinkle

1 Place the sugar in a large bowl with 125 ml (4 fl oz/½ cup) warm water and stir until dissolved. Stir in the yeast, then add the plain flour and mix until smooth. Cover with a plate and leave for 30 minutes, or until frothy and trebled in size.

2 Place the bread flour in a bowl with 1 teaspoon salt. Add the olive oil, 270 ml (9½ fl oz) warm water and the yeast mixture. Mix to a loose dough. Turn out onto a lightly floured surface and knead for 15 minutes. Add minimal flour as the dough needs to be very soft and moist.

3 Shape into a ball and place in a large oiled bowl. Cover with a clean tea (dish) towel and leave in a warm place for 1 hour, or until trebled in size. Punch down, divide into 6 equal portions and lightly shape into smooth balls, kneading as little as possible. Place these apart on a tray and place the tray in a plastic bag. Leave for 10 minutes.

4 Sprinkle a large baking tray with flour. Roll out three balls of dough to a 15 cm (6 inch) circle and place on the baking tray, leaving room for spreading. Cover the dough with a tea towel and rest for 20 minutes. Preheat the oven to 230°C (450°F/Gas 8) and place another baking tray on the centre rack.

5 Indent the surface of the dough with your finger. Brush with the egg mixture and sprinkle with seeds. Place the tray on the heated tray and bake for 8–10 minutes, or until puffed and golden. Wrap in a tea towel to soften the crusts while cooling. Repeat with the remaining dough.

COOK'S FILE

Note: If bread flour is unavailable, use plain (all-purpose) flour. Start by adding half the water in step 2 then gradually add the rest until a loose, soft dough forms. Bread flour requires more water. The holey texture of pide will be lessened using plain flour.

Leave the flour and yeast mixture to stand until frothy and trebled in size.

Knead the dough for 15 minutes, or until soft and moist.

Indent the surface of the dough with your finger.

PARMESAN AND PROSCIUTTO LOAF

Preparation time: 30 minutes
   + 2 hours rising
Total cooking time: 25 minutes
Serves 6

7 g (¼ oz) dried yeast
1 teaspoon caster (super fine) sugar
125 ml (4 fl oz/½ cup) warm milk
250 g (9 oz/2 cups) plain (all-purpose) flour
1 teaspoon salt
1 egg, lightly beaten
30 g (1 oz) butter, melted and cooled slightly

1 tablespoon milk, extra
60 g (2 oz) sliced prosciutto, finely chopped
35 g (1¼ oz/½ cup) grated Parmesan cheese

1 Grease a baking tray. Mix the yeast, sugar and milk in a bowl. Cover and set aside in a warm place for 10 minutes, or until frothy.
2 Mix the flour and salt in a bowl. Make a well in the centre and add the egg, butter and frothy yeast. Mix to a soft dough and gather into a ball; turn out onto a floured surface and knead for 8 minutes, or until elastic.
3 Put in an oiled bowl, cover loosely with greased plastic wrap and leave in a warm place for 1¼ hours, or until doubled in size.

4 Punch down the dough, turn out onto a floured surface and knead for 30 seconds, or until smooth. Roll out to a rectangle, 30 x 20 cm (12 x 8 inches), and brush with some extra milk. Sprinkle with the prosciutto and Parmesan, leaving a border. Roll lengthways into a log shape.
5 Lay on the baking tray and brush with the remaining milk Using a sharp knife, slash the loaf diagonally at intervals. Leave to rise in a warm place for 30 minutes. Preheat the oven to 220°C (425°F/Gas 7). Bake the loaf for 25 minutes, or until golden.

Sprinkle the prosciutto and Parmesan on the dough, leaving a clear border.

Roll up the dough tightly lengthways into a log shape.

Using a sharp knife, slash the loaf diagonally at intervals.

OLIVE SPIRALS

Preparation time: 25 minutes + 1 hour
  30 minutes rising
Total cooking time: 35 minutes
Makes 12 spirals

7 g (¼ oz) dried yeast
1 teaspoon sugar
600 g (1 lb 5 oz/4 cups) plain
  (all-purpose) flour
1 teaspoon salt
2 tablespoons olive oil
250 g (9 oz/2 cups) pitted black
  olives
50 g (1¾ oz/½ cup) finely grated
  Parmesan cheese
3 garlic cloves, chopped

1 Mix the yeast, sugar and 125 ml (4 fl oz/½ cup) warm water in a bowl. Cover and set aside in a warm place for 10 minutes, or until frothy.
2 Sift flour and salt into a bowl and make a well in the centre. Add the frothy yeast, oil and 250 ml (9 fl oz/ 1 cup) of warm water. Mix to a soft dough and gather into a ball. Turn out onto a floured surface and knead for 10 minutes, or until smooth. Cover loosely with greased plastic wrap and set aside for 1 hour, or until it is well risen.
3 Process the olives, Parmesan and garlic in a food processor until chopped. With the motor running, add 1 tablespoon of oil and process to a paste.

4 Punch down the dough and knead for 1 minute. Roll out to a rectangle 42 x 35 cm (18 x 14 inches). Spread with the olive paste, leaving a plain strip along one of the long sides. Roll up lengthways, ending with the plain long side.
5 Cut into 12 slices and place close together on a greased baking tray. Cover with a damp tea (dish) towel and set aside for 30 minutes, or until well risen. Preheat the oven to 200°C (400°F/Gas 6). Bake for 35 minutes, or until golden brown.

Spread with olive paste and roll up lengthways.

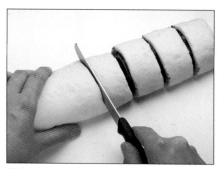

Using a serrated knife, cut the logs into 12 equal slices.

Place the spirals close together on the baking tray.

FOCACCIA

Preparation time: 30 minutes +
  3 hours 40 minutes rising
Total cooking time: 20 minutes
Makes two loaves

½ teaspoon caster (superfine)
  sugar
7 g (¼ oz) sachet dry yeast
1 kg (2 lb 4 oz) bread flour
  (see Note)
3 tablespoons olive oil

1 Mix the sugar, dry yeast and 2 tablespoons warm water in a small bowl. Leave in a warm place for 10 minutes, or until foamy. If it doesn't foam the yeast is dead and you will have to start again.
2 Place the flour in a large bowl with 2 teaspoons salt, and mix well. Add 2 tablespoons of the oil, the yeast mixture and 750 ml (26 fl oz/3 cups) warm water. Mix with a wooden spoon until it comes together in a loose dough; turn out onto a lightly floured surface. Start kneading to form a soft, moist, non-sticky dough, adding a little extra flour or warm water as needed. Knead for 8 minutes, or until smooth.
3 Lightly oil a large bowl. Place the dough in the bowl and roll it around. Cut a cross on top with a sharp knife. Cover the bowl with a tea towel and leave in a dry, warm place for 1 hour 30 minutes, or until doubled in size.
4 Punch down the dough on a lightly floured surface. Divide in half. Roll one portion out to a 28 x 20 cm (11 x 8 inch) rectangle. Use the heels of your hands to work from the middle outwards and shape into a 38 x 28 cm (15¼ x 11 inch) rectangle.

5 Lightly oil a baking tray and dust with flour. Place the dough in the centre and slide the tray inside a plastic bag. Leave in a dry, warm place for 2 hours, or until doubled in size.
6 Preheat the oven to 220°C (425°F/Gas 7). Brush the dough with some of the remaining olive oil and bake for 20 minutes, or until golden. Transfer to a wire rack to cool. Allow plenty of air to circulate under the loaf to keep the crust crisp. Repeat with the remaining dough. Best eaten within 6 hours of baking.

COOK'S FILE

Note: If bread flour is unavailable, you can use plain (all-purpose) flour. It requires less water, so start by adding 250 ml (9 fl oz/1 cup) of the water in step 2, then gradually add more to give a soft but non-sticky dough. The bread will have a denser texture.

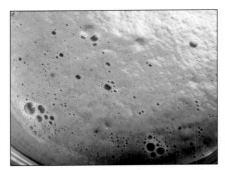

Leave the yeast mixture in a warm place until foamy.

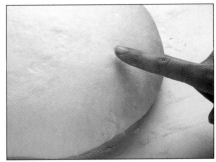

Knead the dough until the impression made by a finger springs out.

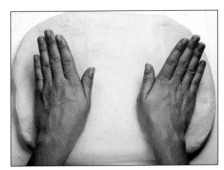

Use the heels of your hands to work from the middle outwards.

PIZZA MARGHERITA

Preparation time: 25 minutes +
  1 hour rising
Total cooking time: 45 minutes
Serves 6–8

225 g (8 oz) white bread
  (strong) flour
1 teaspoon sugar
7 g (¼ oz) sachet dry yeast
2 tablespoons olive oil
90 ml (3 fl oz) milk
1 garlic clove, crushed
425 g (15 oz) tinned tomatoes,
  crushed
1 bay leaf
1 teaspoon chopped fresh thyme
6 fresh basil leaves, chopped
150 g (5½ oz) bocconcini,
  thinly sliced
olive oil, extra, to drizzle

1 Place the flour, sugar, yeast and ½ teaspoon salt in a large bowl. Combine half the olive oil with the milk and 4 tablespoons warm water—add to the dry ingredients. Stir with a wooden spoon to combine.
2 Place on a lightly floured work surface and knead for 5 minutes, or until soft and smooth. Lightly oil a bowl, add the dough and turn to coat in the oil. Leave in a warm place for 1 hour, or until doubled in size. Preheat the oven to 210°C (415°F/ Gas 6–7).
3 Meanwhile, heat the remaining oil in a saucepan over medium heat, add the garlic and cook, stirring, for 30 seconds. Add the tomato, bay leaf, thyme and basil and simmer, stirring occasionally, for 20–25 minutes, or until thick and fragrant. Allow to cool. Remove the bay leaf.
4 Place the dough on a lightly floured work surface, then punch down to expel the air and knead for 5 minutes. Shape the dough into a neat ball and roll out to a 28–30 cm (11–12 inch) diameter. Lightly oil a 28–30 cm (11–12 inch) pizza tray and place the dough on the tray. Spread the tomato sauce over the dough, leaving a 3 cm (1¼ inch) border. Arrange bocconcini over the sauce, drizzle with olive oil and bake for 15 minutes, or until crisp and bubbling.

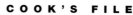
COOK'S FILE

Note: The red, white and green toppings of this pizza symbolize the Italian flag.

Roll the pizza dough out to a 28 x 30 cm (11 x 12 inch) diameter.

Arrange the bocconcini slices over the tomato sauce.

PISSALADIERE

Preparation time: 30 minutes
  + 15 minutes standing + 1 hour
  30 minutes rising
Total cooking time: 1 hour 25 minutes
Serves 4–6

7 g (¼ oz) sachet dry yeast
175 g (6 oz/1¼ cup) plain
  (all-purpose) flour
1 egg, beaten
1 tablespoon olive oil

Topping
3 tablespoons olive oil
2 garlic cloves
1 sprig fresh thyme
4 large onions (800 g/1 lb 12 oz),
  thinly sliced
pinch ground nutmeg
30 g (1 oz) drained anchovy
  fillets, halved lengthways
16 pitted black olives

1 Place the yeast in a bowl with 2 tablespoons lukewarm water. Leave in a warm place for 15 minutes, or until foamy.

2 Sift the flour and ¼ teaspoon salt into a large bowl, make a well in the centre and add the yeast mixture, egg, oil and 2 tablespoons warm water. Bring together with a wooden spoon and when clumped together, transfer to a lightly floured surface. Knead to a soft, pliable dough, adding a little more water or flour as needed. Continue kneading for 6–8 minutes, or until smooth and elastic. Lightly oil a clean large bowl and place the dough in it. Roll the dough around to coat with oil, cover the bowl with a dry tea (dish) towel and place in a warm place for 1 hour, or until doubled in size.

3 To make the topping, heat the oil in a large frying pan, add the garlic, thyme and onion and cook, stirring occasionally, over low heat for 1 hour, or until the onion is soft and buttery but not brown. Discard the garlic and thyme, add the nutmeg and season.

4 Brush a 30 cm (12 inch) round pizza tray with oil. Punch down the dough and lightly knead into a ball. Roll out to a 30 cm (12 inch) circle and place over the oiled tray. Spread the onion over the surface, leaving a 1 cm (½ inch) border. Make a diamond cross-hatch pattern on top with the anchovies. Intersperse with the olives. Slide the tray into a large plastic bag and leave to rise again for 30 minutes. Preheat the oven to 200°C (400°F/Gas 6).

5 Bake for 20–25 minutes, or until the dough is cooked and golden. Reduce the heat to 190°C (375°F/Gas 5) if the crust over browns towards the end of baking. Serve in slices.

Using a rolling pin, roll the dough out to a 30 cm (12 inch) circle.

Arrange the anchovies and olives over the top of the onion mixture.

SEMI-DRIED TOMATO AND SALAMI PIZZA

Preparation time: 40 minutes
Total cooking time: 35–45 minutes
Serves 4

1 green capsicum (pepper)
1 red or yellow capsicum
  (pepper)
125 g (4½ oz/½ cup) grated
  Cheddar cheese
100 g (3⅓ oz) salami, sliced
1 red onion, thinly sliced into
  rings
90 g (3¼ oz/½ cup) black olives,
  pitted and sliced
150 g (4¾ oz) bocconcini

Pizza base
7 g (¼ oz) sachet dried yeast
½ teaspoon salt
½ teaspoon sugar
250 g (9 oz/2½ cups) plain
  (all-purpose) flour
160 g (5¼ oz/1 cup) semi-dried
  (sun-blushed) tomatoes,
  finely chopped
80 g (2¾ oz/½ cup) pine nuts,
  finely chopped

1 Cut the capsicums into large flat pieces; remove the membrane and seeds. Place, skin-side-up, under a hot grill (broiler) and cook until the skin blackens and blisters. Cool under a tea (dish) towel. Peel away the skin and cut the flesh into thin strips. Set aside.
2 To make pizza base, mix the yeast, salt, sugar and 250 ml (9 fl oz/1 cup) warm water in a small bowl. Cover with plastic wrap and leave in a warm place for 10 minutes, until foamy. Sift the flour into a bowl, make a well in the centre and add the yeast mixture, semi-dried tomatoes and pine nuts. Mix to a dough.

3 Preheat the oven to 200°C (400°F/ Gas 6). Knead the dough on a lightly floured surface for about 10 minutes, or until smooth and elastic. Roll out to a 35 cm (14 inch) round. Place on a 30 cm (12 inch) non-stick pizza tray, folding the edge over to form a rim.
4 Sprinkle the pizza base with grated cheese. Top with salami, red onion, olives and roasted capsicum. Bake for 30–40 minutes, or until the base is cooked. Top with thinly sliced bocconcini and bake for a further 5 minutes, or until just melted.

Leave the yeast mixture in a warm place until it becomes foamy.

Top the base with grated cheese, onion, salami, olives and roasted capsicum.

CALZONE WITH OLIVES, CAPERS AND ANCHOVIES

Preparation time: 35 minutes + 1 hour
  45 minutes rising
Total cooking time: 15 minutes
Serves 4

1 tablespoon caster (superfine)
  sugar
7 g (¼ oz) sachet dry yeast
540 g (1 lb 3 oz/4⅓ cups) plain
  (all-purpose) flour
3 tablespoons olive oil
polenta (cornmeal), for dusting

Filling
2 tablespoons olive oil
200 g (7 oz) mozzarella cheese,
  cut into 1 cm (½ inch) cubes
2 medium tomatoes, juice
  squeezed out and cut into
  1 cm (½ inch) dice
12 basil leaves, torn into pieces
20 pitted black olives
2 teaspoons baby capers
12 anchovy fillets, cut into thin
  strips 2 cm (¾ inch) long

1 Place the sugar, yeast and 4 tablespoons warm water in a small bowl. Leave in a warm place for 15 minutes, or until foamy. If it does not foam in 5 minutes the yeast is dead and you must start again.
2 Sift the flour into a large bowl with ½ teaspoon salt. Add the yeast mixture, olive oil and 170 ml (5½ fl oz/⅔ cup) warm water. Mix with a wooden spoon until the dough loosely clumps together. Turn it out onto a lightly floured surface and knead to form a soft, moist but non-sticky dough. Add a little extra flour or warm water as needed. Knead for 15–20 minutes, or until smooth and elastic, and a finger imprint springs straight out.
3 Oil the sides of a large bowl with olive oil. Roll the ball of dough around in the bowl to coat the surface with oil, then cut a shallow cross on the top of the ball with a sharp knife. Cover the bowl with a tea (dish) towel and leave in a warm place for up to 1 hour 30 minutes, or until the dough has doubled in size.
4 Preheat the oven to 230°C (450°F/ Gas 8). Lightly oil 2 pizza or baking trays and dust with polenta. Punch down the dough. Place it on a lightly floured work surface and divide into two portions. One or both portions can be frozen at this stage for future use. Shape one portion into a ball. Roll it out to a circle of roughly 25 cm (10 inch). Using the heels of your hands and working from the centre outwards, press the circle to a diameter of 32 cm (13 inch). Transfer to the tray. Brush the surface lightly with olive oil.
5 Scatter half the mozzarella over one half of the dough, leaving a 1 cm (½ inch) border at the outer edge. Scatter half the tomato and basil over the cheese. Season. Distribute half the olives, capers and anchovies over the top. Fold the undressed half of dough over the filling to form a half-moon shape. Press together firmly to seal. Turn the cut edge up and over on itself and press into a scroll pattern to further seal in the filling. Brush the surface with a little more olive oil. Repeat with the remaining ingredients to make a second calzone. Bake for 10–15 minutes, or until puffed and golden brown.

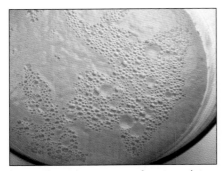

Leave the yeast, sugar and water mixture in a warm place until foamy.

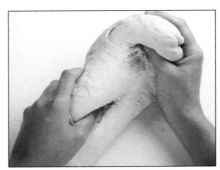

Knead the dough to form a soft, moist but non-sticky dough.

Place the dough on a lightly floured work surface and divide in half.

Press the dough out to a 32 cm (13 inch) circle using the heels of your hands.

Distribute half the filling ingredients over the dough.

Press the edges together in a scroll pattern to fully seal.

Pizzettas

SEMI-DRIED TOMATO PESTO AND ARTICHOKE

Preheat the oven to 200°C (400°F/Gas 6). To make pesto, place 75 g (2½ oz/½ cup) whole semi-dried (sun-blushed) tomatoes, 2 tablespoons pine nuts, 2 garlic cloves and 2 tablespoons grated Parmesan cheese in a food processor. Process until smooth. Divide the pesto among 4 individual pizza bases. Slice 4 marinated artichoke hearts and place on top of the pesto. Sprinkle with 150 g (5½ oz/1 cup) grated mozzarella cheese. Bake for 15–20 minutes, or until the base is crisp and the cheese has melted. Serves 4.

BOCCONCINI AND TOMATO

Preheat the oven to 200°C (400°F/Gas 6). Combine 3 tablespoons olive oil with 8 crushed garlic cloves. Drizzle the mixture over 4 individual pizza bases. Bake for 10 minutes. Slice 4 Roma (plum) tomatoes and place on the pizza bases. Top with 4 sliced fresh bocconcini, cracked black pepper and salt. Return to the oven and cook for a further 6 minutes, or until the cheese has melted. Sprinkle pizzettas with 30 g (1 oz/½ cup) shredded basil. Serves 4.

CHAR-GRILLED CAPSICUM AND PROSCIUTTO

Preheat the oven to 200°C (400°F/Gas 6). Spread 250 g (9 oz/1 cup) ready-made pizza sauce over 4 individual pizza bases. Cut 1 red and 1 green capsicum (pepper) into large, flattish pieces and place, skin-side-up, under a hot grill (broiler). Cook until the skin blackens and blisters. Remove from the heat and cover with a tea (dish) towel; leave to cool. Peel away the skin and cut the flesh into thin strips. Divide among the pizza bases. Cut 12 thin slices of prosciutto into strips and place on top of the capsicum. Top the prosciutto with 125 g (4½ oz/⅔ cup) good-quality black olives, pitted and sliced. Drizzle with extra virgin olive oil. Bake for 10–15 minutes, or until the crusts are golden. Serves 4.

SWEET POTATO AND SCALLOP

Preheat the oven to 200°C (400°F/Gas 6). Drizzle 4 individual pizza bases with olive oil. Clean and cut in half 250 g (8 oz) scallops and arrange on the bases. Very thinly slice 375 g (12 oz) orange sweet potato and deep- fry until golden and crisp; drain well. Thinly slice 1 red onion. Top the scallops with sweet potato and onion and drizzle with extra virgin olive oil. Bake for 10–15 minutes. Sprinkle with 2 tablespoons chopped fresh thyme to serve. Serves 4.

HERBED TOMATO AND ROCKET

Preheat the oven to 200°C (400°F/Gas 6). Heat 1 tablespoon olive oil in a pan. Add 1 finely chopped onion and 2 crushed garlic cloves and cook over medium heat for 3–4 minutes. Peel and chop 500 g (1 lb) ripe Roma (plum) tomatoes and add to the pan with 2 tablespoons chopped fresh herbs. Cook over high heat for 5–7 minutes, or until the mixture is quite thick; spread over 4 individual pizza bases. Bake for 10–15 minutes, or until the bases are crisp. Remove from the oven and top with 40 g (1½ oz/2 cups) torn rocket (arugula) leaves. Sprinkle with shavings of Parmesan and season with cracked black pepper. Serves 4.

CARAMELIZED ONION AND GOAT'S CHEESE

Preheat the oven to 200°C (400°F/Gas 6). Slice 4 onions very finely. Heat 2 tablespoons olive oil in a large pan; cook the onion over high heat for 2–3 minutes, or until starting to brown. Reduce the heat and cook for 15 minutes, or until the onion is soft. Spread the onion over 4 individual pizza bases. Top with 125 g (4 oz) goat's cheese, crumbled or thinly sliced. Bake for 10–15 minutes, or until the crusts are golden. Remove from the oven and sprinkle with 2 tablespoons chopped fresh oregano. Serves 4.

Pizzettas from left: Semi-dried Tomato Pesto and Artichoke; Bocconcini and Tomato; Char-grilled Capsicum and Prosciutto; Sweet Potato and Scallop; Herbed Tomato and Rocket; Caramelized Onion and Goat's Cheese

ROASTED TOMATO AND EGGPLANT PIZZA

Preparation time: 40 minutes
Total cooking time: 1 hour 45 minutes
Serves 4

500 g (1 lb) Roma (plum)
    tomatoes
1 large eggplant (aubergine)
olive oil, for frying
200 g (6½ oz) mozzarella
    cheese, grated
3 tablespoons grated Parmesan
    cheese
1 tablespoon chopped fresh
    oregano

Pizza base
1 teaspoon dried yeast
¼ teaspoon salt
¼ teaspoon sugar
155 g (5 oz/1¼ cups) plain
    (all-purpose) flour
6 garlic cloves, crushed

1 Preheat the oven to 150°C (300°F/ Gas 2). Cut the tomatoes in half and place in one layer on a baking tray, cut-side-up. Sprinkle with salt and roast for 1 hour 15 minutes. Set aside to cool.

2 To make pizza base, put yeast, salt, sugar and 125 ml (4 fl oz/½ cup) warm water in a small bowl. Leave, covered with plastic wrap, in a warm place for 10 minutes, or until foamy. Sift the flour into a large bowl, make a well in the centre and add the yeast mixture and garlic. Mix to form a dough. Knead on a lightly floured surface for 10 minutes, or until smooth and elastic. Roll out to fit a 30 cm (12 inch) greased or non-stick pizza tray.

3 Preheat the oven to 200°C (400°F/ Gas 6). Thinly slice the eggplant. Drizzle a chargrill (griddle) or large frying pan with olive oil until nearly smoking. Add the eggplant in batches and cook, turning once, until soft. Drain on paper towel. Arrange the eggplant on the pizza base. Top with tomatoes and sprinkle with the combined mozzarella and Parmesan. Bake for 20–30 minutes, or until the base is cooked and the cheese melted and golden. Sprinkle with fresh oregano to serve.

Cut the tomatoes in half and sprinkle with sea salt.

Make a well in the centre of the flour and add the yeast and garlic.

Cook the eggplant in batches, turning once until soft.

Put the eggplant on the pizza base and top with the tomatoes.

POTATO ONION PIZZA

Preparation time: 40 minutes
Total cooking time: 40 minutes
Serves 4

7 g (¼ oz) sachet dry yeast
½ teaspoon sugar
185 g (6½ oz/1½ cups) plain
    (all-purpose) flour
150 g (5½ oz/1 cup) wholemeal
    (whole-wheat) plain
    (all-purpose) flour
1 tablespoon olive oil

Topping
1 large red capsicum (pepper)
1 potato, peeled
1 large onion, sliced

125 g (4 oz) soft goat's cheese,
    crumbled
3 tablespoons capers
1 tablespoon dried oregano
1 teaspoon cracked pepper
1 teaspoon olive oil

1 Mix the yeast, sugar, a good pinch of salt and 250 ml (9 fl oz/1 cup) warm water in a bowl. Cover with plastic wrap and leave in a warm place for 10 minutes, or until foamy. Sift both flours into a bowl. Make a well in the centre, add the yeast mixture and mix to a firm dough. Knead on a lightly floured surface for 5 minutes, or until smooth. Roll out to a 35 cm (14 inch) round. Brush a 30 cm (12 inch) pizza tray with oil; put the dough on the tray and tuck the edge over to form a rim.

Preheat the oven to 200°C (400°F/ Gas 6).
2 To make topping, cut the capsicum into large flat pieces; remove the seeds. Place, skin-side-up, under a hot grill (broiler) until blackened. Cool under a tea (dish) towel, peel away the skin and cut the flesh into narrow strips.
3 Slice the potato paper thin and arrange over the base with the onion, capsicum and half the goat's cheese. Sprinkle with capers, oregano and pepper and drizzle with olive oil. Brush the edge of the crust with oil and bake for 20 minutes. Add the remaining goat's cheese and bake for 15–20 minutes, or until the crust has browned. Cut into wedges to serve.

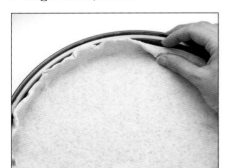

Tuck the edge of the pizza dough over to form a rim.

Remove the skin from the capsicum and cut the flesh into thin strips.

Arrange the onion, capsicum and half the goat's cheese over the base.

HAM AND CHEESE CALZONI

Preparation time: 30 minutes + chilling
Total cooking time: 30 minutes
Makes 4

250 g (9 oz/2 cups) plain
  (all-purpose) flour
100 g (3⅓ oz) butter, chopped
2 egg yolks

Ham and cheese filling
250 g (8 oz) ricotta cheese
50 g (1⅔ oz) Gruyère cheese,
  cubed

50 g (1⅔ oz) ham, finely
  chopped
2 spring onions (scallions),
  chopped
1 tablespoon chopped fresh
  flat-leaf (Italian) parsley
freshly ground black
  pepper, to season

1 Lightly grease a large oven tray. Sift the flour and a pinch of salt into a bowl and rub in the butter. Make a well in the centre, cut in the egg yolks with a knife and add 2–3 tablespoons water, or enough to form a dough. Gather together into a ball, cover with plastic wrap and chill for 20 minutes.

Preheat the oven to 200°C (400°F/Gas 6).
2 To make filling, combine the cheeses, ham, spring onions, parsley and black pepper in a bowl.
3 Roll out a quarter of the dough to make a large round 2–3 mm (⅛ inch) thick, trimming any uneven edges. Spoon a quarter of the filling mixture into the centre, brush the edge very lightly with water and fold over to enclose the filling, pressing the edge to seal. Repeat with the remaining dough and filling. Place the calzoni on the oven tray, brush with a little olive oil and bake for 30 minutes, or until well browned and crisp.

Use a knife to cut the egg yolks into the flour and butter mixture.

Mix together the cheeses, ham, spring onions, parsley and pepper in a bowl.

Brush the edge of the pastry with water, then fold over to enclose the filling.

SEMI-DRIED TOMATO ROLLS

Preparation time: 20 minutes + resting
Total cooking time: 40 minutes
Makes 16 rolls

3 tablespoons olive oil
2 red onions, sliced
1 tablespoon tomato paste
  (concentrated purée)
110 g (3¾ oz/⅔ cup) semi-dried
  (sun-blushed) tomatoes,
  chopped
1 tablespoon chopped fresh
  oregano
2 teaspoons chopped fresh
  rosemary
¼ teaspoon dried chilli flakes
14 g (½ oz) packet dried yeast
750 g (1 lb 10 oz/6 cups) plain
  (all-purpose) flour
3 teaspoons salt
2 tablespoons polenta (cornmeal)
1 egg white, lightly beaten

1 Heat oil in a pan and cook onions until very soft. Stir in tomato paste, tomatoes, herbs and chilli. Cool to room temperature.
2 Put the yeast, 250 ml (9 fl oz/1 cup) warm water and 125 g (4½ oz/1 cup) of the flour in a bowl, then whisk until smooth and leave in a warm place for 20 minutes, or until frothy.
3 Sift remaining flour and salt into a large bowl. Make a well in centre and pour in yeast mixture, 250 ml (9 fl oz/1 cup) warm water and tomato mixture. Gradually mix to form a soft sticky dough. Turn out onto a floured surface and knead for 5 minutes. Place in a greased bowl, cover with greased plastic wrap and leave in a warm place for 1 hour, or until doubled. Grease two 20 cm (8 inch) round shallow cake tins and sprinkle with a little polenta.
4 Punch down dough, then knead on a floured surface for 3 minutes. Roll into 16 balls and arrange in the tins. Make 2–3 cuts on the top of each roll. Leave in a warm place for 20 minutes or until risen; brush with egg white and sprinkle with polenta. Preheat the oven to 200°C (400°F/Gas 6). Bake for 30 minutes (cover with foil if overbrowning). For crusty rolls, spray with a little water three times during baking. Turn out onto a wire rack.

Whisk the yeast, water and flour together and leave in a warm place until frothy.

Add the yeast mixture, warm water and tomato mixture to the flour.

Leave the dough in a warm place for 1 hour, or until doubled in size.

Divide the dough into 16 portions, then roll into balls and put in the tins.

Seafood

MUSSELS IN TOMATO AND HERB SAUCE

Preparation time: 30 minutes
Total cooking time: 35 minutes
Serves 4

Tomato and herb sauce
4 tablespoons olive oil
3 garlic cloves, finely chopped
¼ teaspoon dried chilli flakes
2 x 425 g (15 oz) tinned
    tomatoes, crushed
1 teaspoon caster (superfine)
    sugar

8 slices crusty Italian bread
2 tablespoons olive oil
2 large garlic cloves, halved
1 kg (2 lb 4 oz) black mussels
2 tablespoons olive oil, extra
1 red onion, finely chopped
6 sprigs fresh flat-leaf (Italian)
    parsley
2 sprigs fresh thyme
2 sprigs fresh oregano
250 ml (9 fl oz/1 cup) dry
    white wine
1 tablespoon chopped fresh
    flat-leaf (Italian) parsley
2 teaspoons fresh thyme
    leaves
2 teaspoons chopped fresh
    oregano leaves

1 Preheat the oven to 160°C (315°F/ Gas 2–3). To make the tomato sauce, heat the oil in a saucepan, add the garlic and chilli flakes, and cook over low heat for 30 seconds without browning. Add the tomato, sugar and 4 tablespoons water. Season and simmer, stirring often, for 15 minutes, or until reduced and thickened.

2 Lightly brush the bread with olive oil. Place in a single layer on a baking tray and bake for 10 minutes, or until crisp and golden. While still warm, rub one side with the garlic.

3 Meanwhile, scrub the mussels with a stiff brush and pull out the hairy beards. Discard any broken mussels or ones that don't close when tapped on the bench. Rinse well.

4 Heat extra oil in a large saucepan, add the onion and cook over medium heat for 3 minutes, or until softened but not browned. Add the parsley, thyme, oregano and wine. Bring to the boil, then reduce the heat and simmer for 5 minutes. Season with pepper.

5 Add the mussels, stir to coat, and cook, covered, for 3–4 minutes. Shake the pan often. Remove the mussels as they open. Discard any unopened mussels.

6 Strain the wine mixture into the tomato sauce, discarding the onion and herbs. Return to the large saucepan and reheat. Add the mussels and toss well to coat in the mixture. Pile into a serving bowl and scatter with the chopped parsley, thyme and oregano. Arrange the bread slices around the bowl.

Pull the hairy beards out of the scrubbed mussels.

Remove the mussels as they open and discard any that don't open.

INSALATA DI FRUTTI DI MARE

Preparation time: 45 minutes
+ 40 minutes marinating
Total cooking time: 10 minutes
Serves 4

500 g (1 lb 2 oz) small calamari (squid)
1 kg (2 lb 4 oz) large clams
1 kg (2 lb 4 oz) black mussels
500 g (1 lb 2 oz) raw medium prawns (shrimp), peeled and deveined, tails intact
5 tablespoons finely chopped fresh flat-leaf (Italian) parsley

Dressing
2 tablespoons lemon juice
4 tablespoons olive oil
1 garlic clove, crushed

1 Grasp the body of the calamari in one hand and the head and tentacles in the other. Gently pull apart to separate. Cut the tentacles from the head by cutting below the eyes. Discard the head. Push out the beak and discard. Pull the quill from inside the body of the calamari and discard. Under cold running water, pull away all the skin (the flaps can be used). Rinse well, then slice the calamari into 7 mm (⅜ inch) rings.

2 Scrub the clams and mussels and remove the beards. Discard any that are cracked or don't close when tapped. Rinse under cold running water. Fill a large saucepan with 2 cm (¾ inch) water, add the clams and mussels, cover, bring to the boil and cook for 4–5 minutes, or until the shells open. Remove, reserving the liquid. Discard any that do not open. Remove the mussels and clams from their shells and place in a large bowl.

3 Pour 1 litre (4 cups) water into the pan, bring to the boil and add the prawns and calamari. Cook for 3–4 minutes, or until the prawns turn pink and the calamari is tender. Drain and add to the clams and mussels.

4 To make the dressing, combine the lemon juice, olive oil and garlic in a small bowl and whisk together. Season with salt and freshly ground black pepper. Pour the dressing over the seafood, add 4 tablespoons of the parsley and toss to coat. Adjust the seasoning if necessary. Cover and marinate in the refrigerator for 30–40 minutes to allow the flavours to develop. Sprinkle with the remaining parsley and serve with slices of fresh crusty bread.

Remove the transparent quill from inside the body of the calamari.

Gently pull the mussels and clams out of their shells.

TUNA AND WHITE BEAN SALAD

Preparation time: 25 minutes
Total cooking time: 5 minutes
Serves 4–6

400 g (14 oz) tuna steaks
1 small red onion, thinly sliced
1 tomato, deseeded and chopped
1 small red capsicum (pepper), thinly sliced
2 x 400 g (14 oz) tinned cannellini beans
2 garlic cloves, crushed
1 teaspoon chopped fresh thyme

4 tablespoons finely chopped fresh flat-leaf (Italian) parsley
1½ tablespoons lemon juice
4 tablespoons extra virgin olive oil
1 teaspoon honey
olive oil, for brushing
100 g (3½ oz) rocket (arugula) leaves
1 teaspoon honey lemon zest

1 Place the tuna on a plate; sprinkle with pepper on both sides. Cover with plastic and chill until needed.
2 Combine the onion, tomato and capsicum in a bowl. Rinse the beans under running water for 30 seconds,
drain. Add to the bowl with the garlic, thyme and 3 tablespoons of parsley.
3 Place the lemon juice, oil and honey in a small saucepan, bring to the boil, then simmer, stirring, for 1 minute, or until the honey dissolves. Remove from the heat.
4 Brush a barbecue or chargrill (griddle) with olive oil, and heat until very hot. Cook tuna for 1 minute on each side. The meat should still be pink in the middle. Slice into 3 cm (1¼ inch) cubes and combine with the salad. Pour on the dressing and toss well to combine.
5 Place the rocket on a platter. Top with the salad, season and garnish with the zest and parsley. Serve.

Add the beans, garlic, thyme and parsley to the bowl and mix well.

Heat the lemon juice, honey and oil in a saucepan until the honey dissolves.

Cook the tuna until still pink in the middle, and cut into 3 cm (1¼ inch) cubes.

INVOLTINI OF SWORDFISH

Preparation time: 30 minutes
Total cooking time: 10 minutes
Serves 4

1 kg (2 lb 4 oz) swordfish, skin
    removed, cut into four 5 cm
    (2 inch) pieces
3 lemons
4 tablespoons olive oil
1 small onion, chopped
3 garlic cloves, chopped
2 tablespoons chopped capers
2 tablespoons chopped pitted
    Kalamata olives
4 tablespoons finely grated
    Parmesan cheese
120 g (4¼ oz/1½ cups) fresh
    bread crumbs
2 tablespoons chopped fresh
    parsley
1 egg, lightly beaten
24 fresh bay leaves
2 small white onions, quartered
    and separated into pieces
2 tablespoons lemon juice, extra

1 Cut swordfish pieces horizontally into 4 slices to give you 16 slices. Place each piece between two pieces of plastic wrap and roll gently with a rolling pin to flatten without tearing. Cut pieces in half to give 32 pieces.
2 Peel the lemons with a vegetable peeler; cut the peel into 24 pieces. Juice the lemon to give 3 tablespoons.
3 Heat 2 tablespoons olive oil, add the onion and garlic, and cook over medium heat for 2 minutes. Place in a bowl with the capers, olives, Parmesan, breadcrumbs and parsley. Season, add the egg and mix to bind.
4 Divide the stuffing among the fish pieces and, with oiled hands, roll up to form parcels. Thread 4 rolls onto each of 8 skewers, alternating with the bay leaves, lemon peel and onion.
5 Mix the remaining oil and the lemon juice. Barbecue or grill (broil) the skewers for 3–4 minutes each side, basting with the oil and lemon mix. Drizzle with extra lemon juice.

Roll the swordfish out between two pieces of plastic wrap.

Roll the fish pieces and filling up to form neat parcels.

Thread the rolls, bay leaves, lemon peel and onion onto skewers.

Remove the clear quills from inside the calamari and purple skin from outside.

Add the breadcrumbs, parsley and Parmesan and mix until well combined.

Divide the filling among the calamari tubes but don't fill them completely.

Shallow-fry in batches for 3–4 minutes on each side.

STUFFED CALAMARI

Preparation time: 30 minutes
Total cooking time: 20 minutes
Serves 4

8 medium calamari tubes
40 g (1⅓ oz) butter
8 slices pancetta, finely chopped
400 g (12⅔ oz) raw prawns
   (shrimp), peeled, deveined
   and finely chopped
80 g (2¾ oz/1 cup) fresh
   breadcrumbs
3 tablespoons chopped fresh
   parsley
100 g (3⅓ oz/1 cup) grated
   Parmesan cheese
100 g (3⅓ oz) butter, extra
3 garlic cloves, crushed
1 tablespoon chopped fresh
   parsley, extra

1 Rinse the calamari under cold water. Put your hand in and remove the insides and quill. Then remove the purple skin from the outside. Rinse and pat dry with paper towel.
2 Melt the butter in a small frying pan; cook the pancetta and prawns over high heat until the prawns are just cooked. Transfer to a bowl; add the breadcrumbs, parsley and Parmesan and mix well.
3 Divide the filling among the calamari tubes. Melt the extra butter with the garlic in a large frying pan and cook the stuffed calamari, in batches, for 3–4 minutes on each side, or until just cooked. Stir through the extra parsley. Place two stuffed calamari on each plate and spoon over a little of the garlic butter.

COOK'S FILE

Note: You will only need to fill each calamari tube three-quarters-full—the tubes shrink a little when cooked and if there is too much filling it will ooze out from the top.

PRAWN SAFFRON RISOTTO

Preparation time: 20 minutes
Total cooking time: 40 minutes
Serves 4

¼ teaspoon saffron threads
500 g (1 lb) raw prawns (shrimp)
4 tablespoons olive oil
2 garlic cloves, crushed

3 tablespoons chopped parsley
3 tablespoons dry sherry
3 tablespoons white wine
6 cups (1.5 litres) fish stock
1 onion, diced
440 g (15½ oz/2 cups) arborio rice

1 Soak the saffron threads in 3 tablespoons water. Peel the prawns and devein, leaving the tails intact. Heat 2 tablespoons of the olive oil in a pan. Add the garlic, parsley and prawns and season with salt and pepper. Cook for 2 minutes, then add sherry, wine and saffron threads with their liquid. Remove the prawns with a slotted spoon. Simmer until the liquid has reduced by half. Add the fish stock and 250 ml (9 fl oz/1 cup) water and leave to simmer.

2 In a separate large, heavy-based pan heat the remaining oil. Add the onion and rice and cook for 3 minutes. Keeping the pan of stock constantly at simmering point, add 125 ml (4 fl oz/½ cup) hot stock to the rice mixture. Stir constantly over low heat, with a wooden spoon, until all the liquid has been absorbed. Add another half cupful of stock and repeat the process until all the stock has been added and the rice is tender and creamy—this will take 25–30 minutes.

3 Stir in the prawns, warm through and serve, perhaps with freshly grated Parmesan cheese.

Cook the prawns for 2 minutes, then remove with a slotted spoon.

Keep the stock simmering in a separate pan and add a little at a time.

TUNA SKEWERS WITH MOROCCAN SPICES AND CHERMOULA

Preparation time: 20 minutes
+ 10 minutes marinating
Total cooking time: 5 minutes
Serves 4

800 g (1 lb 12 oz) tuna
  steaks, cut into 3 cm
  (1¼ inch) cubes
2 tablespoons olive oil
½ teaspoon ground cumin
2 teaspoons grated lemon zest

Chermoula
3 teaspoons ground cumin
½ teaspoon ground coriander
2 teaspoons paprika
pinch cayenne pepper
4 garlic cloves, crushed
15 g (½ oz/½ cup) chopped fresh
  flat-leaf (Italian) parsley
25 g (1 oz/½ cup) chopped fresh
  coriander (cilantro)
4 tablespoons lemon juice
125 ml (4 fl oz/½ cup) olive oil

1 If using wooden skewers, soak for 30 minutes to prevent burning. Place the tuna in a shallow non-metallic dish. Combine the olive oil, ground cumin and lemon zest, and pour over the tuna. Toss to coat and leave to marinate for 10 minutes.
2 To make the chermoula, place the cumin, coriander, paprika and cayenne in a frying pan and cook over medium heat for 30 seconds, or until fragrant. Combine with the remaining ingredients and leave for the flavours to develop.
3 Thread the tuna onto the skewers. Lightly oil a chargrill (griddle) or barbecue, and cook the skewers for 1 minute on each side for rare and 2 minutes for medium. Serve on couscous with the chermoula drizzled over the skewers.

Pour the combined olive oil, cumin and lemon zest over the tuna cubes.

Combine the chermoula ingredients in a small bowl.

Thread the tuna onto the skewers and grill (broil) until done to your liking.

SALAD NICOISE

Preparation time: 30 minutes
Total cooking time: 15 minutes
Serves 4

3 eggs
2 vine-ripened tomatoes
175 g (6 oz) baby green beans, trimmed
125 ml (4 fl oz/½ cup) olive oil
2 tablespoons white wine vinegar
1 large garlic clove, halved
325 g (11½ oz) iceberg lettuce heart, cut into 8 wedges
1 small red capsicum (pepper), deseeded and thinly sliced
1 celery stalk, cut into 5 cm (2 inch) thin strips
1 Lebanese (short) cucumber, cut into thin 5 cm (2 inch) lengths
¼ large red onion, thinly sliced
2 x 185 g (6¾ oz) tinned tuna, drained, broken into chunks
12 Kalamata olives
45 g (1½ oz) tinned anchovy fillets, drained
2 teaspoons baby capers
12 small fresh basil leaves

1 Place the eggs in a saucepan of cold water. Bring slowly to the boil, then reduce the heat and simmer for 10 minutes. Stir during the first few minutes to centre the yolks. Cool under cold water, then peel and cut into quarters. Meanwhile, score a cross in the base of each tomato. Place in boiling water for 1 minute, then plunge into cold water; peel the skin away from the cross. Cut into eighths.

2 Cook the beans in a saucepan of boiling water for 2 minutes, then refresh quickly under cold water and drain. Place the oil and vinegar in a jar and shake to combine.

3 Rub the garlic halves over the base and sides of a large salad serving platter. Arrange the lettuce wedges evenly over the base. Layer the tomato, capsicum, celery, cucumber, beans and egg quarters over the lettuce. Scatter with the onion and tuna. Arrange the olives, anchovies, capers and basil leaves over the top, pour the dressing over the salad and serve immediately.

Using a sharp knife, cut the celery stalk into long, thin strips.

Cut the peeled tomatoes into quarters, and again into eighths.

Layer the tomato, capsicum, celery, cucumber, beans and egg over the lettuce.

SPAGHETTI AND MUSSELS IN TOMATO AND HERB SAUCE

Preparation time: 15 minutes
Total cooking time: 30 minutes
Serves 4

1.5 kg (3 lb 5 oz) mussels in the shell
2 tablespoons olive oil
1 onion, thinly sliced
2 garlic cloves, crushed
425 g (15 oz) tinned tomatoes, crushed

250 ml (9 fl oz/1 cup) white wine
1 tablespoon chopped fresh basil
2 tablespoons chopped fresh parsley
500 g (1 lb 2 oz) spaghetti

1 Remove beards from the mussels and wash away any grit. Set aside.
2 Heat the oil in a large pan. Add the onion and garlic, and stir over low heat until the onion is tender. Add the crushed tomatoes, wine and herbs. Season with salt and pepper. Bring to the boil, reduce the heat, then simmer for 15–20 minutes, or until the sauce begins to thicken.

3 Add the mussels to the pan. Cook, covered, for about 5 minutes, shaking the pan occasionally. Discard any mussels that do not open during cooking. Meanwhile, add the spaghetti to a large pan of rapidly boiling water and cook until just tender. Drain immediately. Serve the mussels and sauce over the pasta.

COOK'S FILE

Hints: Serve with crusty bread and a crisp green salad.
If fresh herbs are unavailable you can substitute with about one-third the amount of dried.

PASTA MARINARA

Preparation time: 10 minutes
Total cooking time: 20 minutes
Serves 4

250 g (9 oz) boneless fish fillets
1 large calamari (squid) tube
1 tablespoon olive oil
1 onion, sliced
1 garlic clove, crushed
125 ml (4 fl oz/½ cup) red wine
2 tablespoons tomato paste (concentrated purée)
425 g (15 oz) tinned tomatoes

1 tablespoon chopped fresh basil

¼ teaspoon dried oregano
150 g (5½ oz) medium raw prawns (shrimp), peeled and deveined (tails intact)
125 g (4½ oz) scallops, halved
125 g (4½ oz) mussel meat (optional)
500 g (1 lb 2 oz) linguine

1 Cut fish fillets into small even-sized pieces. Thinly slice calamari. Heat the oil in a large frying pan. Add the onion and garlic; stir over low heat until onion is tender. Stir in the wine and tomato paste to combine. Simmer until the liquid is reduced by half. Stir in the crushed tomatoes.

2 Add the basil, oregano and season. Simmer gently for 10 minutes, stirring occasionally.
3 Add the fish, calamari, prawns, scallops and mussel meat to the sauce. Simmer, stirring, for 2–3 minutes, or until the flesh changes colour. Meanwhile, add the pasta to a large saucepan of rapidly boiling water and cook until just tender. Drain well. Serve the sauce over the pasta.

COOK'S FILE

Hints: Marinara mix is an economical method of preparing this dish and is readily available from fish shops. Overcooking of seafood will cause it to toughen.

Spaghetti and Mussels in Tomato and Herb Sauce (top) and Pasta Marinara

BAKED FISH WITH TAHINI SAUCE

Preparation time: 30 minutes
Total cooking time: 30 minutes
Serves 4

1 kg (2 lb 4 oz) whole
    white-fleshed fish, (snapper,
    bream or barramundi), scaled
    and cleaned
3 garlic cloves, crushed
2 teaspoons harissa
2 tablespoons olive oil
1 lemon, thinly sliced
1 onion, thinly sliced
2 large firm, ripe tomatoes,
    sliced
4 sprigs fresh thyme

Tahini sauce
2 teaspoons olive oil
1 garlic clove, crushed
3 tablespoons light tahini
2½ tablespoons lemon
    juice
1½ tablespoons chopped fresh
    coriander (cilantro) leaves

1 Preheat the oven to 200°C (400°F/ Gas 6). Lightly grease a large baking dish. Make 3–4 diagonal cuts on each side of the fish through the thickest part of the flesh and to the bone to ensure even cooking. Combine the garlic, harissa and olive oil in a small dish. Place 2 teaspoons in the cavity and spread the remainder over both sides of the fish, rubbing it into the slits. Place 2 lemon slices in the cavity of the fish.
2 Arrange the onion in a layer on the baking dish. Top with the tomato, thyme and remaining lemon slices. Place the fish on top and bake, uncovered, for about 25–30 minutes, or until the fish flesh is opaque.
3 Meanwhile, to make the sauce, heat the olive oil in a small saucepan over low heat and cook the garlic over medium heat for 30 seconds, then stir in the tahini, lemon juice and 125 ml (4 fl oz/½ cup) water. Add more water, if necessary, to make a smooth, but fairly thick sauce. Cook for 2 minutes, then remove from the heat and stir in the coriander. Season.
4 Transfer the onion and tomato to a serving dish. Place the fish on top and season with salt. Pour the sauce into a dish and serve on the side.

Spread the remaining harissa mixture over the sides of the fish.

Bake the fish in a moderately hot oven until the flesh is opaque.

Add some water to the tahini sauce, if necessary, to make it smooth but thick.

STUFFED SQUID

Preparation time: 50 minutes
Total cooking time: 50 minutes
Serves 4

500 g (1 lb 2 oz) firm ripe
   tomatoes
100 ml (3½ fl oz) olive oil
1 large onion, finely chopped
2 garlic cloves, crushed
160 g (5½ oz/1 cup) fresh bread
   crumbs
1 egg, lightly beaten
60 g (2¼ oz) kefalotyri cheese,
   grated
60 g (2¼ oz) haloumi cheese,
   grated
4 large or 8 small squid (1 kg/
   2 lb 4 oz), cleaned (see Note)
1 small onion, finely chopped,
   extra
2 garlic cloves, crushed, extra
150 ml (5½ fl oz) good-quality
   red wine
1 tablespoon chopped fresh
   oregano
1 tablespoon chopped fresh
   flat-leaf (Italian) parsley

1 Score a cross in the base of each tomato. Place the tomatoes in a bowl of boiling water for 1 minute, then plunge into cold water and peel the skin from the cross. Dice the flesh.
2 Heat 2 tablespoons of the oil in a frying pan, add the onion and cook over medium heat for 3 minutes. Remove. Combine with the garlic, breadcrumbs, egg and cheese. Season.
3 Pat the squid hoods dry with paper towels and, using a teaspoon, fill three-quarters full with the stuffing. Do not pack too tightly or the mixture will swell and burst out during cooking. Secure with toothpicks.
4 Heat the remaining oil in a large frying pan, add the squid and cook for 1–2 minutes on all sides. Remove. Add the extra onion and cook over medium heat for 3 minutes, or until soft, then add the extra garlic and cook for a further 1 minute. Stir in the tomato and wine, and simmer for 10 minutes, or until thick and pulpy, then stir in the herbs. Return the squid to the pan and cook, covered, for 20–25 minutes, or until tender. Serve warm with the tomato sauce or cool with a salad.

COOK'S FILE

Note: Ask the fishmonger to clean the squid. Or, discard the tentacles and cartilage. Rinse the hoods under running water and pull off the skin.

Fill the squid tubes three-quarters full with the stuffing.

Cook the stuffed squid tubes on all sides in a frying pan.

Add the squid to the tomato mixture and cook until tender.

ZARZUELA DE PESCADO

Preparation time: 30 minutes
Total cooking time: 40 minutes
Serves 6–8

300 g (10½ oz) red mullet fillets
400 g (14 oz) firm white fish
   fillets
300 g (10½ oz) cleaned calamari
   (squid)
1.5 litres (6 cups) fish stock
4 tablespoons olive oil
1 onion, chopped
6 garlic cloves, chopped
1 small red chilli, chopped
1 teaspoon paprika
pinch saffron threads
150 ml (5 fl oz) white wine
425 g (15 oz) tinned tomatoes,
   crushed
16 raw medium prawns
   (shrimp), peeled, deveined,
   tails intact
2 tablespoons brandy
24 black mussels, cleaned
1 tablespoon chopped fresh
   parsley

Picada
2 tablespoons olive oil
2 slices day-old bread, cubed
2 garlic cloves
5 blanched almonds, toasted
2 tablespoons fresh flat-leaf
   (Italian) parsley

1 Cut the fish and calamari into 4 cm (1½ inch) pieces. Place the stock in a large pan, bring to the boil and boil for 15 minutes, or until reduced by half.
2 To make the picada, heat the oil in a frying pan, cook the bread, stirring, for 2–3 minutes, or until golden, adding the garlic in the last minute.

Place the nuts, bread, garlic and parsley in a food processor and process. Add enough stock for a smooth paste.
3 Heat 2 tablespoons of the oil in a large saucepan, add the onion, garlic, chilli and paprika, and cook, stirring, for 1 minute. Add the saffron, wine, tomatoes and stock. Bring to the boil, then reduce the heat and simmer.
4 Heat the remaining oil in a frying pan and quickly fry the fish and calamari for 3–5 minutes. Remove

from the pan. Add the prawns, cook for 1 minute, then pour in the brandy. Carefully ignite the brandy with a match and let the flames burn down. Remove from the pan.
5 Add the mussels to the stock and simmer, covered, for 2–3 minutes, or until opened—discard any mussels that remain unopened. Add all the seafood and the picada to the pan, stirring until the sauce has thickened and the seafood is cooked. Season. Sprinkle with parsley; serve.

Process the nuts, bread, garlic, parsley and stock to a smooth paste.

Quickly cook the fish and calamari in a frying pan.

Add the mussels to the stock and simmer until they open.

GREEK OCTOPUS IN RED WINE STEW

Preparation time: 25 minutes
Total cooking time: 1 hour 10 minutes
Serves 4–6

1 kg (2 lb 4 oz) baby octopus
2 tablespoons olive oil
1 large onion, chopped
3 garlic cloves, crushed
1 bay leaf
750 ml (26 fl oz/3 cups) red
　　wine
3 tablespoons red wine vinegar
400 g (14 oz) tinned tomatoes,
　　crushed
1 tablespoon tomato paste
　　(concentrated purée)
1 tablespoon chopped fresh
　　oregano
¼ teaspoon ground cinnamon
small pinch ground cloves
1 teaspoon sugar
2 tablespoons finely chopped
　　fresh flat-leaf (Italian)
　　parsley

1 Cut between the head and tentacles of the octopus, just below the eyes. Grasp the body and push the beak out and up through the centre of the tentacles with your fingers. Cut the eyes from the head by slicing a small round off. Discard the eye section. Carefully slit through one side, avoiding the ink sac, and remove any gut from inside. Rinse the octopus well under running water.

2 Heat the oil in a large saucepan, add the onion and cook over medium heat for 5 minutes, or until starting to brown. Add the garlic and bay leaf, and cook for 1 minute further. Add the octopus and stir to coat in the onion mixture.

3 Stir in the wine, vinegar, tomato, tomato paste, oregano, cinnamon, cloves and sugar. Bring to the boil, then reduce the heat and simmer for 1 hour, or until the octopus is tender and the sauce has thickened slightly. Stir in the parsley and season to taste with salt and ground black pepper. Serve with a Greek salad and crusty bread to mop up the delicious juices.

Cut between the head and the tentacles of the octopus.

Slit the head section and remove any gut from the inside.

Add the octopus to the pan and stir to coat in the onion mixture.

Simmer until the octopus is tender and the sauce has thickened slightly.

CREAMY SEAFOOD RAVIOLI

Preparation time: 45 minutes +
  30 minutes standing
Total cooking time: 15 minutes
Serves 4

Pasta
250 g (9 oz/2 cups) plain
  (all-purpose) flour
pinch of salt
3 eggs
1 tablespoon olive oil
1 egg yolk, extra

Filling
50 g (1⅔ oz) butter, softened
3 garlic cloves, finely chopped
2 tablespoons finely chopped
  flat-leaf (Italian) parsley
100 g (3⅓ oz) scallops, cleaned
  and finely chopped
100 g (3⅓ oz) raw prawn
  (shrimp) meat, finely chopped

Sauce
3 tablespoons butter
3 tablespoons plain
  (all-purpose) flour
375 ml (13 fl oz/1½ cups) milk
300 ml (9½ fl oz) cream
125 ml (4 fl oz/½ cup) white
  wine
50 g (1¾ oz/½ cup) grated
  Parmesan cheese
2 tablespoons chopped flat-leaf
  (Italian) parsley

1 To make pasta, sift the flour and salt into a bowl and make a well in the centre. Whisk the eggs, oil and 1 tablespoon water in a bowl, then add gradually to the flour and mix to a firm dough. Gather into a ball.

2 Knead on a lightly floured surface for 5 minutes, or until smooth and elastic. Place in a lightly oiled bowl, cover with plastic wrap and set aside for 30 minutes.

3 To make filling, mix together the butter, garlic, parsley, scallops and prawns. Set aside.

4 Roll out a quarter of the pasta dough at a time until very thin (each portion of dough should be roughly 10 cm/4 inches wide when rolled). Place 1 teaspoonful of filling at 5 cm (2 inch) intervals down one side of each strip. Whisk the extra egg yolk with 3 tablespoons water. Brush along one side of the dough and between the filling. Fold dough over the filling to meet the other side. Repeat with the remaining filling and dough. Press the edges of the dough together firmly to seal closed.

5 Cut between the mounds with a knife or a fluted pastry cutter. Cook in batches in a large pan of rapidly boiling water for 6 minutes each batch (while the pasta is cooking make the sauce). Drain well and return to the pan to keep warm.

6 To make sauce, melt the butter in a pan, add the flour and cook over low heat for 2 minutes. Remove from the heat and gradually stir in the combined milk, cream and white wine. Cook over low heat until the sauce begins to thicken, stirring constantly to prevent lumps forming. Bring to the boil and simmer gently for 5 minutes. Add the Parmesan cheese and parsley and stir until combined. Remove from the heat, add to the ravioli and toss well to combine.

Add the combined egg, oil and water gradually to the flour.

Knead on a lightly floured surface until smooth and elastic.

Mix together the butter, garlic, parsley, scallops and prawns.

Place a teaspoon of filling at intervals down one side of the pasta.

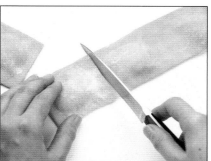

Cut between each mound of filling with a sharp knife.

Gradually stir in the combined milk, cream and white wine.

BAKED TROUT WITH FENNEL AND WATER CHESTNUTS

Preparation time: 20 minutes
Total cooking time: 20–30 minutes
Serves 4

4 whole small trout, cleaned and gutted

1 tablespoon sea salt
1 teaspoon cracked black pepper
2 fennel bulbs, trimmed and thinly sliced
230 g (7⅓ oz) tinned water chestnuts, drained
125 ml (4 fl oz/½ cup) fresh lemon juice
125 ml (4 fl oz/½ cup) dry white wine

1 Preheat the oven to 180°C (350°F/ Gas 4). Arrange the trout, side by side, in a large baking dish, and sprinkle with sea salt and pepper.
2 Top with the sliced fennel and water chestnuts. Pour over the lemon juice and wine and cover with foil.
3 Bake for 20–30 minutes, or until the fish flakes with a fork and the fennel is tender, then remove the foil and serve immediately.

Trim the stalk and base from the fennel bulbs and thinly slice.

Arrange the trout, side-by-side, in a dish and sprinkle with salt and pepper.

Top the trout with fennel and chestnuts, then pour over the lemon juice and wine.

MOROCCAN SALMON WITH COUSCOUS

Preparation time: 15 minutes +
  2 hours marinating
Total cooking time: 20 minutes
Serves 4

4 salmon fillets (about 170–
  200 g or 6–7 oz each),
  skinned and pin boned (see
  below image)
2 garlic cloves, crushed
4 tablespoons chopped coriander
  (cilantro) leaves
2 tablespoons chopped flat-leaf
  (Italian) parsley
¼ preserved lemon, pith
  discarded
½ teaspoon paprika
2 tablespoons chopped mint
2 teaspoons ground cumin
2 teaspoons ground turmeric
2 tablespoons lemon juice
¼ teaspoon crushed dried
  chillies
2 tablespoons olive oil
2 tablespoons niçoise olives
400 g (14 oz) instant couscous

1 Pat the salmon dry with paper towel, then place in a non-metallic dish. Place the garlic, coriander leaves, parsley, preserved lemon, paprika, mint, ground cumin, ground turmeric, lemon juice, chilli, 2 tablespoons of the olive oil and 2 tablespoons water in a food processor and pulse to blend. Do not over-process; it should remain chunky. Spread on the fish and marinate for at least 2 hours.

2 Preheat the oven to 190°C (375°F/ Gas 5). Cut out four squares of foil large enough to enclose each fillet of fish. Place a fillet (flat-side down), some of the marinade and olives on each piece of foil, then season well. Bring up the sides of the foil and fold in the ends to form a neat parcel. Place on a baking tray and bake for 20 minutes.

3 Place the couscous in a large heatproof bowl. Add the remaining oil and 500 ml (17 fl oz/2 cups) boiling water, then cover and leave for 5 minutes. Fluff up with a fork. Divide the couscous among the serving plates. Remove the salmon from the foil and place on top of the couscous. Spoon on the cooking juices and olives.

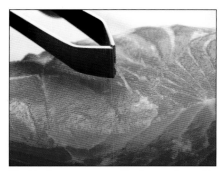

To pin bone, remove the bones from the salmon fillets with a pair of tweezers.

Evenly spread the chunky sauce on the salmon and leave to marinate.

BAKED FISH WITH GARLIC BREADCRUMBS

Preparation time: 15 minutes
Total cooking time: 20 minutes
Serves 4

4 fillets firm white fish (about
    200 g/6½ oz each)
75 g (2½ oz) butter, melted
3 garlic cloves, crushed
160 g (5½ oz/2 cups) fresh white
    breadcrumbs (made from
    Italian bread)

1 tablespoon finely chopped
    parsley
lemon wedges, to serve

1 Preheat the oven to 200°C (400°F/ Gas 6). Brush an ovenproof dish with olive oil and arrange the fish in a single layer.
2 Mix together the butter and garlic in a bowl and set aside. Mix together the bread crumbs and parsley and scatter in a thick layer over the fish. Drizzle with the garlic butter.
3 Bake for 20 minutes, or until the fish is white and flakes easily, and the

crumbs are golden brown. If the crumbs are not golden but the fish is cooked, flash under a hot grill for a couple of minutes. Don't take your eyes off it as it can burn very quickly. Serve with lemon wedges.

COOK'S FILE

Note: Fresh bread crumbs are very simple to make. Remove the crusts from slightly stale (at least one-day old) slices of bread. Put the bread in a food processor and mix until crumbs form. Use ordinary bread or, as in this recipe, Italian bread.

Brush an ovenproof dish with olive oil and arrange the fish in a single layer.

Mix together the fresh breadcrumbs and parsley and scatter over the fish.

Bake until the fish is white and can be easily flaked with a fork.

FISH IN PARCHMENT

Preparation time: 20 minutes
Total cooking time: 20 minutes
Serves 4

4 deep sea perch fillets (about
    150–200 g/5–6 oz each)
1 leek, white part only, cut into
    julienne strips (see Note)
4 spring onions (scallions), cut
    into julienne strips
2 teaspoons finely chopped
    chives, optional

30 g (1 oz) butter
1 lemon, cut into 12 very
    thin slices
juice of 1 lemon, extra

1 Preheat the oven to 180°C (350°F/ Gas 4). Place each fish fillet in the centre of a piece of baking paper large enough to enclose the fish.
2 Scatter over the leek, spring onion and chives. Top each with a teaspoon of butter and 3 slices of lemon. Squeeze over the extra lemon juice. Bring the top and bottom edges of the paper together and fold over, then

scrunch over the sides to make a parcel. Put on a baking tray and bake for 20 minutes.
3 Check to see that the fish is cooked (it should be white and easily flaked with a fork) and then serve. You can either let each person open their own parcel or take out the fish with an egg slice and serve on warm plates. Good with mixed wild and brown rice.

COOK'S FILE

Note: Julienne strips are thin, regular, matchstick-sized pieces of vegetables. They cook quickly and look attractive.

Slice the leek and the spring onions very finely to make julienne strips.

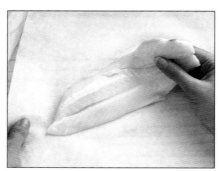
Place each fish fillet in the centre of a piece of baking paper.

Scatter over the julienne vegetables and top with butter and lemon slices.

Baked Fish with Garlic Breadcrumbs (top) and Fish in Parchment

SPAGHETTI WITH OLIVE, CAPER AND ANCHOVY SAUCE

Preparation time: 15 minutes
Total cooking time: 20 minutes
Serves 6

375 g (13 oz) spaghetti
4 tablespoons olive oil
2 onions, finely chopped
3 garlic cloves, finely chopped

½ teaspoon chilli flakes
6 large ripe tomatoes, diced
4 tablespoons capers in brine, rinsed, drained
7–8 anchovies in oil, drained, minced
150 g (5½ oz) Kalamata olives
3 tablespoons chopped fresh flat-leaf (Italian) parsley

1 Bring a large saucepan of salted water to the boil, add the spaghetti and cook until al dente. Drain.

2 Meanwhile, heat the oil in a sauce pan, add the onion and cook over medium heat for 5 minutes. Add the garlic and chilli flakes, and cook for 30 seconds, then add the tomatoes, capers and anchovies. Simmer over low heat for 5–10 minutes, or until thick and pulpy, then stir in the olives and parsley.

3 Stir the pasta through the sauce. Season with salt and freshly ground black pepper and serve immediately with crusty bread.

Mince the drained anchovies in a mortar and pestle.

Cook the spaghetti in a pan of lightly salted boiling water until al dente.

Simmer the tomato and caper mixture over low heat until thick and pulpy.

CAPONATA WITH CHARGRILLED TUNA

Preparation time: 25 minutes + 1 hour standing + cooling
Total cooking time: 50 minutes
Serves 6

Caponata
500 g (1 lb 2 oz) ripe tomatoes
750 g (1 lb 10 oz) eggplant (aubergine), cut into 1 cm (½ inch) cubes
4 tablespoons olive oil
2 tablespoons olive oil, extra
1 onion, chopped
3 celery stalks, chopped
2 tablespoons drained capers
90 g (3¼ oz/½ cup) green olives, pitted
1 tablespoon sugar
125 ml (4 fl oz/½ cup) red wine vinegar

olive oil, for brushing
6 x 200 g (7 oz) tuna steaks

1 To make the caponata, score a cross in the base of each tomato. Place in a bowl of boiling water for 1 minute, remove, then plunge into cold water and peel skin away from the cross. Cut into 1 cm (½ inch) cubes.

2 Sprinkle the eggplant with salt and leave for 1 hour. Place in a colander, rinse under cold running water and pat dry. Heat half the oil in a frying pan, add half the eggplant and cook for 4–5 minutes, or until golden and soft. Remove. Repeat with the remaining oil and eggplant. Remove.

3 Heat the extra oil in the same pan, add the onion and celery, and cook for 3–4 minutes, or until golden. Reduce the heat to low, add the tomato and simmer for 15 minutes, stirring occasionally. Stir in the capers, olives, sugar and vinegar, season and simmer, stirring occasionally, for 10 minutes, or until slightly reduced. Stir in the eggplant. Remove from the heat and allow to cool.

4 Heat a chargrill plate (griddle) and brush lightly with olive oil. Cook the tuna for 2–3 minutes each side, or until cooked to your liking. Serve immediately with the caponata.

Cook the eggplant in two batches until golden and soft.

Add the capers, olives, sugar and vinegar to the tomato mixture.

Cook the tuna on a chargrill plate (griddle) until cooked to your liking.

Cut open the octopus heads and discard the guts.

Remove the beaks from the octopus and cut the tentacles into sections.

Toss the octopus over high heat until it becomes opaque.

When most of the liquid has evaporated add the tomato and onions.

OCTOPUS IN FRESH TOMATO SAUCE

Preparation time: 20 minutes
Total cooking time: 1 hour 10 minutes
Serves 4–6

1 kg (2 lb) baby octopus
2 tablespoons olive oil
4 tablespoons dry white
　wine
500 g (1 lb) ripe tomatoes,
　peeled and chopped
4 pickling onions, peeled and
　quartered
1 garlic clove, chopped
2 tablespoons chopped fresh
　flat-leaf (Italian) parsley

1 Wash the octopus and cut the heads off. Cut open the heads and remove the guts. Wash the heads and drain. Remove the beaks and cut the tentacles into sets of four.
2 Heat the oil in a large pan until very hot, add the octopus and toss over high heat for about 10 minutes, or until the octopus is opaque and the pan almost dry. Add the wine and simmer, uncovered, until most of the liquid has evaporated, then add the tomato and onions. Bring to the boil, then reduce the heat and simmer over low heat for 45 minutes to 1 hour, or until tender.
3 Serve hot or warm, sprinkled with the combined chopped garlic and parsley and lots of black pepper.

COOK'S FILE

Note: To peel tomatoes, cut a cross in the base, plunge in boiling water then into cold. Peel the skin from the cross.

PAN-FRIED FISH

Preparation time: Nil
Total cooking time: 8 minutes
Serves 4

plain (all-purpose) flour,
   for dusting
olive oil

4 white fish steaks, such as
   swordfish or blue-eyed cod

1 Sift the flour together with a little salt and pepper onto a dinner plate. Coat both sides of the fish steaks with seasoned flour, shaking off the excess.
2 Heat about 3 mm (⅛ inch) oil in a frying pan until very hot. Put the fish into the hot oil immediately and cook for 3 minutes on one side, then turn and cook the other side for 2 minutes, or until the coating is crisp and well browned. Reduce the heat to low and cook for a further 2–3 minutes, until the flesh flakes easily with a fork.
3 Remove from the pan and drain briefly on paper towels, then serve straight away, perhaps with lemon wedges, sautéed potatoes and a salad.

Coat both sides of the fish with seasoned flour and shake off the excess.

Cook the fish for 3 minutes, then turn over. Cook in batches if necessary.

Remove from the pan and drain briefly on paper towels.

TROUT WITH LEEK AND CAPER SAUCE

Preparation time: 10 minutes
Total cooking time: 10 minutes
Serves 4

45 g (1½ oz) melted
   butter
4 thick ocean trout fillets
   (about 155 g/5 oz each)

Leek and caper sauce
50 g (1⅔ oz) butter

1 leek, chopped
250 ml (9 fl oz/1 cup) white
   wine (riesling or chardonnay)
2 tablespoons capers, drained
1 tablespoon chopped flat-leaf
   (Italian) parsley

1 Brush a shallow oven tray with melted butter and put the fish on the tray. Brush fish with melted butter and grill (broil) under moderate heat, without turning, until the fish is just cooked. Remove and cover loosely with foil to keep warm while making the sauce.

2 To make leek and caper sauce, melt the butter in a pan and cook the leek gently until soft, but not brown. Add the wine and simmer for 3–4 minutes. Add the capers, parsley and salt and pepper to taste, then remove from the heat.

3 Spoon the hot sauce over the fish and serve immediately.

COOK'S FILE

Variation: Use salmon fillets or cutlets or any thick white fish.

Cut down the sides of the leek (not all the way to the base) to wash thoroughly.

Brush the trout with melted butter and grill until almost cooked.

Add the capers, parsley, salt and pepper, then remove from the heat.

Once the mussels have cooled a little, remove them from their shells.

Mix the tomato paste with water and whisk into the simmering liquid.

Gradually add the milk, stirring constantly over low heat until thickened.

Spoon the white sauce over the mussels and tomato sauce.

MUSSELS IN TWO SAUCES

Preparation time: 25 minutes
Total cooking time: 45 minutes
Serves 4

3 tablespoons olive oil
1.25 kg (2½ lb) mussels in
    shells, scrubbed
3 tablespoons mozzarella, grated
2 tablespoons Parmesan, grated

Tomato sauce
2 cloves garlic, crushed
125 ml (4 fl oz/½ cup) white
    wine
3 tablespoons tomato paste
    (concentrated purée)

White sauce
25 g (¾ oz) butter
3 tablespoons plain
    (all purpose) flour
250 ml (9 fl oz/1 cup) milk

1 Heat half the oil in a large pan. Add the mussels and cook over high heat, shaking the pan, for 5 minutes until opened. Discard any that do not open. Strain the liquid and reserve. Let the mussels cool, then remove from their shells. Preheat oven to 190°C (375°F/Gas 5).

2 To make tomato sauce, heat the remaining oil in a pan. Add the garlic and fry until golden. Add the wine and reserved liquid and simmer gently for 5 minutes. Mix the tomato paste with 3 tablespoons water, then whisk into the simmering liquid. Simmer for a further 10 minutes and season to taste with salt and pepper.

3 To make white sauce, melt the butter in a pan. Add the flour and cook for 1 minute. Very gradually stir in the milk over low heat until the sauce thickens. Season.

4 Combine the tomato sauce and mussels and pour into four 250 ml (9 fl oz/1 cup) ramekins. Spoon over the white sauce. Sprinkle with the combined cheeses and bake for 20 minutes. Serve with crusty bread.

Meat and poultry

LAMB TAGINE

Preparation time: 15 minutes + 1 hour
   marinating
Total cooking time: 1 hour 45 minutes
Serves 6–8

1.5 kg (3 lb 5 oz) leg or shoulder
   lamb, cut into 2.5 cm (1 inch)
   pieces
3 garlic cloves, chopped
4 tablespoons olive oil
2 teaspoons ground cumin
1 teaspoon ground ginger
1 teaspoon ground turmeric
1 teaspoon paprika
½ teaspoon ground cinnamon
2 onions, thinly sliced
600 ml (21 fl oz) beef stock
¼ preserved lemon, pulp
   discarded, rind rinsed and cut
   into thin strips
425 g (15 oz) tinned chickpeas,
   drained
35 g (1¼ oz) cracked green
   olives
3 tablespoons chopped fresh
   coriander (cilantro) leaves

1 Place the lamb in a non-metallic bowl, add garlic, 2 tablespoons olive oil, ground cumin, ginger, turmeric, paprika, cinnamon, and ½ teaspoon ground black pepper and 1 teaspoon salt. Mix well to coat and leave to marinate for 1 hour.
2 Heat the remaining oil in a large saucepan, add the lamb in batches and cook over high heat for 2–3 minutes, or until browned. Remove from the pan. Add the onion and cook for 2 minutes, return the meat to the pan and add the beef stock. Reduce the heat and simmer, covered, for 1 hour. Add the preserved lemon, chickpeas and olives, and cook, uncovered, for a further 30 minutes, or until the meat is tender and the sauce reduced and thickened. Stir in the coriander. Serve in bowls with couscous.

COOK'S FILE

Note: If you prefer, you can bake this lamb in the oven in a covered casserole dish. Preheat the oven to 190°C (375°F/ Gas 5) and cook the tagine for about 1 hour, adding the lemon, chickpeas and olives after 40 minutes.

Coat the lamb in the spice marinade, then leave for 1 hour.

Cook the lamb in batches over high heat until browned.

Add the preserved lemon, chickpeas and cracked green olives to the pan.

LAMB KEFTA

Preparation time: 30 minutes
Total cooking time: 40 minutes
Serves 4

1 kg (2 lb 4 oz) minced (ground)
    lamb
1 onion, finely chopped
2 garlic cloves, finely chopped
2 tablespoons finely chopped
    fresh flat-leaf (Italian)
    parsley
2 tablespoons finely chopped
    fresh coriander (cilantro)
    leaves
½ teaspoon cayenne pepper
½ teaspoon ground allspice
½ teaspoon ground ginger
½ teaspoon ground cardamom
1 teaspoon ground cumin
1 teaspoon paprika

Sauce
2 tablespoons olive oil
1 onion, finely chopped
2 garlic cloves, finely chopped
2 teaspoons ground cumin
½ teaspoon ground cinnamon
1 teaspoon paprika
2 x 425 g (15 oz) tinned
    tomatoes, chopped
2 teaspoons harissa
4 tablespoons chopped fresh
    coriander (coriander)
    leaves

1 Preheat the oven to 180°C (350°F/ Gas 4). Lightly grease two baking trays. Place the lamb, onion, garlic, herbs and spices in a bowl and mix together well. Season to taste. Roll tablespoons of the mixture into balls and place on the prepared trays. Bake for 18–20 minutes, or until browned.

2 Meanwhile, to make the sauce, heat the oil in a large saucepan, add the onion and cook over medium heat for 5 minutes, or until soft. Add the garlic, cumin, cinnamon and paprika, and cook for 1 minute, or until fragrant.

3 Stir in the tomato and harissa, and bring to the boil. Reduce the heat and simmer for 20 minutes, then add the meatballs and simmer for 10 minutes, or until cooked through. Stir in the coriander, season well and serve.

Roll tablespoons of the lamb mixture into balls.

Add the spices to the onion and cook until fragrant.

Simmer the meatballs in the tomato sauce until cooked through.

SPRING CHICKEN WITH HONEY GLAZE

Preparation time: 15 minutes
Total cooking time: 55 minutes
Serves 6–8

2 small (1.5 kg/3 lb) chickens
1 tablespoon light olive oil

Honey glaze
3 tablespoons honey
juice and finely grated zest
    of 1 lemon

1 tablespoon finely chopped
    rosemary
1 tablespoon dry white wine
1 tablespoon white wine vinegar
2 teaspoons Dijon mustard
1½ tablespoons olive oil

1 Preheat the oven to 180°C (350°F/ Gas 4). Halve the chickens by cutting down either side of the backbone. Discard the backbone. Cut the chickens into quarters; brush with oil and season lightly. Place on a rack in a roasting pan, skin-side-down, and roast for 20 minutes.

2 To make honey glaze, combine all the ingredients in a small pan. Bring to the boil, reduce the heat and simmer for 5 minutes.

3 After cooking one side, turn the chickens over and baste well with the warm glaze. Return to the oven and roast for 20 minutes. Baste once more and cook for a further 15 minutes. Serve hot or cold.

COOK'S FILE

Note: To test if the chicken is cooked, pierce the meat at its thickest point. The juices should run clear.

Halve each chicken by cutting down either side of the backbone.

Cut the chickens into quarters—you will find kitchen scissors easier than a knife.

Cook one side of the chicken, then turn over and baste with warm glaze.

PORK WITH MUSTARD AND CREAM SAUCE

Preparation time: 10 minutes
Total cooking time: 25 minutes
Serves 4

2 tablespoons olive oil
4 pork leg steaks
1 onion, sliced into rings

2 garlic cloves, crushed
125 ml (4 fl oz/½ cup) white wine
250 ml (9 fl oz/1 cup) cream
2 tablespoons wholegrain mustard
2 tablespoons chopped parsley

1 Heat the oil in a large frying pan; cook the pork for 3–4 minutes each side. Transfer to a plate and set aside.

2 Reduce the heat and add the onion. Cook until soft, then add the garlic and cook for a further minute. Add the wine and simmer until the liquid is reduced by half.

3 Stir in the cream and mustard and simmer gently for 5 minutes. Add the pork and simmer for a further 5 minutes. Stir in the parsley and season to taste. Serve immediately, with the sauce spooned over the pork.

Fry the pork in oil for 3–4 minutes on each side, until browned.

Cook the onion and garlic until soft and golden, then add the wine and simmer.

Add the pork and then simmer gently for 5 minutes. Stir in the fresh parsley.

BEEF WITH PROSCIUTTO AND MUSHROOMS

Preparation time: 15 minutes
Total cooking time: 25 minutes
Serves 4

2 tablespoons olive oil
200 g (6½ oz) button
  mushrooms, stalks trimmed
60 g (2 oz) sliced prosciutto, cut
  into wide strips
4 thick slices beef scotch fillet
  or eye fillet steaks

2 garlic cloves, crushed
2 tablespoons chopped fresh
  flat-leaf (Italian) parsley
3 tablespoons dry white
  wine
125 ml (4 fl oz/½ cup) cream

1 Preheat oven to 200°C (400°F/Gas 6). Heat the oil in a deep ovenproof frying pan (large enough to hold the beef steaks in one layer, without overlapping). Add the mushrooms and prosciutto and toss until the mushrooms start to brown.
2 Layer steaks over the mushrooms,

sprinkle with garlic and parsley, then pour over the wine. Bring to the boil, reduce the heat, then cover the pan (with a lid or tightly with foil) and bake for 10–15 minutes, or until the steaks are cooked to taste.
3 Set the steaks aside to keep warm. Heat the pan on the hotplate, add the cream and boil for 3–5 minutes, or until thickened slightly; pour over the steaks and serve immediately.

Add the mushrooms and prosciutto to the oil and toss until starting to brown.

Sprinkle the steaks with garlic and parsley and then pour in the wine.

Add the cream to the pan and boil for 3–5 minutes, or until slightly thickened.

Trim away any fat from the veal cutlets, then toss them in flour.

Cook the veal cutlets in a single layer until browned on both sides.

Once most of the wine has evaporated, pour in the beef stock and add pepper.

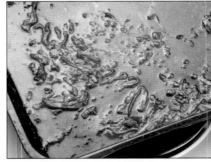

If the pan juices need thickening, simmer them for a while, uncovered.

VEAL CUTLETS WITH SAGE

Preparation time: 25 minutes
Total cooking time: 1 hour 20 minutes
Serves 4–6

8 veal cutlets
2–3 tablespoons plain
   (all-purpose) flour
30 g (1 oz) butter
2 tablespoons olive oil
75 g (2½ oz) sliced ham, cut into
   strips
125 ml (4 fl oz/½ cup) dry white
   wine
8 fresh sage leaves, shredded
2 teaspoons chopped fresh
   rosemary
250 ml (9 fl oz/1 cup) beef stock
freshly ground black pepper

1 Trim any fat from the veal cutlets and then toss in flour. Shake off the excess flour.
2 Heat the butter and 1 tablespoon of the oil in a large baking dish. When foaming, add the veal cutlets in a single layer and cook until browned on both sides. Drain on paper towel. Wipe the pan clean, then add the remaining oil and the ham; toss over the heat for a few minutes.
3 Return the cutlets to the pan, then pour in the wine with the herbs. Simmer, uncovered, until most of the liquid has evaporated. Add the stock and black pepper. Bring back to the boil, reduce the heat and simmer, covered (with foil if necessary), for about 1 hour, or until the cutlets are tender, turning once during cooking.
4 Transfer the cutlets to a serving dish and keep warm. If the pan juices are very thin, simmer uncovered until thickened. Season with salt to taste, if necessary, then pour over the cutlets. Garnish with fresh sage.

CHICKEN TORTELLINI WITH TOMATO SAUCE

Preparation time: 30 minutes + resting
Total cooking time: 30 minutes
Serves 4

Pasta
250 g (9 oz/2 cups) plain
    (all-purpose) flour
pinch of salt
3 eggs
1 tablespoon olive oil

Filling
20 g (⅔ oz) butter
80 g (2⅔ oz) skinless, boneless
    chicken breasts, cubed
2 slices pancetta, chopped
50 g (1¾ oz/½ cup) grated
    Parmesan cheese
½ teaspoon nutmeg
1 egg, lightly beaten

Tomato sauce
4 tablespoons olive oil
1.5 kg (3 lb) fresh ripe tomatoes,
    peeled and chopped
3 tablespoons chopped fresh
    oregano
50 g (1¾ oz/½ cup) grated
    Parmesan cheese
100 g (3⅓ oz) fresh bocconcini,
    thinly sliced, to serve

1 To make pasta, sift the flour and salt into a bowl and make a well in the centre. In a jug, whisk together the eggs, oil and 1 tablespoon water. Add the egg mixture gradually to the flour, mixing to a firm dough. Gather together into a ball, adding a little extra water if necessary.
2 Knead on a lightly floured surface for 5 minutes, or until the dough is smooth and elastic. Place in a lightly oiled bowl, cover with plastic wrap and leave for 30 minutes.
3 To make filling, heat the butter in a frying pan; add the chicken and cook until golden brown, then drain. Process the chicken and pancetta in a food processor or mincer until finely chopped. Transfer to a bowl and add the cheese, nutmeg, egg, and salt and pepper to taste. Set aside.
4 Roll out the dough very thinly on a lightly floured surface. Using a floured cutter, cut into 5 cm (2 inch) rounds. Spoon about ½ teaspoon of filling into the centre of each round. Fold the rounds in half to form semi-circles, pressing the edges together firmly. Wrap each semi-circle around your finger to form a ring and then press the ends of the dough together firmly.
5 To make tomato sauce, place the oil, tomatoes and oregano in a frying pan and cook over high heat for 10 minutes. Stir through the Parmesan cheese, then set aside.
6 Cook the tortellini in two batches in a large pan of rapidly boiling water for about 6 minutes each batch, or until just tender. Drain well and return to the pan. Reheat the tomato sauce, add to the tortellini and toss to combine. Divide the tortellini among individual bowls, top with bocconcini and allow the cheese to melt a little before serving.

Gather together the dough into a ball with your hand.

Place the dough in a lightly oiled bowl, cover with plastic wrap and leave.

Add the cheese, nutmeg, egg and seasoning to the processed filling mixture.

Roll out the dough very thinly and cut into rounds with a floured pastry cutter.

Wrap the semi-circles around your finger to make a ring. Press the ends together.

Stir the grated Parmesan into the tomato sauce.

MOROCCAN LAMB SALAD

Preparation time: 30 minutes + 1 hour
marinating
Total cooking time: 10 minutes
Serves 4

500 g (1 lb) lamb backstrap
  (tender eye of the lamb loin)
1 teaspoon ground cumin
½ teaspoon turmeric
2 teaspoons harissa (see Note)
2 tablespoons oil
3 oranges, segmented
1 red onion, sliced
¼ preserved lemon, zest only,
  finely chopped

2 tablespoons shredded mint
3 tablespoons coriander
  (cilantro) leaves
2 small red chillies, cut into very
  thin strips, to garnish

Dressing
2 garlic cloves, crushed
½ teaspoon ground cumin
1 tablespoon lemon juice
3 tablespoons olive oil

1 Trim any excess fat or sinew from
the lamb and place in a shallow dish.
Combine the cumin, turmeric,
harissa and oil, pour over the lamb
and toss to coat. Cover and refrigerate
for 1 hour.

2 To make the dressing, whisk all the
ingredients together in a bowl.
3 Combine the orange, onion, lemon
zest and herbs. Drizzle with the
dressing, mix gently and refrigerate.
4 Cook the marinated lamb on a
preheated barbecue grill or in a
chargrill (griddle) pan for 5 minutes
on each side, or until medium rare.
Leave for 10 minutes before slicing.
Divide the salad among four plates,
top with the sliced lamb, garnish with
the chilli strips and serve.

COOK'S FILE

Note: Harissa is made of spices, chilli
peppers, garlic and oil. It is available
from supermarkets and delicatessens.

*Peel and segment the oranges using a small
sharp knife.*

*Combine the orange segments, red onion,
preserved lemon zest and herbs.*

*Cook the marinated lamb for 5 minutes on
each side.*

MADRID CHICKEN

Preparation time: 10 minutes
Total cooking time: 1 hour
Serves 4

1 orange
1 tablespoon olive oil
4 chicken breasts on the bone,
  skin and excess fat removed
2 chorizo sausages (about 200 g/
  7 oz), cut into 1 cm (½ inch)
  slices (see Note)
250 ml (9 fl oz/1 cup) chicken
  stock

250 ml (9 fl oz/1 cup) bottled
  tomato pasta sauce
12 Kalamata olives
Kalamata olives, extra, to
  garnish
flat-leaf (Italian) parsley, to
  garnish

1 Using a vegetable peeler, cut off 4 thin strips of orange zest. Remove the peel from the orange and segment.
2 Heat the oil in a frying pan and brown the chicken and chorizo slices, in batches if necessary. (Leave the meat side of the chicken browning for 5 minutes.) Add the stock, tomato sauce and orange zest. Bring to the boil, then reduce the heat and simmer, covered, for 25 minutes.
3 Remove the lid, turn the chicken over and continue to simmer, uncovered, for about 25 minutes, or until the chicken is tender and the sauce reduced. Season with salt and freshly ground black pepper and stir through the olives and reserved orange segments. Garnish with extra olives and flat-leaf parsley.

COOK'S FILE

Note: Chorizo sausages can be replaced with any spicy sausages.

1

2

3

SPAGHETTI CARBONARA

Preparation time: 10 minutes
Total cooking time: 25 minutes
Serves 4–6

8 rashers bacon
500 g (1 lb 2 oz) spaghetti
4 eggs
50 g (1¾ oz/½ cup)
    freshly grated Parmesan
    cheese
300 ml (10½ fl oz/1¼ cups)
    cream

1 Remove rind from the bacon and discard. Cut bacon into thin strips. Add to a heavy-based frying pan and cook over medium heat until crisp. Remove and drain on paper towel.
2 Add pasta to a large pan of rapidly boiling water and cook until just just tender. Drain in a colander and return to the pan. Set aside.
3 While pasta is cooking, beat eggs, Parmesan and cream in a small bowl. Add bacon to the bowl and pour the mixture over the hot pasta; toss well. Return pan to heat and cook mixture, over very low heat, for ½–1 minute, or until mixture just thickens. Add the pepper and serve immediately. May be garnished with sprigs of fresh herbs, if desired.

COOK'S FILE

Storage time: Best cooked just before serving.
Hint: Take care not to overcook sauce as it can curdle. Make sure the heat is very low after you have combined pasta with sauce. If you are using an electric element you can turn the heat off at this stage.

1

2

3

TAGLIATELLE WITH CHICKEN LIVERS AND CREAM

Preparation time: 20 minutes
Total cooking time: 15 minutes
Serves 4

300 g (10½ oz) chicken livers
2 tablespoons olive oil
1 onion, finely chopped
1 garlic clove, crushed
250 ml (9 fl oz/1 cup) cream
1 tablespoon snipped chives
1 teaspoon seeded mustard

2 eggs, beaten
375 g (13 oz) tagliatelle
2 tablespoons freshly grated
  Parmesan cheese, for serving
snipped chives, for serving

1 Trim the chicken livers and chop them into small pieces.
2 Heat the oil in a large frying pan. Add the onion and garlic and stir over low heat until the onion is tender. Add the chicken livers to pan, then cook gently for 2–3 minutes. Remove from the heat. Stir the cream, chives and mustard into the chicken livers. Season to taste with salt and freshly ground black pepper. Return the pan to the heat. Bring to the boil.
3 Add the beaten eggs and stir quickly to combine. Remove the pan from the heat. Meanwhile, add the tagliatelle to a large pan of rapidly boiling water and cook until just tender. Drain well and return to the pan. Add sauce to hot pasta and toss well to combine. Serve in warmed pasta bowls. Sprinkle with the Parmesan cheese and snipped chives.

COOK'S FILE

Hint: Snip chives with kitchen scissors.

CABBAGE ROLLS

Preparation time: 30 minutes
Total cooking time: 1 hour 35 minutes
Makes 12 large rolls

1 tablespoon olive oil
1 onion, finely chopped large
    pinch allspice
1 teaspoon ground cumin
large pinch ground nutmeg
2 bay leaves
1 large head of cabbage
500 g (1 lb 2 oz) minced
    (ground) lamb
220 g (7¾ oz/1 cup) short-grain
    white rice
4 garlic cloves, crushed
4 tablespoons pine nuts, toasted
2 tablespoons finely chopped
    fresh mint
2 tablespoons finely chopped
    fresh flat-leaf (Italian)
    parsley
1 tablespoon finely chopped
    raisins
250 ml (9 fl oz/1 cup) olive oil,
    extra
4 tablespoons lemon juice
extra virgin olive oil, to drizzle
lemon wedges, to serve

1 Heat the oil in a saucepan, add the onion and cook over medium heat for 10 minutes, or until golden. Add the allspice, cumin and nutmeg, and cook for 2 minutes, or until fragrant. Remove from the pan.
2 Bring a very large saucepan of water to the boil and add the bay leaves. Remove the tough outer leaves and about 5 cm (2 inch) of the core from the cabbage with a sharp knife, then place the cabbage into the boiling water. Cook for 5 minutes, then carefully loosen a whole leaf with tongs and remove. Continue to cook and remove the leaves until you reach the core. Drain, reserving the cooking liquid and set aside to cool.
3 Take 12 equal-size leaves and cut a small 'v' from the core end of each leaf to remove the thickest part, then trim the firm central veins so that the leaf is as flat as possible. Place three quarters of the remaining leaves into a very large sauce pan to prevent the rolls catching on the base.

4 Combine meat, onion mixture, rice, garlic, pine nuts, mint, parsley and raisins. Season. With the core end of the leaf closest to you, form 2 tablespoons of the mixture into an oval and place in the centre of the leaf. Roll up, tucking in the sides to enclose the filling. Repeat with the other 11 leaves and filling. Place the rolls tightly in a single layer in the lined saucepan, seam-side down.
5 Combine 625 ml (21½ fl oz/2½ cups)

of the cooking liquid with the extra olive oil, lemon juice and 1 teaspoon salt, and pour over the rolls (the liquid should just come to the top of the rolls). Lay the remaining leaves on top. Cover and bring to the boil, then reduce the heat and simmer for 1 hour 15 minutes, or until the filling is cooked. Remove with a slotted spoon and drizzle with extra virgin olive oil. Serve with lemon wedges.

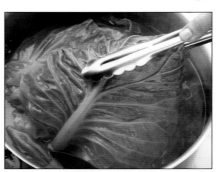

Cook the cabbage in boiling water and remove the outer leaves as they cook.

Roll up the cabbage leaf, tucking in the sides, to enclose the filling.

TURKISH LAMB AND RICE PILAU

Preparation time: 20 minutes + 1 hour standing
Total cooking time: 35 minutes
Serves 4–6

1 large eggplant (aubergine) (500 g/1 lb 2 oz), cut into 1 cm (½ inch) cubes
125 ml (4 fl oz/½ cup) olive oil
1 large onion, finely chopped
1 teaspoon ground cinnamon
2 teaspoons ground cumin
1 teaspoon ground coriander
300 g (10½ oz) long-grain rice
500 ml (17 fl oz/2 cups) chicken stock
500 g (1 lb 2 oz) minced (ground) lamb
½ teaspoon allspice
2 tablespoons olive oil, extra
2 tomatoes, cut into wedges
3 tablespoons pistachios, toasted
2 tablespoons currants
2 tablespoons chopped fresh coriander (cilantro) leaves

1 Place the eggplant in a colander, sprinkle generously with salt and leave to stand for 1 hour. Rinse well and squeeze dry in a tea (dish) towel. Heat 2 tablespoons oil in a large, deep frying pan with a lid, and cook the eggplant over medium heat for 5–8 minutes, or until golden and cooked. Drain.
2 Heat the remaining oil in the pan and cook the onion for 2–3 minutes, or until soft but not brown. Stir in ½ teaspoon cinnamon, 1 teaspoon cumin and ½ teaspoon ground coriander. Stir in the rice, then add the stock, season and bring to the boil.

Reduce the heat and simmer, covered, for 15 minutes, adding more water if the pilau starts to dry out.
3 Meanwhile, place the meat in a bowl with the allspice and remaining cumin, cinnamon and coriander. Season and mix together well. Roll into walnut-size balls. Heat the extra oil in the frying pan, add the meatballs in batches and cook over medium heat for 5 minutes, or until lightly browned and cooked through. Remove and drain on paper towel. Add the tomato to the pan and cook for 3–5 minutes or until turning lightly golden. Remove.
4 Stir the eggplant, pistachios, currants and meatballs through the rice (this should be quite dry). Spoon onto plates, place the cooked tomato around the edges and garnish with the coriander leaves.

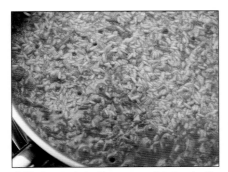

Add the stock to the pan and bring to the boil.

Roll the lamb mixture into walnut-size balls.

Stir the eggplant, pistachios, currants and meatballs through the rice.

179

BEEF OLIVES WITH ARTICHOKE STUFFING

Preparation time: 20 minutes
Total cooking time: 50 minutes
Serves 4

8 slices beef topside (about 80g/
    2⅔ oz each slice)
100 g (3⅓ oz) prosciutto, finely
    chopped
50 g (1⅔ oz) butter, melted
4 artichoke hearts
2 tablespoons chopped fresh
    thyme
plain (all-purpose) flour, for
    coating
4 tablespoons dry white wine
125 ml (4 fl oz/½ cup) beef
    stock

1 Flatten each beef slice with a meat mallet (or rolling pin) until wafer thin. Mix together the prosciutto and 1 tablespoon of the butter and spread over the beef slices. Roughly chop each artichoke into quarters and arrange the pieces evenly over the prosciutto. Sprinkle with thyme and salt and pepper to taste.
2 Roll up the beef slices around the stuffing. Tie each beef olive with string to hold it together.
3 Heat the remaining butter in a frying pan. Roll the beef olives in a little flour, shake off the excess and fry until browned. Add the wine and the beef stock, then cover and cook for 45 minutes, or until tender. Turn the meat several times during cooking.
4 Remove the beef olives with a slotted spoon, cover and keep warm. Return the pan to the heat and reduce the sauce until slightly thickened. Season to taste with salt and black pepper. Remove the string from the beef olives and pour the sauce over before serving.

C O O K ' S   F I L E

Note: To make beef stock at home, bake 2 kg (4 lb) beef bones at 210°C (415°F/Gas 6–7) for 30 minutes, then simmer in a large pan with chopped carrots, onions, celery, bouquet garni and 3 litres (12 cups) water for 4 hours.

Cover the beef with a sheet of plastic wrap and flatten with a meat mallet.

Roll the beef around the filling and then secure with string.

Add the wine, a little more salt and black pepper and the beef stock.

Remove the beef olives from the pan, then reduce the sauce to thicken.

CHICKEN MARSALA

Preparation time: 10 minutes
Total cooking time: 25 minutes
Serves 4

4 skinless, boneless chicken
   breasts
2 tablespoons oil
60 g (2 oz) butter
1 garlic clove, crushed
500 ml (16 fl oz/2 cups) chicken
   stock
4 tablespoons Marsala
2 teaspoons plain (all-purpose)
   flour
3 tablespoons cream
2 teaspoons Worcestershire
   sauce

1 Trim the chicken of excess fat and sinew. Heat the oil in a heavy-based frying pan and add the chicken. Cook over medium heat for 4 minutes on each side, or until cooked through and lightly golden. Remove the chicken, cover loosely with foil and keep warm. Drain off any fat from the pan.
2 Add the butter and garlic to the pan and stir over medium heat for 2 minutes. Add the combined stock and Marsala and bring to the boil. Reduce the heat and simmer for 10 minutes, or until the liquid has reduced by half.
3 Blend together the flour, cream and Worcestershire sauce; add a little of the hot liquid and blend to a paste. Add this to the pan and then stir over medium heat until the sauce boils and

thickens. Season to taste with salt and black pepper and then pour over the chicken fillets. Delicious with pasta.

COOK'S FILE

Variation: Marsala is a sweet wine and so makes a sweet-tasting sauce. Port or any dry red wine can be used instead. Boiling wine evaporates the alcohol, leaving the flavour but not the intoxicating qualities. Chicken thighs or drumsticks can be used instead of breast fillets.
Hint: Blending the flour to a paste first prevents lumps forming when it is added to the sauce.

Cook the chicken in a frying pan until lightly golden on each side.

Mix together the stock and Marsala, then add to the pan and bring to the boil.

Add the flour, cream and Worcestershire sauce and stir over heat until thickened.

HOMESTYLE MEATBALLS WITH FUSILLI

Preparation time: 25 minutes
Total cooking time: 35 minutes
Serves 4

1 onion
750 g (1 lb 10 oz) minced (ground) pork and veal or beef
80 g (2¾ oz/1 cup) fresh breadcrumbs
3 tablespoons freshly grated Parmesan cheese
2 tablespoons chopped fresh parsley
1 egg, beaten
1 garlic clove, crushed
zest and juice of ½ lemon
3 tablespoons plain (all-purpose) flour, seasoned
2 tablespoons olive oil
500 g (1 lb 2 oz) fusilli or spiral pasta

Sauce
425 g (15 oz) tinned puréed tomato
125 ml (4 fl oz/½ cup) beef stock
125 ml (4fl oz/½ cup) red wine
2 tablespoons chopped fresh basil
1 garlic clove, crushed

1 Peel onion and chop very finely. In a large bowl, combine the meat, breadcrumbs, Parmesan, onion, parsley, egg, garlic and lemon zest and juice. Season with salt and pepper. Roll tablespoonsful of mixture into balls and roll balls in seasoned flour.
2 Place oil in a large frying pan and fry the meatballs until golden. Remove from the pan and drain on paper towel.

Set aside. Remove the excess fat and meat juices from the pan.
3 To make sauce, in the same pan, combine puréed tomato, stock, wine, basil and garlic. Season to taste with salt and pepper. Bring to the boil.
4 Reduce the heat and return the meatballs to pan. Allow to simmer for

10–15 minutes. Meanwhile, add fusilli to a large pan of rapidly boiling water and cook until just tender. Drain well. Serve fusilli with meatballs and sauce over the top.

1

2

3

RIGATONI WITH CHORIZO AND TOMATO

Preparation time: 15 minutes
Total cooking time: 20–25 minutes
Serves 4

250 g (9 oz) chorizo sausage
   (see Note)
1 onion, sliced
2 tablespoons olive oil
425 g (15 oz) tinned tomatoes,
   crushed
125 ml (4 fl oz/½ cup) dry white
   wine

½–1 teaspoon chopped chilli,
   optional
375 g (13 oz) rigatoni
2 tablespoons chopped fresh
   parsley, for serving
2 tablespoons freshly grated
   Parmesan cheese, for
   serving

1 Cut the chorizo sausage into slices. Heat oil in a large frying pan. Add onion and stir over low heat until tender.
2 Add the sausage to the pan; cook, turning frequently, for 2–3 minutes. Add tomatoes, wine and chilli. Season

with salt and ground black pepper and stir. Bring to boil and reduce heat; simmer for 15–20 minutes.
3 Meanwhile, add the rigatoni to a large pan of rapidly boiling water and cook until just tender. Drain well and return to the pan. Add the sauce to the hot pasta with half of the combined parsley and Parmesan cheese. Toss to combine well. Serve sprinkled with remaining combined parsley and Parmesan cheese.

COOK'S FILE

Variation: Use different spicy sausage in place of chorizo.

1

2

3

Coat the pork fillet pieces in the ground coriander and pepper.

Heat some oil in a frying pan and cook the pork in batches until brown.

Remove the meat from the pan and keep warm.

Boil the liquid until reduced and slightly thickened.

CYPRIOT PORK AND CORIANDER STEW

Preparation time: 15 minutes +
  overnight marinating
Total cooking time: 1 hour 20 minutes
Serves 4–6

1½ tablespoons coriander seeds
800 g (1 lb 12 oz) pork fillet, cut
  into 2 cm (¾ inch) dice
1 tablespoon plain (all-purpose)
  flour
3 tablespoons olive oil
1 large onion, thinly sliced
375 ml (13 fl oz/1½ cups) red
  wine
250 ml (9 fl oz/1 cup) chicken
  stock
1 teaspoon sugar
fresh coriander (cilantro) sprigs,
  to garnish

1 Crush the coriander seeds in a mortar and pestle. Combine the pork, crushed seeds and ½ teaspoon cracked pepper in a bowl. Cover and marinate overnight in the fridge.

2 Combine the flour and pork and toss. Heat 2 tablespoons oil in a frying pan and cook the pork in batches over high heat for 1–2 minutes, or until brown. Remove.

3 Heat the remaining oil, add the onion and cook over medium heat for 2–3 minutes, or until just golden. Return the meat to the pan, add the red wine, stock and sugar, and season. Bring to the boil, then reduce the heat and simmer, covered, for 1 hour.

4 Remove the meat. Return the pan to the heat and boil over high heat for 3–5 minutes, or until reduced and slightly thickened. Pour over the meat and top with the coriander.

Using a small, sharp knife, remove the chokes from the artichokes.

Fill each artichoke with some of the lamb mixture.

Deep-fry the stuffed artichokes until golden brown.

Remove the artichokes from the cooking liquid with a slotted spoon.

MIDDLE EASTERN STUFFED ARTICHOKES

Preparation time: 1 hour 30 minutes
Total cooking time: 1 hour 25 minutes
Serves 6

140 ml (4½ fl oz) lemon juice
12 globe artichokes
500 g (1 lb 2 oz) minced
　(ground) lamb
40 g (1½ oz/½ cup) fresh
　breadcrumbs
1 egg, lightly beaten
1 tablespoon chopped fresh
　thyme
olive oil, for deep-frying
125 ml (4 fl oz/½ cup) extra
　virgin olive oil
375 ml (13 fl oz/1½ cups)
　chicken stock
½ teaspoon ground turmeric
1 bay leaf
40 g (1½ oz) butter
2 tablespoons plain (all-purpose)
　flour

1 Fill a large bowl with water and add 3 tablespoons lemon juice. Peel the outer leaves from the artichokes, trimming the base and stem to reveal the bottom. Cut the tops off to reveal the chokes and remove. Place all the artichokes in the bowl of lemon water.
2 Place the lamb, breadcrumbs, egg and thyme in a bowl, season and mix well. Pat the artichokes dry with paper towel. Fill each artichoke with 2 tablespoons of the lamb mixture.
3 Fill a large heavy-based saucepan one-third full of oil and heat to 180°C (350°F), or until a cube of bread browns in 15 seconds. Cook the artichokes in batches for 5 minutes, or until golden brown. Drain.
4 Place the extra virgin olive oil, 250 ml (9 fl oz/l cup) stock, turmeric, bay leaf and remaining lemon juice in a 1.25 litre (5 cup) casserole dish. Season. Bring to the boil, add the artichokes and simmer, covered, for 1 hour, or until tender, adding more stock if needed. Turn the artichokes twice during cooking. Remove the artichokes and keep warm. Reserve the liquid.
5 Melt the butter in a saucepan, add the flour and stir for 1 minute, or until pale and foamy. Remove from the heat and gradually stir in the reserved liquid. Return to the heat and stir until the sauce boils and thickens, then reduce the heat and simmer for 2 minutes. Serve immediately with the artichokes.

185

PASTICCIO

Preparation time: 25 minutes +
    15 minutes resting
Total cooking time: 2 hours
Serves 4–6

3 tablespoons olive oil
1 onion, finely chopped
2 garlic cloves, crushed
80 g (2¾ oz) pancetta, finely
    chopped
500 g (1 lb 2 oz) minced
    (ground) beef
1 teaspoon chopped fresh
    oregano
60g (2¼ oz) small button
    mushrooms, sliced
115 g (4 oz) chicken
    livers, trimmed and finely
    chopped
¼ teaspoon ground nutmeg
pinch cayenne pepper
3 tablespoons dry white wine
2 tablespoons tomato paste
    (concentrated purée)
375 ml (13 fl oz/½ cups) beef
    stock
2 tablespoons grated Parmesan
    cheese
1 egg, beaten
150 g (5 oz) macaroni
100 g (3½ oz) ricotta cheese
2 tablespoons milk
pinch cayenne pepper, extra
pinch ground nutmeg, extra
1 egg, beaten, extra
100 g (3½ oz/1 cup) grated
    Parmesan cheese, extra

Béchamel sauce
40 g (1½ oz) butter
1½ tablespoons plain
    (all-purpose) flour
pinch ground nutmeg

300 ml (10½ fl oz) milk
1 small bay leaf

1 Preheat the oven to 180°C (350°F/
Gas 4). Grease a 1.5 litre (6 cup)
ovenproof dish. Heat the oil in a large
frying pan over medium heat and cook
the onion, garlic and pancetta, stirring,
for 5–6 minutes, or until the onion is
golden. Add the beef, increase the heat
and stir for 5 minutes, or until browned.
2 Add the oregano, mushrooms,
chicken livers, nutmeg and cayenne,
season and cook for 2 minutes, or until
the livers change colour. Add the wine
and cook over high heat for 1 minute,
or until evaporated. Stir in the tomato
paste and stock. Reduce the heat and
simmer for 45 minutes, or until
thickened. Beat the Parmesan and egg
together, and quickly stir through the
sauce.
3 Cook the macaroni in lightly salted
boiling water until al dente.
Meanwhile, blend the ricotta, milk,
extra cayenne, extra nutmeg, extra
egg and 3 tablespoons extra Parmesan.
Season. Drain the macaroni, add to the
ricotta mixture and mix well.
4 To make the béchamel sauce, melt
the butter in a small saucepan. Stir in
the flour and cook over low heat until
just golden; stir in the nutmeg. Take
off the heat and gradually stir in the
milk. Add the bay leaf. Season. Return
to low heat and simmer, stirring, until
thickened. Discard the bay leaf.
5 Spread half the meat sauce in the
dish, top with half the pasta and half
the remaining Parmesan. Layer with
the remaining meat sauce and pasta;
press down with the back of a spoon.
Spread the béchamel on top, then top
with remaining Parmesan. Bake for
45–50 minutes, or until golden. Rest
for 15 minutes before serving.

*Cook the mixture for 2 minutes, or until
the chicken livers change colour.*

*Add the tomato paste and stock, then
simmer until thickened.*

*Stir the cooked, drained macaroni through
the ricotta mixture.*

Gradually add the milk to the butter and flour to make the béchamel sauce.

Spoon half the pasta and ricotta mixture over the meat sauce.

Pour the béchamel sauce evenly over the top pasta layer.

ROAST GARLIC CHICKEN WITH VEGETABLES

Preparation time: 20 minutes
Total cooking time: 1 hour 20 minutes
Serves 4

315 g (10 oz) orange sweet potatoes, peeled and cut into wedges
315 g (10 oz) pontiac potatoes, peeled and cut into wedges
315 g (10 oz) pumpkin, peeled and cut into wedges

1 chicken, cut into 8 pieces, or 1.5 kg (3 lb) chicken pieces
3 tablespoons olive oil
1 tablespoon fresh thyme leaves
20 large garlic cloves, unpeeled (see Note)
½ teaspoon sea salt

1 Preheat the oven to hot 220°C (425°F/Gas 7). Bring a large pan of salted water to the boil and cook the sweet potatoes, pontiac potatoes and pumpkin for 5 minutes. Drain well.
2 Put the chicken and vegetables in a baking dish, drizzle with olive oil and scatter with thyme leaves and garlic cloves. Sprinkle with the sea salt.
3 Roast for 1 hour 15 minutes, turning every 20 minutes or so, until the chicken, potatoes and pumpkin become well browned and crisp at the edges. Serve immediately.

COOK'S FILE

Note: This may seem a lot of garlic, but it loses its pungency when cooked, becoming sweet and mild. To eat the garlic, squeeze the creamy roasted flesh from the skins and over the chicken and vegetables.

Boil the sweet and pontiac potatoes and pumpkin for 5 minutes, then drain.

Drizzle the chicken and vegetables with oil then sprinkle with garlic and thyme.

Turn the chicken and vegetables every 20 minutes, until browned and crisp.

Use a meat mallet to flatten the veal steaks. Nick the edges to prevent curling.

Press the crumb mixture firmly onto the steaks with your fingers to make it stick.

Cook the steaks in batches until golden brown, then drain on paper towels.

Top with the Parmesan and mozzarella and bake until golden brown.

VEAL PARMIGIANA

Preparation time: 30 minutes + chilling
Total cooking time: 30 minutes
Serves 4

4 thin veal steaks
100 g (3½ oz/1 cup) dry
    breadcrumbs
½ teaspoon dried basil
3 tablespoons finely grated fresh
    Parmesan cheese
plain (all-purpose) flour, for
    coating
1 egg, lightly beaten
1 tablespoon milk
olive oil, for frying
250 g (9 oz/1 cup) good-quality
    ready-made tomato pasta
    sauce
50 g (1¾ oz/½ cup) finely grated
    fresh Parmesan cheese, extra
100 g (3⅓ oz) mozzarella,
    thinly sliced

1 Trim the meat of any excess fat and sinew. Place between sheets of plastic wrap and flatten with a meat mallet to 5 mm (¼ inch) thick. Nick the edges to prevent curling. Combine the breadcrumbs, basil and Parmesan on a sheet of greaseproof paper.
2 Coat the veal steaks in flour, shaking off the excess. Working with one at a time, dip the steaks into the combined egg and milk, then coat with the breadcrumb mixture. Lightly shake off the excess. Refrigerate for 30 minutes to firm the coating.
3 Preheat the oven to 180°C (350°F/ Gas 4). Heat the oil in a frying pan and brown the veal steaks over medium heat for 2 minutes each side, in batches if necessary. Remove from the pan and drain on paper towel.
4 Spread half the pasta sauce into a shallow ovenproof dish. Arrange the veal steaks on top in a single layer and spoon over the remaining sauce. Top with the Parmesan cheese

and mozzarella and bake for 20 minutes, or until the cheeses are melted and golden brown. Serve immediately.

LEG OF LAMB WITH PANCETTA STUFFING

Preparation time: 30 minutes
Total cooking time: 1 hour 45 minutes
Serves 6

60 g (2 oz) pancetta, chopped
60 g (2 oz) mild Provolone
   cheese, chopped
2 tablespoons grated Parmesan
4 tablespoons fresh breadcrumbs
3 tablespoons chopped fresh
   flat-leaf (Italian) parsley
2 teaspoons rosemary, chopped
2 spring onions (scallions),
   chopped
1 egg plus 1 yolk, lightly beaten
1.5 kg (3 lb) boned leg of lamb
   (ask your butcher to do this)
3 tablespoons olive oil
1 onion, chopped
1 carrot, chopped
1 celery stalk, chopped
250 ml (9 fl oz/1 cup) dry
   white wine
1 tablespoon plain (all-purpose)
   flour

1 Preheat oven to 200°C (400°F /Gas 6). Combine the pancetta, cheeses, breadcrumbs, herbs, spring onions and enough beaten egg to form a stuffing that just comes together. Season with pepper.

2 Fill the lamb leg with stuffing, fold over the ends and secure with wooden skewers or string.

3 Heat oil in a deep pan and brown the lamb all over. Transfer to a baking dish and sprinkle with salt and pepper. Reheat the pan and add onion, carrot and celery; toss over the heat for 2 minutes. Add wine, let the bubbles subside, then pour over the lamb. Bake for 1½ hours, or until tender, turning once or twice.

4 Remove the meat from the dish and leave, loosely covered, for 10 minutes before slicing. Strain the pan juices into a jug and skim off the fat; add water to make up 375 ml (13 fl oz/1½ cups). Heat the flour in a small pan until beginning to brown, remove from the heat and slowly whisk in the pan juices until smooth. Return to the heat and whisk until the sauce boils and thickens. Return the vegetables to the sauce and drizzle over the meat.

Add enough beaten egg to the stuffing mixture to make it just stick together.

Carefully stuff the leg of lamb, pushing the pancetta filling into the cavity.

Skewer together the open ends of the leg of lamb, or tie with string.

Use a large deep pan to brown the lamb as the fat will tend to spit.

VEAL SCALOPPINI WITH LEMON SAUCE

Preparation time: 5 minutes
Total cooking time: 5 minutes
Serves 4

3 tablespoons olive oil
60 g (2 oz) butter
8 thin veal steaks
plain (all-purpose) flour, for
    coating
2 tablespoons lemon juice

2 tablespoons finely chopped
    parsley
lemon slices, to garnish

1 Heat the oil and half the butter in a large frying pan until quite hot. Coat the veal steaks in the flour and add to the pan, cooking in batches if necessary. Cook until lightly browned on one side, then turn over and brown the other side. The veal steaks should take only 1 minute on each side—cooking longer will toughen the meat. Transfer to a warm plate and season.

2 Lower the heat and add the lemon juice, parsley and remaining butter to the pan, stirring to combine. Add the veal steaks, turning them in the sauce.
3 Serve the veal steaks with the sauce. Garnish with lemon slices.

COOK'S FILE

Note: For thin veal steaks, cover them with plastic wrap and beat with a rolling pin or meat mallet.

Coat the veal steaks in flour, shaking off any excess.

Lightly brown the veal steaks on either side, cooking in batches if necessary.

Return all the veal steaks to the pan, turning to coat them in sauce.

CHICKEN AND PORK PAELLA

Preparation time: 30 minutes
Total cooking time: 1 hour
Serves 6

3 tablespoons olive oil
1 large red capsicum (pepper), deseeded and cut into 5 mm (¼ inch) strips
600 g (1 lb 5 oz) skinless, boneless chicken thighs, cut into 3 cm (1¼ inch) cubes
200 g (7 oz) chorizo sausage, cut into 2 cm (¾ inch) slices
200 g (7 oz) mushrooms, thinly sliced
3 garlic cloves, crushed
1 tablespoon lemon zest
700 g (1 lb 9 oz) tomatoes, roughly chopped
200 g (7 oz) green beans, cut into 3 cm (1¼ inch) lengths
1 tablespoon chopped fresh rosemary
2 tablespoons chopped fresh flat-leaf (Italian) parsley
¼ teaspoon saffron threads dissolved in 3 tablespoons hot water
440 g (15½ oz/2 cups) short-grain rice
750 ml (26 fl oz/3 cups) hot chicken stock
6 lemon wedges

1 Heat the oil in a large, deep frying or paella pan over medium heat. Add capsicum and cook for 6 minutes, or until softened. Remove from pan.
2 Add chicken to the pan and cook for 10 minutes, or until brown on all sides. Remove. Add the sausage to the pan and cook for 5 minutes, or until golden on all sides. Remove.
3 Add the mushrooms, garlic and lemon zest, and cook over medium heat for 5 minutes. Stir in the tomato and capsicum, and cook for a further 5 minutes, or until the tomato is soft.
4 Add the beans, rosemary, parsley, saffron mixture, rice, chicken and sausage. Stir briefly and add the stock. Do not stir at this point. Reduce the heat and simmer for 30 minutes. Remove from the heat, cover and leave to stand for 10 minutes. Serve with lemon wedges

COOK'S FILE

Note: Paellas are not stirred right to the bottom of the pan during cooking in the hope that a thin crust of crispy rice will form. This is considered one of the best parts of the paella. For this reason, it is important not to use a non-stick frying pan. Paellas are traditionally served at the table from the pan.
Variation: Try adding shellfish such as prawns (shrimp) 5–10 minutes after adding the stock.

Cut the chorizo sausage into 2 cm (¾ inch) thick slices.

Add the tomato and capsicum and cook until the tomato is soft.

Pour the chicken stock into the pan and do not stir.

CHICKEN WITH PRESERVED LEMON AND OLIVES

Preparation time: 10 minutes
Total cooking time: 1 hour
Serves 4

3 tablespoons olive oil
1.6 kg (3 lb 8 oz) free-range
   chicken
1 onion, chopped
2 garlic cloves, chopped
600 ml (21 fl oz) chicken stock
½ teaspoon ground ginger
1½ teaspoons ground cinnamon
pinch saffron threads
100 g (3½ oz) green olives
¼ preserved lemon, pulp
   removed, rind washed and cut
   into slivers
2 bay leaves
2 chicken livers
3 tablespoons chopped fresh
   coriander (cilantro) leaves

1 Preheat the oven to 180°C (350°F/ Gas 4). Heat 2 tablespoons oil in a large frying pan, add the chicken and brown on all sides. Place in a deep baking dish.
2 Heat the remaining oil, add the onion and garlic and cook over medium heat for 3–4 minutes, or until softened. Add the stock, ginger, cinnamon, saffron, olives, lemon and bay leaves and pour around the chicken. Bake for 45 minutes, adding a little more water or stock if the sauce gets too dry.
3 Remove the chicken from the dish, cover with foil and leave to rest. Discard the bay leaves. Pour the contents of the baking dish into a frying pan, add the chicken livers and mash into the sauce as they cook. Cook for 5–6 minutes, or until the sauce has reduced and thickened. Add the coriander. Cut the chicken into four and serve with the sauce.

Pour the chicken stock mixture around the chicken.

Bake the chicken for 45 minutes, adding stock or water if it is too dry.

Mash the chicken livers into the sauce so they thicken it as they cook.

LAYERED LAMB AND BURGHUL

Preparation time: 30 minutes +
  30 minutes soaking +
  10 minutes cooling
Total cooking time: 50 minutes
Serves 4–6

350 g (12 oz/2 cups) burghul
  (bulgar)
400 g (14 oz) minced (ground)
  lamb
1 large onion, finely chopped
1 tablespoon ground cumin
1 teaspoon allspice
olive oil, for brushing

Filling
1 tablespoon olive oil, plus extra
  for brushing
1 onion, finely chopped
1 teaspoon ground cinnamon
1 tablespoon ground cumin
500 g (1 lb 2 oz) minced
  (ground) lamb
80 g (2¾ oz/½ cup) raisins
100 g (3½ oz) pine nuts, toasted

1 Soak the burghul in cold water for 30 minutes, drain and squeeze out excess water. Place the lamb, onion, cumin, allspice, salt and pepper in a food processor, and process until combined. Add the burghul and process to a paste. Refrigerate until needed. Preheat the oven to 180°C (350°F/Gas 4). Grease a 20 x 30 cm (8 x 12 inch) roasting tin.
2 To make the filling, heat the oil in a large frying pan over medium heat and cook the onion for 5 minutes, or until softened. Add the cinnamon and cumin, and stir for 1 minute, or until fragrant. Add the lamb, stirring to break up any lumps, and cook for 5 minutes, or until the meat is brown. Stir in the raisins and nuts and season.
3 Press half the burghul mixture into the base of the tin, smoothing the surface with wetted hands. Spread the filling over the top, then cover with the remaining burghul, again smoothing the surface.

4 Score a diamond pattern in the top of the mixture with a sharp knife and brush lightly with olive oil. Bake for 35–40 minutes, or until the top is brown and crisp. Cool for 10 minutes before cutting into diamond shapes. Serve with yoghurt and salad.

Process the meat mixture and the burghul to a paste.

Spread the meat filling over the burghul layer.

Using a sharp knife, score a diamond pattern into the top.

SOUVLAKE

Preparation time: 20 minutes +
  overnight marinating + 30 minutes
  standing
Total cooking time: 10 minutes
Serves 4

1 kg (2 lb 4 oz) boned leg lamb,
  trimmed, cut into 2 cm
  (¾ inch) cubes
3 tablespoons olive oil
2 teaspoons finely grated
  lemon zest
4 tablespoons lemon juice

2 teaspoons dried oregano
125 ml (4 fl oz/½ cup) dry white
  wine
2 large garlic cloves, finely
  chopped
2 fresh bay leaves
250 g (9 oz/1 cup) Greek-style
  plain yoghurt
2 garlic cloves, crushed, extra

1 Place the lamb in a non-metallic bowl with 2 tablespoons olive oil, lemon zest and juice, oregano, wine, garlic and bay leaves. Season with black pepper and toss to coat. Cover and refrigerate overnight.

2 Place the yoghurt and extra garlic in a bowl, mix together well and leave for 30 minutes.

3 Drain the lamb and pat dry. Thread onto 8 skewers and cook on a barbecue or chargrill plate (griddle), brushing with the remaining oil, for 7–8 minutes, or until brown on the outside and still a little rare in the middle. Drizzle with the garlic yoghurt and serve with warm pitta bread and a salad.

COOK'S FILE

Note: If using wooden skewers, soak them in water for 30 minutes to prevent burning during cooking.

Toss the lamb to coat well with the spicy marinade.

Pat the drained lamb dry and thread onto eight skewers.

Brush the remaining oil over the lamb skewers during cooking.

CHICKEN CACCIATORE

Preparation time: 20 minutes
Total cooking time: 1 hour
Serves 6

3 tablespoons olive oil
12 small chicken drumsticks
1 large onion, finely chopped
3 garlic cloves, crushed
440 g (14 oz) tinned tomatoes,
   crushed
90 g (3 oz/½ cup) black olives

250 ml (9 fl oz/1 cup) tomato
   purée
125 ml (4 fl oz/½ cup) white
   wine
125 ml (4 fl oz/½ cup) chicken
   stock
125 g (4 oz) button mushrooms,
   quartered
1 tablespoon chopped fresh
   oregano
2 teaspoons chopped fresh
   thyme
2 teaspoons soft brown
   sugar

1 Heat half the oil in a large heavy-based pan and brown the drumsticks in small batches over high heat.
2 Heat the remaining oil in a frying pan and cook the onion and garlic for 10 minutes, or until golden. Remove from the pan and add to the chicken.
3 Add the remaining ingredients to the frying pan. Bring to the boil, reduce the heat and then simmer for 10 minutes. Season to taste with salt and pepper. Pour over the chicken, stir to combine, cover and simmer for 35 minutes, or until very tender.

Cut the mushrooms into quarters and finely chop the onion.

Cook the drumsticks in batches so they brown—if overcrowded they will stew.

Simmer the tomato mixture, then pour over the chicken and mix together.

LAMB SHANKS WITH LENTILS

Preparation time: 20 minutes
Total cooking time: 2 hours
Serves 2

250 g (9 oz/1 cup) red lentils,
   rinsed and drained
½ teaspoon salt
2 celery stalks, diced
1 green capsicum (pepper),
   diced
2 cloves garlic, finely chopped
2 onions, finely chopped

4 small lamb shanks
800 g (1 lb 10 oz) tinned
   tomatoes, crushed
3 bay leaves
3 teaspoons chopped fresh
   marjoram
3 teaspoons chopped thyme

1 Preheat the oven to 180°C (350°F/Gas 4). Spread the lentils in the base of a large ovenproof casserole dish and sprinkle with salt.
2 Add the celery, capsicum, garlic and onion. Layer the lamb shanks over the top, then pour over the tomatoes. Add the bay leaves, fresh marjoram and

thyme. Cover the dish (with foil if you don't have a lid) and bake for 2 hours.
3 Skim off any fat which may have formed on the surface. Remove the bay leaves and stir together the lentils, meat and vegetables before serving.

COOK'S FILE

Note: Red lentils are smaller and softer than green or brown lentils and so do not need to be soaked before cooking.
Variation: Lamb shanks are a very economical cut of meat—use chump chops if shanks are not available.

Spread the lentils in a large dish and sprinkle with salt.

Place the vegetables over the lentils, layer the lamb on top and add the tomatoes.

Remove the bay leaves and give the dish a quick stir before serving.

Chicken Cacciatore (top) and
Lamb Shanks with Lentils

WARM CHICKEN AND PASTA SALAD

Preparation time: 15 minutes
Cooking time: 15 minutes
Serves 4

375 g (13 oz) penne
100 ml (3½ fl oz) olive oil
4 slender eggplants
   (aubergines), thinly sliced
   on the diagonal
2 skinless, boneless chicken
   breasts
2 teaspoons lemon juice
15 g (½ oz/½ cup) chopped fresh
   flat-leaf (Italian) parsley
270 g (9¾ oz) chargrilled red
   capsicum (pepper), drained
   and sliced (see Note)
155 g (5½ oz) fresh asparagus,
   trimmed, blanched and cut
   into 5 cm (2 inch) lengths
85 g (3 oz) semi-dried
   (sun-blushed) tomatoes,
   finely sliced

1 Cook the pasta in a large saucepan of boiling water until al dente. Drain, return to the pan and keep warm. Heat 2 tablespoons of the oil in a large frying pan over high heat and cook the eggplant for 4–5 minutes, or until golden and cooked through.
2 Heat a lightly oiled chargrill pan (griddle) over high heat and cook the chicken for 5 minutes each side, or until browned and cooked through. Cut into thick slices. Put the lemon juice, parsley and remaining oil in a small jar and shake well. Return the pasta to the heat, toss through the dressing, chicken, eggplant, capsicum asparagus and tomato until well mixed and warmed through. Season with black pepper. Serve warm with grated Parmesan, if desired.

COOK'S FILE

Note: Jars of chargrilled capsicum can be bought at the supermarket; otherwise, visit your local deli.

1

2

PASTA GNOCCHI WITH SAUSAGE AND TOMATO

Preparation time: 15 minutes
Cooking time: 20 minutes
Serves 4–6

500 g (1 lb 2 oz) pasta gnocchi
2 tablespoons olive oil
400 g (14 oz) thin Italian
    sausages
1 red onion, finely chopped
2 garlic cloves, finely chopped
2 x 400 g (14 oz) tinned
    tomatoes, chopped

1 teaspoon caster (superfine)
    sugar
35 g (1¼ oz) fresh basil, torn
45 g (1½ oz/½ cup) grated
    Pecorino cheese

1 Cook the pasta in a large saucepan of boiling water until al dente. Drain and return the pasta to the pan. Meanwhile, heat 2 teaspoons of the oil in a large frying pan. Add the sausages and cook, turning, for 5 minutes, or until well browned and cooked through. Drain on paper towel, then slice when they have cooled enough to touch. Keep warm.

2 Wipe clean the frying pan and heat the remaining oil. Add the onion and garlic and cook over medium heat for 2 minutes, or until the onion has softened. Add the tomato, sugar and 250 ml (9 fl oz/l cup) water and season well with ground black pepper. Reduce the heat and simmer for 12 minutes, or until thickened and reduced a little.

3 Pour the sauce over the cooked pasta and stir through the sausage, then the basil and half of the cheese. Divide among serving plates and serve hot with the remaining cheese sprinkled over the top.

OSSO BUCCO DI GREMOLATA

Preparation time: 30 minutes
Total cooking time: 2 hours
  20 minutes
Serves 4–6

12 meaty pieces veal shank,
  osso bucco style
4 tablespoons plain (all-purpose)
  flour, seasoned
20 g (½ oz) butter
4 tablespoons olive oil
1 onion, diced
1 carrot, diced
1 celery stalk, diced
1 bay leaf

1 garlic clove, crushed
500 ml (17 fl oz/2 cups) veal or
  chicken stock
250 ml (9 fl oz/1 cup) white
  wine
4 tablespoons lemon juice

Gremolata
12 g (¼ oz/⅔ cup) fresh flat-leaf
  (Italian) parsley, finely
  chopped
2 garlic cloves, finely chopped
1 tablespoon grated lemon zest

1 Lightly dust the veal shanks in the seasoned flour. Heat the butter and 3 tablespoons oil in a large deep-sided frying pan over high heat until sizzling. Add the veal and cook in batches for 5 minutes, or until brown all over. Remove from the pan.

2 Heat the remaining oil in a large saucepan and add the onion, carrot, celery and bay leaf, and cook for 10 minutes, or until softened and starting to brown. Stir in the garlic, stock, wine and lemon juice, scraping the bottom of the pan to remove any sediment. Add the veal, bring to the boil then reduce the heat to low, cover and simmer for 1½–2 hours, or until the veal is very tender and falling off the bone and the sauce has reduced. Season to taste.

3 To make the gremolata, combine the parsley, garlic and zest. Sprinkle over the osso bucco just before serving. Serve with soft polenta.

Cook the veal shank pieces in batches until well browned.

Cook the onion, carrot, celery and bay leaf until softened.

Simmer until the veal is very tender and the sauce has reduced.

MOUSSAKA

Preparation time: 20 minutes
  + 40 minutes standing
Total cooking time: 1 hour 50 minutes
Serves 6

2 large ripe tomatoes
1.5 kg (3 lb 5 oz) eggplant
    (aubergines), cut into 5 mm
    (¼ inch) slices
125 ml (4 fl oz/½ cup) light
    olive oil
1 tablespoon olive oil
2 onions, finely chopped
2 large garlic cloves, crushed
½ teaspoon ground allspice
1¼ teaspoons ground cinnamon
750 g (1 lb 10 oz) minced
    (ground) lamb
2 tablespoons tomato paste
    (concentrated purée)
125 ml (4 fl oz/½ cup) white
    wine
3 tablespoons chopped fresh
    flat-leaf (Italian) parsley

White sauce
50 g (1¾ oz) butter
60 g (2¼ oz/½ cup) plain
    (all-purpose) flour
600 ml (21 fl oz) milk
pinch ground nutmeg
4 tablespoons finely grated
    kefalotyri or Parmesan
    cheese
2 eggs, lightly beaten

1 Preheat the oven to 180°C (350°F/ Gas 4). Score a cross in the base of each tomato. Place in a bowl of boiling water for 1 minute, remove, then plunge into cold water. Peel the skin away from the cross. Roughly chop. Lay the eggplant on a tray, sprinkle with salt and leave to stand for 30 minutes. Rinse and pat dry

2 Heat 2 tablespoons olive oil in a frying pan, and cook the eggplant in 4–5 batches for 1–2 minutes each side, or until golden and soft. Add more oil when needed.

3 Heat the oil in a saucepan and cook the onion over medium heat for 5 minutes. Add the garlic, allspice and cinnamon and cook for 30 seconds. Add the meat and cook for 5 minutes, or until browned, breaking up any lumps. Add the tomato, tomato paste

and wine, and simmer over low heat for 30 minutes, or until the liquid has evaporated. Stir in parsley and season.
4 Meanwhile, to make the white sauce, melt the butter in a saucepan over medium heat. Add the flour and cook for 1 minute. Remove from the heat and gradually stir in the milk and nutmeg. Return to the heat and simmer for 2 minutes. Add 1 tablespoon of the cheese and stir well. Stir in the egg just before using.

5 Line the base of a 3 litre (12 cup) 25 x 30 cm (10 x 12 inch) ovenproof dish with a third of the eggplant. Spoon on half the meat and cover with a second layer of eggplant. Top with remaining meat and eggplant. Pour on the white sauce and sprinkle with remaining cheese. Bake for 1 hour. Leave for 10 minutes before slicing.

Cook the tomato and mince mixture until the liquid has evaporated.

Pour the white sauce over the final layer of eggplant.

DUCK BREAST WITH WALNUT AND POMEGRANATE SAUCE

Preparation time: 15 minutes +
   5 minutes resting
Total cooking time: 25 minutes
Serves 4

4 large duck breasts
1 onion, finely chopped
250 ml (9 fl oz/1 cup)

fresh pomegranate juice
   (see Note)
2 tablespoons lemon juice
2 tablespoons soft brown sugar
1 teaspoon ground cinnamon
185 g (6½ oz/1½ cups) chopped
   walnuts
pomegranate seeds,
   to garnish, optional

1 Preheat the oven to 180°C (350°F/ Gas 4). Score the duck breasts 2 or 3 times with a sharp knife. Place in a non-stick frying pan and cook over high heat, skin-side-down, for 6 minutes, or until crisp and it has rendered most of its fat. Place in a baking dish.

2 Remove all but 1 tablespoon of fat from the pan. Add the onion to the pan and cook over medium heat for 2–3 minutes, or until golden. Add the pomegranate and lemon juice, sugar, cinnamon and 125 g (4½ oz/1 cup) walnuts and cook for 1 minute. Pour over the duck breasts and bake for 15 minutes.

3 Leave the duck breasts to rest for 5 minutes while you skim any excess fat from the sauce. Slice the duck breasts and serve with a little of the sauce. Garnish with the pomegranate seeds and remaining walnuts, if desired.

COOK'S FILE

Note: If fresh pomegranate juice is not available, combine 3 tablespoons pomegranate concentrate with 185 ml (6 fl oz/¾ cup) water.

Score the duck breasts 2 or 3 times with a sharp knife.

Pour the pomegranate sauce over the duck breasts.

OLIVE AND LEMON LAMB CUTLETS

Preparation time: 15 minutes +
    marinating
Total cooking time: 10 minutes
Serves 4

12 lamb cutlets
2 tablespoons olive oil
juice and zest of 1 lemon
1 garlic clove, crushed
**1 teaspoon finely chopped fresh
    rosemary leaves**
1 teaspoon butter
16 black olives, cut into strips
2 tablespoons chopped parsley

1 Trim the lamb cutlets of fat and place in a dish. Pour over 1 tablespoon of the oil, the lemon juice and zest, garlic and chopped rosemary. Leave to marinate for at least 30 minutes.

2 Heat the remaining oil and the butter in a large frying pan. Drain the cutlets, reserving the marinade, and fry over medium heat until cooked through, turning once. Remove from the pan and set aside.

3 Drain the excess fat from the pan and add the olives, parsley and remaining marinade. Bring to the boil and cook for 2 minutes. Season to taste with salt and pepper, pour over the cutlets and serve with mashed or roasted potatoes.

Trim the fat away from the lamb cutlets, leaving just the meat and bone.

Pour over 1 tablespoon of oil, the lemon juice and zest, garlic and rosemary.

Fry the cutlets over medium heat until they are cooked through, turning once.

Add the olives, parsley and remaining marinade and cook for 2 minutes.

CLASSIC LASAGNE

Preparation time: 25 minutes
Total cooking time: 1 hour 15 minutes
Serves 4–6

250 g (9 oz) packet instant
  lasagne sheets
75 g (2½ oz/½ cup) freshly
  grated mozzarella cheese
60 g (2¼ oz/½ cup) freshly
  grated Cheddar cheese
125 ml (4 fl oz/½ cup) cream
3 tablespoons freshly grated
  Parmesan cheese

Cheese sauce
60 g (2¼ oz) butter or margarine
4 tablespoons plain (all-purpose)
  flour
500 ml (17 fl oz/2 cups) milk
120 g (4¼ oz/1 cup) freshly
  grated Cheddar cheese

Meat sauce
1 tablespoon olive oil
1 onion, finely chopped
1 garlic clove, crushed
500 g (1 lb 2 oz) minced
  (ground) beef
2 x 425 g (15 oz) tinned
  tomatoes
3 tablespoons red wine
½ teaspoon ground oregano
¼ teaspoon ground basil

1 Preheat oven to 180°C (350°F/
Gas 4). Brush a shallow oblong
ovenproof dish (about 24 x 30 cm/9½
x 12 inch) with melted butter or oil.
Line with lasagne sheets, breaking
them to fill any gaps. Set aside.
2 To make cheese sauce, melt butter
in a medium saucepan. Add the flour
and stir for 1 minute. Remove from
heat. Gradually add the milk, stirring
until the mixture is smooth. Return to
the heat. Cook, stirring constantly,

over medium heat until the sauce boils
and thickens. Reduce heat and simmer
for 3 minutes. Remove from heat, add
cheese and season to taste with salt
and freshly ground black pepper; stir
until well combined. Set aside.
3 To make meat sauce, heat the oil in
a large pan. Add the onion and garlic
and stir over low heat until onion
softens. Add the meat. Brown well,
breaking up with a fork as it cooks.

Stir in undrained, crushed tomatoes, wine, oregano and basil. Season with salt and freshly ground black pepper. Bring to boil. Reduce heat; simmer 20 minutes.

4 Spoon one-third of the meat sauce over lasagne sheets. Top with one-third of the cheese sauce. Arrange layer of lasagne sheets over top.

5 Continue layering, finishing with lasagne sheets. Sprinkle with combined mozzarella and Cheddar cheese.

6 Pour cream over. Sprinkle with Parmesan. Bake for 35–40 minutes, or until bubbling and golden.

COOK'S FILE

Note: Cheese sauce is a variation of Béchamel Sauce. A true Béchamel uses milk infused with flavourings such as bay leaf, cloves, peppercorns, parsley sprig and cinnamon stick. To do this, bring milk to boiling point (without boiling—known as scalding) with one or more of the flavourings and allow to stand for 10 minutes before straining. To prevent sauce forming a skin, cover the surface completely with plastic wrap or greased greaseproof paper until required.

Sauces are easier to handle if allowed to cool before layering.

LAMB SALAD WITH HUMMUS DRESSING

Preparation time: 20 minutes
Total cooking time: 25 minutes
Serves 4

2 tablespoons olive oil
250 g (9 oz) lamb fillets
250 g (9 oz) slender eggplant (aubergine)
1 red capsicum (pepper), quartered
1 green or yellow capsicum (pepper), quartered

3 tablespoons flat-leaf (Italian) parsley leaves

Hummus dressing
3 tablespoons lemon juice
3 tablespoons olive oil
1 teaspoon sugar
1 tablespoon hummus

1 Heat half the oil in a pan, add the lamb and cook until browned all over and still pink in the centre. Remove and drain on paper towel.
2 Halve eggplant lengthways. Lightly brush eggplant and capsicum with remaining oil. Cook under a hot grill (broiler) until eggplant is brown and tender and capsicum is blackened and blistered. Cool capsicum under a tea (dish) towel or in a plastic bag, then peel away the skin and cut flesh into thick strips.
3 To make the dressing, whisk the ingredients in a jug until smooth.
4 Slice the lamb diagonally into long thin strips. Combine with the eggplant, capsicum and parsley in a bowl, then pile onto serving plates. Drizzle with the dressing just before serving.

Lightly brush the eggplant and capsicum with the remaining olive oil.

Slice the grilled (broiled), peeled capsicum into thick strips.

Whisk the lemon juice, olive oil, sugar and hummus together until smooth.

CHERMOULA CHICKEN

Preparation time: 10 minutes +
  2 hours marinating
Total cooking time: 15 minutes
Serves 4

10 g (¼ oz/½ cup) flat-leaf
  (Italian) parsley
3 tablespoons coriander
  (cilantro) leaves
2 garlic cloves, roughly chopped
3 tablespoons lemon juice
3 teaspoons ground cumin
1 tablespoon chopped preserved
  lemon

125 ml (4 fl oz/½ cup) olive oil
4 skinless, boneless chicken
  breasts, flattened

1 To make the marinade, combine the parsley, coriander, garlic, lemon juice, cumin and preserved lemon in a food processor or blender and process until well combined. While the motor is running, gradually add the oil in a thin stream until smooth. Season.
2 Place the chicken in a large, flat dish and pour over the marinade. Marinate for 2 hours, or overnight if time permits.
3 Grease four sheets of foil and place a chicken breast in the centre of each.

Spoon any extra marinade over the chicken. Fold over the foil and secure the ends. Place the parcels under a hot griller (broiler) and cook for 10–12 minutes without turning, or until cooked through. Remove from the foil parcels, cut into slices and serve with couscous.

COOK'S FILE

Note: To flatten chicken breast fillets, put them between two pieces of plastic wrap and hit with a meat mallet or the palm of your hand.

COQ AU VIN

Preparation time: 15 minutes
Total cooking time: 1 hour 40 minutes
Serves 4–6

30 g (1 oz) butter
125 g (4½ oz) bacon,
    chopped

1.5 kg (3 lb 5 oz) skinless
    chicken pieces
350 g (12 oz) baby onions
2 tablespoons plain (all-purpose)
    flour
750 ml (26 fl oz/3 cups) red
    wine
250 g (9 oz) field mushrooms,
    sliced
1 tablespoon thyme leaves

1 Preheat the oven to 180°C (350°F/ Gas 4). Melt the butter in a large ovenproof casserole dish. Add the bacon and cook until golden, then remove. Add the chicken and cook, in batches, for 4–5 minutes, or until browned. Remove. Add the onions and cook for 2–3 minutes, or until browned, then remove from the pan.

2 Stir in the flour to the pan, remove from the heat and slowly pour in the wine, while stirring. Return to the heat, bring to the boil and return the bacon and chicken to the pan. Cover and bake for 1 hour. Return the onions to the pan and add the mushrooms. Cook for a further 30 minutes. Season with salt and freshly ground black pepper and garnish with the thyme. Serve with mashed potato, if desired.

1

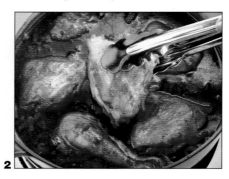

2

SPICY LAMB PIE

Preparation time: 40 minutes
Total cooking time: 1 hour 15 minutes
Serves 6

1 tablespoon oil
1 large onion, chopped
2 garlic cloves, crushed
500 g (1 lb) minced (ground)
   lamb
1 teaspoon ground cinnamon
2 teaspoons ground cumin
1 teaspoon curry powder
3 tablespoons red wine
3 tablespoons tomato paste

4 tablespoons currants
500 g (1 lb) English spinach
   leaves, shredded
2 tablespoons marmalade
3 tablespoons beef stock
12 sheets filo pastry
80 g (2⅔ oz) butter, melted

1 Preheat the oven to 180°C (350°F/ Gas 4). Brush a 21 cm (8½ inch) round pie dish with butter. Heat oil in a pan. Add onion and garlic; and stir for 2 minutes. Add lamb mince and stir for 5 minutes, breaking up any lumps with a fork.

2 Add spices, wine, tomato paste, currants, spinach, marmalade and stock. Simmer, uncovered, for 20 minutes, or until all the liquid has evaporated. Season with salt and pepper. Allow to cool.

3 Remove 1 sheet of pastry and cover the rest with a damp tea (dish) towel to prevent drying out. Brush the sheet of filo lightly with butter and cover with another 2 sheets; brush each with butter. Cut in half, crossways, and line the pie dish with the 2 halves of pastry, leaving any overhanging edges. Spoon lamb mixture into dish. Brush remaining sheets of pastry with butter, scrunch each into a ball and place on top of the pie. Bake for 45 minutes, until pastry turns golden.

Add the spices, red wine, tomato paste, currants, spinach, marmalade and stock.

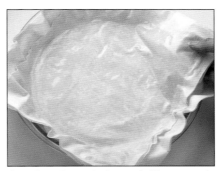

Cut the 3-layered sheet of filo pastry in half and line a pie dish with the 2 halves.

Scrunch the remaining 9 filo sheets into balls and place on top of the pie.

PESTO LAMB CUTLETS

Preparation time: 40 minutes + chilling
Total cooking time: 20 minutes
Serves 4

12 lamb cutlets
1 egg
3 tablespoons pesto
1 teaspoon wholegrain mustard
2 tablespoons cornflour
   (cornstarch)

80 g (2¾ oz/1 cup) fresh
   breadcrumbs
4 tablespoons grated Parmesan
   cheese
4 tablespoons pine nuts, finely
   chopped

1 Trim any fat from the cutlets and scrape the flesh from the bone to give them a nice shape. Whisk together the egg, pesto, mustard and cornflour.
2 Mix the bread crumbs, Parmesan and pine nuts in a bowl. Dip each cutlet into the pesto then breadcrumb mixtures. Chill for 30 minutes.
3 Shallow-fry the cutlets in oil, in batches, for 5 minutes each side.

COOK'S FILE

Note: To make pesto, process 2 bunches basil leaves, 4 tablespoons toasted pine nuts, 2 crushed garlic cloves and 4 tablespoons grated Parmesan until finely chopped. Slowly add 4 tablespoons olive oil.

Whisk together the egg, pesto, mustard and cornflour.

Dip the cutlets in the pesto mixture, then the breadcrumb mixture.

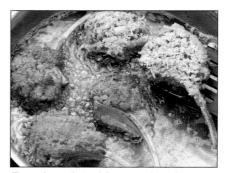

Turn the cutlets with a spatula, taking care not to dislodge the crumb coating.

SPAGHETTI WITH CHICKEN MEATBALLS

Preparation time: 30 minutes + chilling
Total cooking time: 1 hour 30 minutes
Serves 4–6

500 g (1 lb) minced (ground) chicken
60 g (2 oz) freshly grated Parmesan cheese
160 g (5¼ oz/2 cups) fresh white breadcrumbs
2 garlic cloves, crushed
1 egg
freshly ground black pepper
1 tablespoon chopped fresh flat-leaf (Italian) parsley
1 tablespoon chopped fresh sage
3 tablespoons vegetable oil

500 g (1 lb) spaghetti
2 tablespoons chopped fresh oregano, to serve

Tomato sauce
1 tablespoon olive oil
1 onion, finely chopped
2 kg (4 lb) ripe tomatoes, coarsely chopped
2 bay leaves
30 g (1 oz/1 cup) fresh basil leaves, loosely packed
1 teaspoon coarse ground black pepper

1 In a large bowl, mix together the mince, Parmesan, breadcrumbs, garlic, egg, pepper and herbs. Shape tablespoonsful of the mixture into small balls and chill for 30 minutes to firm. Heat the oil in a shallow pan and fry the balls in batches until golden brown; turn often by shaking the pan. Drain on paper towel.

2 To make tomato sauce. Heat the oil in a large pan, add the onion and fry for 1–2 minutes. Add the tomato and bay leaves, cover and bring to the boil, stirring occasionally. Reduce the heat to low, partially cover and cook for 50–60 minutes.

3 Add the meatballs, basil leaves and pepper and simmer for 10–15 minutes, uncovered. Cook the spaghetti in boiling water until just tender. Drain; return to the pan. Add some sauce to the pasta and toss. Serve the pasta in individual bowls with sauce and meatballs, sprinkled with fresh oregano and perhaps extra Parmesan.

Shape tablespoonsful of the mixture into small balls.

Partially cover the pan and cook for 50–60 minutes.

Add the meatballs, basil and pepper to the tomato mixture.

SLOW-COOKED LAMB SHANKS WITH SOFT POLENTA

Preparation time: 20 minutes
Total cooking time: 2 hours
 20 minutes
Serves 4

3 tablespoons olive oil
8 French trimmed lamb
 shanks
3 tablespoons seasoned plain
 (all-purpose) flour
2 onions, sliced
3 garlic cloves, crushed
1 celery stalk, cut into 2.5 cm
 (1 inch) lengths
2 long thin carrots, cut into 3 cm
 (1¼ inch) chunks
2 parsnips, peeled and cut into
 3 cm (1¼ inch) chunks
250 ml (9 fl oz/1 cup) red
 wine
750 ml (26 fl oz/3 cups) chicken
 stock
250 ml (9 fl oz/1 cup) Italian
 tomato passata (puréed
 tomatoes)
1 bay leaf
1 sprig thyme
zest of half an orange (without
 pith), cut into thick strips
1 sprig parsley
sprigs of thyme, to garnish

Polenta
500 ml (17 fl oz/2 cups) chicken
 stock
150 g (5½ oz/1 cup) fine instant
 polenta (cornmeal)
50 g (1¾ oz) butter
pinch paprika, for sprinkling

1 Preheat the oven to 160°C (315°F/ Gas 2–3). Heat the oil in a large heavy-based flameproof casserole dish, big enough to fit the shanks in a single layer. Lightly dust the shanks with seasoned flour then brown them in batches on the stovetop. Remove from the casserole dish.

2 Add the onion, reduce the heat and cook gently for 3 minutes. Stir in the garlic, celery, carrot and parsnip. Pour in the wine and simmer for 1 minute, then return the shanks to the casserole dish. Add the stock, tomato passata, bay leaf, thyme, orange zest and parsley. Cover and bake for 2 hours, or until the meat is very tender.

3 To make the polenta, place the stock and 500 ml (17 fl oz/2 cups) water in a large saucepan and bring to the boil. Gradually stir in the polenta using a wooden spoon. Reduce the heat and simmer over low heat, stirring often, for 5–6 minutes, or until the mixture thickens and starts to leave the side of the pan. Remove from the heat, add the butter and season with salt and pepper. Stir until the butter melts. Spoon into a warm dish and sprinkle with paprika.

4 Gently remove the shanks from the pan. Arrange on a warm serving platter. Discard the herbs and zest, then spoon vegetables and gravy over the shanks. Garnish with the thyme sprigs. Serve with the soft polenta.

Cook the seasoned lamb shanks in hatches until brown all over.

Bake the lamb shanks and vegetables until the meat is very tender.

212

FISH FILLETS WITH RATATOUILLE

Preparation time: 15 minutes
Total cooking time: 25 minutes
Serves 4

4 large fish fillets
1 medium leek
2 medium zucchini (courgettes)
1 medium red capsicum (pepper)
1 medium eggplant (aubergine)
2 tablespoons oil
2 garlic cloves, crushed
425 g (15 oz) tinned tomatoes, undrained, crushed
125 ml (4 fl oz/½) cup water

1–2 tablespoons chopped fresh oregano
freshly ground black pepper
2 tablespoons oil, extra
2 tablespoons lemon juice
2 tablespoons chopped fresh parsley

1 Rinse fish under cold water. Pat dry with paper towel. Thinly slice leek and zucchini. Chop capsicum and eggplant into small cubes.

2 Heat oil in a large pan. Add leek, cook over medium heat for 5 minutes, stirring occasionally. Add zucchini, capsicum, eggplant, garlic, tomatoes, water and oregano. Bring to boil, cover. Reduce heat to low, simmer, covered, for 15 minutes or until vegetables are tender; stir occasionally.

3 Sprinkle fish fillets on both sides with pepper. Heat extra oil in medium frying pan. Add fish and cook over medium heat for 3 minutes on each side or until just cooked through. Place fish on serving plates and spoon ratatouille on top. Sprinkle with lemon juice and chopped parsley.

COOK'S FILE

Storage time: Ratatouille can be made up to 2 days ahead; reheat just before serving. Cook the fish just before serving.

1

2

3

CANNELLONI

Preparation time: 35 minutes
Total cooking time: 1 hour 10 minutes
Serves 4–6

Beef and spinach filling
1 tablespoon olive oil
1 onion, chopped
1 garlic clove, crushed
500 g (1 lb 2 oz) minced
    (ground) beef
250 g (9 oz) packet frozen
    spinach, thawed
4 tablespoons tomato paste
    (concentrated purée)
125 g (4½ oz/½ cup) ricotta
    cheese
1 egg
½ teaspoon ground oregano

Béchamel sauce
250 ml (9 fl oz/1 cup) milk
1 sprig fresh parsley
5 peppercorns
30 g (1 oz) butter or margarine
1 tablespoon plain (all-purpose)
    flour
125 ml (4 fl oz/½ cup) cream

Tomato sauce
425 g (15 oz) tinned puréed
    tomatoes
2 tablespoons chopped fresh
    basil
1 garlic clove, crushed
½ teaspoon sugar
12–15 instant cannelloni tubes
150 g (5½ oz/1 cup) freshly
    grated mozzarella cheese
50 g (1¾ oz/½ cup) freshly
    grated Parmesan cheese

1 Preheat oven to 180°C (350°F/ Gas 4). Lightly oil a large shallow casserole dish. Set aside.

2 To make beef and spinach filling, heat oil in a frying pan. Add onion and garlic and stir over low heat until onion is soft. Add beef and brown well, breaking up with a spoon or fork as it cooks. Add the spinach and tomato paste. Cook, stirring, for 1 minute. Remove from heat. In a small bowl, mix the ricotta, egg and oregano. Season to taste with salt and freshly ground black pepper. Add to beef mixture; stir to combine. Set aside.

3 To make béchamel sauce, place milk, parsley and peppercorns in a small pan. Bring to the boil. Remove from heat. Allow to stand for 10 minutes. Strain, discard flavourings. Melt butter in a small pan. Add flour. Cook, stirring, for 1 minute. Remove from heat. Gradually blend in strained milk, stirring until mixture is smooth. Return to heat. Cook, stirring constantly over medium heat, until sauce boils and thickens. Reduce heat and simmer for 3 minutes. Add cream and season to taste, then stir.

4 To make tomato sauce, place tomato puree, basil, garlic and sugar in a medium pan and stir to combine. Bring to the boil. Reduce heat. Simmer for 5 minutes.

5 Spoon the beef and spinach filling into a piping bag and fill the cannelloni tubes or fill using a teaspoon.

6 Spoon a little of the tomato sauce in the base of the prepared casserole dish. Arrange cannelloni on top.

7 Pour the béchamel sauce over the cannelloni, followed by the remaining tomato sauce. Sprinkle combined cheeses over the top. Bake, uncovered, for 30–35 minutes, or until golden.

4

5

6

SPAGHETTI BOLOGNESE

Preparation time: 10 minutes
Cooking time: 55 minutes
Serves 4

1 tablespoon olive oil
1 large onion, diced
2 garlic cloves,
   crushed

600 g (1 lb 5 oz) minced
   (ground) beef (or minced
   beef and veal)
125 ml (4 fl oz/½ cup) red
   wine
125 ml (4 fl oz/½ cup) beef
   stock
2 x 400 g (14 oz) tinned
   tomatoes, chopped
1 carrot, grated
350 g (12 oz) spaghetti

1 Heat the oil over medium heat in a large saucepan, add the onion and garlic and cook for 1–2 minutes, or until soft. Add the meat and cook, stirring to break up any lumps, for 5 minutes, or until the meat is browned. Pour in the wine and simmer for 2–3 minutes, or until reduced slightly, then add the stock and simmer for 2 minutes. Add the tomato and carrot and season well. Cook over low heat for 40 minutes.

2 About 15 minutes before serving, cook the pasta in a large saucepan of boiling water until al dente. Drain well and keep warm. Divide the pasta evenly among four serving bowls and pour the meat sauce over the pasta. Garnish with parsley, if desired.

COOK'S FILE

Hint: Delicious with grated Parmesan cheese.

216

BUCATINI WITH SAUSAGE AND FENNEL SEED

Preparation time: 10 minutes
Cooking time: 40 minutes
Serves 4

500 g (1 lb 2 oz) good-quality
　　Italian sausages
2 tablespoons olive oil
3 garlic cloves, chopped
1 teaspoon fennel seeds
½ teaspoon chilli flakes

2 x 425 g (15 oz) tinned
　　tomatoes, crushed
500 g (1 lb 2 oz) bucatini
1 teaspoon balsamic vinegar
3 tablespoons loosely packed
　　fresh basil, chopped

1 Heat a frying pan over high heat, add the sausages and cook, turning, for 8–10 minutes, or until well browned and cooked through. Remove, cool slightly and slice on the diagonal into 1 cm (½ inch) pieces.
2 Heat the oil in a saucepan, add the garlic and cook over medium heat for 1 minute. Add the fennel seeds and chilli flakes and cook for 1 minute. Stir in the tomato and bring to the boil, then reduce the heat and simmer, covered, for 20 minutes. Cook the pasta in a large saucepan of boiling water until al dente. Drain. Return to the pan to keep warm.
3 Add the sausages to the sauce and cook, uncovered, for 5 minutes to heat through. Stir in the vinegar and basil. Divide the pasta among four bowls, top with the sauce and serve.

Sweet finishes

Biscuits

FLORENTINES

Preheat the oven to 180°C (350°F/Gas 4). Line an oven tray with baking paper. Sift 3 tablespoons plain (all- purpose) flour into a bowl. Add 2 tablespoons each o chopped walnuts, chopped flaked almonds, finely chopped glacé cherries and finely chopped mixed peel, and stir to combine. Combine 75 g (2½ oz) butter and 3 tablespoons soft brown sugar in a pan, stirring over low heat until the butter has melted and the sugar dissolved. Add to the bowl and mix until just combined. Drop heaped teaspoonsful of the mixture onto the tray, leaving about 6 cm (2½ inches) between each. Press into neat 5 cm (2 inch) rounds. Bake for 7 minutes, then cool on the tray for 5 minutes. Lift carefully onto a wire rack to allow to cool completely. Repeat with the remaining mixture. Spread one side o each Florentine with melted dark chocolate and leave until set. Makes 24.

PANFORTE

Preheat the oven to 180°C (350°F/Gas 4). Brush a 20 cm (8 inch) round cake tin with oil or melted butter and line the base with baking paper. Combine 90 g (3 oz/⅔ cup) each of slivered almonds, chopped macadamia nuts and chopped walnuts in a large bowl with 285 g (9¼ oz/1½ cups) mixed dried fruit. Sift together 85 g (2¾ oz/⅔ cup) plain (all-purpose) flour, 2 tablespoons cocoa powder and 1 teaspoon ground cinnamon and add to the bowl. Stir 60 g (2 oz) butter, 60 g (2 oz) chopped dark chocolate, 4 tablespoons caster (superfine) sugar and 3 tablespoons honey together in a small pan over low heat until melted and combined. Add to the dry ingredients and stir until just combined. Spoon into the tin and smooth the surface. Bake in the preheated oven for 50 minutes and then leave to cool completely in the tin before turning out. Dust with icing (confectioners') sugar and cut into thin wedges to serve. Makes 25 wedges.

Biscuits from left: *Florentines; Panforte; Chocolate Wafers; Biscotti; Amaretti*

BISCOTTI

Preheat the oven to 160°C (315°F/Gas 2–3). Lightly oil a large oven tray and line with baking paper. Beat 3 eggs, 250 g (8 oz/1 cup) caster (super fine) sugar and 1 teaspoon vanilla extract with electric beaters for 2 minutes, or until light and frothy. Sift in 310 g (9¾ oz/2½ cups) plain (all-purpose) flour, 60 g (2 oz/½ cup) self-raising flour, 1 teaspoon bicarbonate of soda (baking soda) and a pinch of salt, and add 115 g (3¾ oz/¾ cup) toasted almonds. Mix with a knife to a soft dough. Divide into 3 portions and roll into log shapes about 20 cm (8 inches) long. Place on the tray and bake for 50 minutes. Cool on a wire rack. Cut the logs into thin slices, place on the tray and bake for 8 minutes each side. Cool and serve. Makes 50.

CHOCOLATE WAFERS

Preheat the oven to 150°C (300°F/Gas 2) and line 3 oven trays with baking paper. Finely chop 100 g (3⅓ oz/⅔ cup) almonds. Finely chop 100 g (3⅓ oz) dark chocolate and add to the almonds with ½ teaspoon each of finely grated orange and lemon zest. Beat 2 egg whites with a pinch of salt until soft peaks form. Gradually add 60 g (2 oz/½ cup) icing (confectioners') sugar, beating well after each addition, until thick and glossy. Fold gently into the nut mixture. Place heaped teaspoonsful of the mixture on the trays and spread into 5 cm (2 inch) rounds. Bake for 20 minutes, until crisp and lightly coloured. Cool on the trays. Makes 30.

AMARETTI

Line 2 baking trays with baking paper. Finely grind 125 g (4 oz) blanched almonds in a food processor and then mix in a bowl with 125 g (4 oz/½ cup) caster (superfine) sugar. Whisk an egg white until frothy and add almost all to the almond mixture; stir to form a dough that is stiff, but soft enough to pipe (add more of the egg white if necessary). Spoon the mixture into a piping bag with a large nozzle and pipe small discs a little apart on the trays. Sift over a little icing (confectioners') sugar and press an almond into the centre of each. Leave, uncovered, for 4 hours at room temperature. Preheat the oven to 150°C (300°F/Gas 2). Bake for 25 minutes, or until lightly browned, and then cool on the trays. Makes about 35.

PEACHES POACHED IN WINE

Preparation time: 20 minutes
Total cooking time: 20 minutes
Serves 4

4 just-ripe yellow-fleshed
    freestone peaches
500 ml (17 fl oz/2 cups) sweet
    white wine such as Sauternes
3 tablespoons orange liqueur
250 g (9 oz 1 cup) sugar
1 cinnamon stick
1 vanilla bean, split
8 fresh mint leaves
mascarpone or crème fraîche,
    to serve

1 Cut a small cross in the base of each peach. Immerse the peaches in boiling water for 30 seconds, then drain and cool slightly. Peel off the skin, cut in half and carefully remove the stones.
2 Place the wine, liqueur, sugar, cinnamon stick and vanilla bean in a deep-sided frying pan large enough to hold the peach halves in a single layer. Heat the mixture, stirring, until the sugar dissolves. Bring to the boil, then reduce the heat and simmer for 5 minutes. Add the peaches to the pan and simmer for 4 minutes, turning them over halfway through. Remove with a slotted spoon and leave to cool. Continue to simmer the syrup for 6–8 minutes, or until thick. Strain and set aside.
3 Arrange the peaches on a serving platter, cut-side-up. Spoon the syrup over the top and garnish each half with a mint leaf. Serve the peaches warm or chilled, with a dollop of mascarpone or crème fraîche.

COOK'S FILE

Note: There are two types of peaches, the freestone and the clingstone. As the names imply, clingstone indicates that the flesh will cling to the stone whereas the stones in freestone peaches are easily removed without breaking up the flesh. Each has a variety with either yellow or white flesh, and all these peaches are equally delicious.

Peel the skin away from the cross cut in the base of the peaches.

Simmer the wine, liqueur sugar cinnamon and vanilla bean.

CASSATA ALLA SICILIANA

Preparation time: 25 minutes +
  overnight refrigeration
Total cooking time: 2 minutes
Serves 6

60 g (2¼ oz) blanched almonds,
  halved
30 g (1 oz) shelled pistachios
650 g (1 lb 7 oz) fresh ricotta
  cheese (see Note)
60 g (2¼ oz/½ cup) icing
  (confectioners') sugar
1½ teaspoons vanilla extract
2 teaspoons finely grated
  lemon zest
50 g (1¾ oz) cedro, chopped into
  5 mm (¼ inch) pieces
  (see Note)
50 g (1¾ oz) glacé orange,
  chopped into 5 mm (¼ inch)
  pieces
60 g (2¼ oz) red glacé cherries,
  halved
375 g (13 oz) ready-made round
  sponge cake, unfilled
125 ml (4 fl oz/½ cup) Madeira
  or malmsey wine
14 blanched almonds, extra
14 red glacé cherries, extra,
  halved
icing (confectioners') sugar, for
  dusting
sweetened whipped cream,
  to serve

1 Dry-fry the almonds and pistachios in a frying pan, tossing, over medium heat for 2 minutes, or until starting to change colour. Cool.
2 Press the ricotta through a sieve over a bowl. Stir in the icing sugar, vanilla, lemon zest, cedro, glacé orange, glacé cherries and nuts. Mix.

3 Grease a 1.25 litre (5 cup) pudding basin. Cut the cake horizontally into 1 cm (½ inch) thick slices. Set aside one round and cut the rest into wedges, trimming the base to make triangles. Sprinkle the cut side of the triangles lightly with Madeira and arrange around the base and side of the bowl, cut-side down, trimming if necessary to fit. Spoon the ricotta mixture into the centre. Top with a layer of cake. Press down firmly and neaten the edges. Chill overnight.
4 Carefully unmould onto a serving plate. Arrange the extra almonds and

cherries on top and dust with icing sugar just before serving. Serve with sweetened whipped cream—piped into patterns for a true Sicilian look.

COOK'S FILE

Note: It is important to use fresh ricotta from the deli so it can be moulded successfully.
Cedro is candied citron peel and is available from most Italian delicatessens. If unavailable, use glacé pineapple and ½ teaspoon finely grated lemon zest.

Arrange the pieces of sponge cake around the base and side of the basin.

Spoon the ricotta mixture into the cake-lined pudding basin.

Top with a layer of sponge cake, press down firmly and neaten any edges.

CHERRY CLAFOUTIS

Preparation time: 15 minutes
Total cooking time: 40 minutes
Serves 6–8

500 g (1 lb 2 oz) fresh cherries
   (see Hint)
90 g (3¼ oz/¾ cup) plain
   (all-purpose) flour
2 eggs, lightly beaten
4 tablespoons caster (superfine)
   sugar
250 ml (9 fl oz/1 cup) milk
3 tablespoons thick (double/
   heavy) cream

50 g (1¾ oz) unsalted butter,
   melted
icing (confectioners') sugar, for
   dusting

1 Preheat the oven to 180°C (350°F/ Gas 4). Lightly brush a 1.5 litre (6 cup) ovenproof dish with melted butter.
2 Carefully pit the cherries, then spread into the dish in a single layer.
3 Sift the flour into a bowl, add the eggs and whisk until smooth. Add the sugar, milk, cream and butter, whisking until just combined, but being careful not to overbeat.
4 Pour the batter over the cherries and bake for 30–40 minutes, or until a

skewer comes out clean when inserted into the centre. Remove from the oven and dust generously with icing sugar. Serve immediately.

COOK'S FILE

Hint: You can use a 720 g (1 lb 9½ oz) jar of cherries. Make sure you thoroughly drain the juice away.
Variation: Blueberries, blackberries, raspberries, or small, well-flavoured strawberries can be used. A delicious version can be made using slices of poached pear.

Add the sugar milk, cream and butter to the flour mixture and whisk well.

Pour the batter over the single layer of cherries.

Cook until the batter is golden brown and nicely set.

FIGS IN HONEY SYRUP

Preparation time: 15 minutes
Total cooking time: 1 hour
Serves 4

100 g (3½ oz) blanched whole
    almonds
12–16 whole fresh figs
    (see Note)
125 g (4½ oz/½ cup) sugar
4 tablespoons honey
2 tablespoons lemon juice
6 cm (2½ inch) sliver of
    lemon zest
1 cinnamon stick
250 g (9 oz/1 cup) plain
    Greek-style yoghurt

1 Preheat the oven to 180°C (350°F/ Gas 4). Place the almonds on a baking tray and bake for 5 minutes, or until golden brown. Cool. Cut the tops off the figs and make a small incision 5 mm (¼ inch) down the top of each one. Push an almond into the base of each fig. Roughly chop the remaining almonds.

2 Place 750 ml (26 fl oz/3 cups) water in a saucepan; stir the sugar over medium heat until it dissolves. Increase the heat and bring to the boil. Stir in the honey, juice, zest and cinnamon. Reduce the heat to medium, gently place the figs in the pan and cook for 30 minutes. Transfer with a slotted spoon to a large serving dish.

3 Boil the liquid over high heat for 15–20 minutes, or until thick and syrupy. Remove the cinnamon and zest. Cool the syrup slightly and pour over the figs. Sprinkle with the remaining almonds. Serve warm or cold with yoghurt.

COOK'S FILE

Note: You can also use 500 g (1 lb 2 oz) dried whole figs. Cover with 750 ml (26 fl oz/3 cups) cold water and soak for 8 hours. Drain, reserving the liquid. Push a blanched almond into the bottom of each fig. Place the liquid in a large saucepan, add the sugar and bring to the boil, stirring as the sugar dissolves. Add the honey, lemon juice, lemon zest and cinnamon stick, and continue the recipe as above.

Make a small crossways incision in the top of each fig.

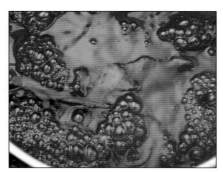

Push a blanched almond into the base of each fig.

Using a slotted spoon, remove the figs from the pan.

Continue to boil the liquid until thick and syrupy.

PANNA COTTA WITH RUBY SAUCE

Preparation time: 20 minutes + chilling
Total cooking time: 20 minutes
Serves 6

375 ml (13 fl oz/1½ cups) milk
3 teaspoons gelatine
375 ml (13 fl oz/1½ cups) cream
4 tablespoons caster (superfine)
   sugar
2 tablespoons Amaretto liqueur

Ruby sauce
250 g (9 oz) caster (superfine)
   sugar
1 cinnamon stick
125g (1½ oz/1 cup) raspberries
125 ml (4 fl oz/½ cup)
   good-quality red wine

1 Use your fingertips to lightly smear the inside of 6 individual 150 ml (5 fl oz) moulds with almond or light olive oil. Place 3 tablespoons milk in a small bowl and sprinkle with gelatine; leave to dissolve for a few minutes.

2 Put the remaining milk in a pan with the cream and sugar and heat gently while stirring, until almost boiling. Remove the pan from the heat; whisk the gelatine into the cream mixture and whisk until dissolved. Leave to cool for 5 minutes and then stir in the Amaretto.

3 Pour the mixture into the moulds and chill until set (about 4 hours). Unmould and serve with ruby sauce.

4 To make the ruby sauce, place the sugar and 250 ml (9 fl oz/1 cup) water in a pan and stir over medium heat until the sugar has completely dissolved (do not allow to boil). Add the cinnamon stick and simmer for 5 minutes. Add the raspberries and wine and boil rapidly for 5 minutes. Remove the cinnamon stick and push the sauce through a sieve; discard the seeds. Cool and then chill the sauce in the refrigerator before serving.

Put some of the milk into a small bowl and sprinkle with gelatine.

Whisk the dissolved gelatine into the cream mixture until dissolved.

Pour the mixture into the moulds and then refrigerate until set.

Remove the cinnamon stick and strain the sauce through a sieve.

RICOTTA POTS WITH RASPBERRIES

Preparation time: 20 minutes
Total cooking time: 25 minutes
Serves 4

4 eggs, separated
125 g (4½ oz/½ cup) caster (superfine) sugar
350 g (11¼ oz) fresh ricotta
3 tablespoons pistachio nuts, finely chopped
1 teaspoon grated lemon zest
2 tablespoons lemon juice
1 tablespoon vanilla sugar
200 g (6½ oz) fresh raspberries

1 Preheat the oven to 180°C (350°F/ Gas 4). Beat the egg yolks and sugar in a small bowl until pale and creamy. Transfer to a large bowl and add the ricotta, pistachio nuts, lemon zest and juice and mix well.

2 In a separate bowl, whisk the egg whites until stiff peaks form. Beat in the vanilla sugar, then fold into the ricotta mixture, stirring until just combined.

3 Lightly grease 4 individual, 250 ml (9 fl oz/1 cup) ramekins. Divide the raspberries among the dishes and spoon the ricotta filling over the top. Place on an oven tray and bake for 20–25 minutes, or until puffed and lightly browned. Serve immediately, with a light dusting of icing (confectioners') sugar.

Beat together the egg yolks and sugar until pale and creamy.

Fold in the egg whites with a metal spoon, trying to keep the volume.

Put the raspberries in the ramekins and spoon the ricotta filling over the top.

HONEY AND PINE NUT TART

Preparation time: 25 minutes +
15 minutes refrigeration
Total cooking time: 1 hour
Serves 6

Pastry
250 g (9 oz/2 cups) plain
   (all-purpose) flour
1½ tablespoons icing
   (confectioners') sugar
115 g (4 oz) chilled unsalted
   butter, chopped
1 egg, lightly beaten

Filling
235 g (8½ oz/1½ cups) pine nuts
175 g (6 oz/½ cup) honey
115 g (4 oz) unsalted butter,
   softened
125 g (4½ oz/½ cup) caster
   (superfine) sugar
3 eggs, lightly beaten
¼ teaspoon vanilla extract
1 tablespoon almond liqueur
1 teaspoon finely grated
   lemon zest
1 tablespoon lemon juice
icing (confectioners') sugar, for
   dusting
crème fraîche or mascarpone, to
   serve

1 Preheat the oven to 190°C (375°F/
Gas 5) and place a baking tray on the
middle shelf. Grease a 23 x 3.5 cm
(9 x 1½ inch) deep loose-bottomed
tart tin.
2 To make the pastry, sift the flour
and icing sugar into a large bowl and
add the butter. Rub the butter into the
flour with your fingertips until it
resembles fine bread crumbs. Make a
well in the centre; add the egg and 2
tablespoons cold water. Mix with a
flat-bladed knife, using a cutting
action, until the mixture comes
together in beads.
3 Gather the dough together and lift
out onto a lightly floured work surface.
Press together into a ball, roll out to a
circle 3 mm (about ⅛ inch) thick and
invert into the tin. Use a small ball of
pastry to press the pastry into the tin,
allowing any excess to hang over the
sides. Roll a rolling pin over the tin,
cutting off any excess pastry. Prick

the base all over with a fork and chill
for 15 minutes. Cut 3 leaves 4 cm
(1½ inch) long from the scraps for
decoration. Cover; chill.
4 Line the pastry with baking paper
and fill with pie weights or dried
beans. Bake on the heated tray for
10 minutes, then remove.
5 Reduce the oven to 180°C (350°F/
Gas 4). To make the filling, roast the
pine nuts on a baking tray in the oven
for 3 minutes, or until golden. Heat the
honey in a small sauce pan until
runny. Beat the butter and sugar in a
bowl until smooth and pale. Gradually
add the eggs, beating well after each
addition. Mix in the honey, vanilla,

liqueur, lemon zest and juice and a
pinch of salt. Stir in the pine nuts,
spoon into the pastry case and smooth
the surface. Arrange the reserved
pastry leaves in the centre.
6 Place on the hot tray and bake for
40 minutes, or until golden and set.
Cover the top with foil after
25 minutes. Serve warm or at room
temperature, dusted with icing sugar.
Serve with crème fraîche or
mascarpone.

COOK'S FILE

Note: The filling rises and cracks
during baking but settles down as the
tart cools.

*Use a small ball of pastry to press the
pastry into the tin.*

*Arrange the reserved pastry leaves over the
smoothed pine nut filling.*

BAKLAVA

Preparation time: 40 minutes
Total cooking time: 1 hour 20 minutes
Makes 18 pieces

560 g (1 lb 4 oz/2¼ cups) caster
    (superfine) sugar
1½ teaspoons lemon zest
3 tablespoons honey
3 tablespoons lemon juice
2 tablespoons orange blossom
    water
200 g (7 oz) walnuts, finely
    chopped
200 g (7 oz) shelled pistachios,
    finely chopped
200 g (7 oz) almonds, finely
    chopped
2 tablespoons caster (superfine)
    sugar, extra
2 teaspoons ground cinnamon
200 g (7 oz) unsalted butter,
    melted
375 g (13 oz) filo pastry

1 Place the sugar, lemon zest and 375 ml (13 fl oz/1½ cups) water in a saucepan and stir over high heat until the sugar dissolves, then boil for 5 minutes. Reduce the heat to low and simmer for 5 minutes, or until the syrup has thickened slightly and just coats the back of a spoon. Add the honey, lemon juice and orange blossom water and cook for 2 minutes. Remove from the heat and cool completely
2 Preheat the oven to 170°C (325°F/Gas 3). Combine the nuts, extra sugar and cinnamon. Grease a 30 x 27 cm (12 x 11 inch) baking dish with the melted butter. Cover the base with a single layer of filo pastry and brush lightly with the butter, folding in any overhanging edges. Continue to layer the filo, brushing with butter between each new layer and folding in the edges until 10 of the sheets have been used. Keep the rest of the filo under a damp tea (dish) towel to prevent it drying out.
3 Sprinkle half the nut mixture over the pastry and pat down evenly . Repeat the layering and buttering of 5 more filo sheets, sprinkle with the rest of the nuts, then layer and butter the remaining filo sheets, brushing the top layer with butter. Press down with your hands so that the pastry and nuts

adhere to each other. Using a large sharp knife, cut into diamond shapes, ensuring you cut through to the bottom layer. Pour any remaining butter evenly over the top and smooth over with your hands. Bake the baklava for 30 minutes. Reduce the heat to 150°C (300°F/Gas 2) and cook for 30 minutes more.
4 Immediately cut through the original diamond markings, then

strain the syrup evenly over the top. Cool completely before lifting the diamonds out onto a serving platter.

COOK'S FILE

Note: To achieve the right texture, it is important for the baklava to be piping hot and the syrup cold when you pour the syrup over the top.

Sprinkle the remaining nut mixture over the filo pastry layers.

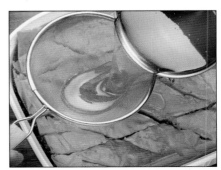

Strain the cooled syrup evenly over the top of the hot baklava.

HAZELNUT PUDDINGS WITH CHOCOLATE CREAM SAUCE AND HONEY ZABAGLIONE

Preparation time: 40 minutes
Total cooking time: 40 minutes
Serves 8

30 g (1 oz) butter, melted
55 g (2 oz/½ cup) ground
    hazelnuts
125 g (4 oz) butter
125 g (4 oz/½ cup) caster
    (superfine) sugar
3 eggs, lightly beaten
250 g (8 oz/2 cups) self-raising
    flour, sifted
4 tablespoons sultanas (golden
    raisin's)
4 tablespoons brandy
4 tablespoons buttermilk
white chocolate shavings, to
    decorate

Chocolate cream sauce
250 ml (8 fl oz/1 cup) cream
30 g (1 oz) butter
200 g (6½ oz) dark chocolate,
    chopped

Honey zabaglione
3 large egg yolks
3 tablespoons honey
2 tablespoons brandy
125 ml (4 fl oz/½ cup) cream

1 Preheat the oven to 180°C (350°F/Gas 4). Brush eight, 125 ml (4 fl oz/½ cup) ovenproof ramekins with melted butter and coat with the ground hazelnuts, shaking off the excess. Beat together the butter and sugar with electric beaters until light and creamy. Add the eggs gradually, beating well after each addition. Fold in the flour, sultanas, brandy and buttermilk. Spoon into the ramekins, cover with greased foil and secure with string.

2 Place the puddings in a large baking dish and pour in enough water to come three-quarters of the way up the sides of the ramekins. Bake for 25 minutes, topping up with more water if necessary. Test with a skewer before removing the ramekins from the pan—the skewer should come out clean when inserted into the centre of the pudding.

3 To make chocolate cream sauce, put the cream, butter and chocolate in a small pan and stir over low heat until melted and smooth. Remove from the heat and set aside.

4 To make honey zabaglione, beat the egg yolks until thick and pale. Place the bowl over a pan of barely simmering water and beat in the honey. Beat for about 5 minutes, until thickened. Remove from the heat, cool to room temperature and stir in the brandy. Beat the cream in a small bowl until firm peaks form, then fold into the egg mixture.

5 Spread chocolate cream sauce over half of each serving plate. Pour zabaglione onto the other half. Unmould the warm pudding onto the centre of the plate and decorate with curls of white chocolate.

COOK'S FILE

Hint: Make chocolate shavings by simply running over the top of the chocolate block with a vegetable peeler.

Brush the ramekins with melted butter then coat with ground hazelnuts.

Beat together the sugar and butter until light and creamy.

Cover the ramekins with foil and secure with string.

Pour water into the baking tray to make a bain-marie.

Put the bowl over a pan of simmering water and beat until thickened.

Unmould the puddings by working around the edges with a sharp knife.

LEMON GRANITA

Preparation time: 15 minutes
  + 2 hours freezing
Total cooking time: 5 minutes
Serves 6

315 ml (10¾ fl oz/1¼ cups)
  lemon juice
1 tablespoon lemon zest

200 g (7 oz) caster (superfine)
  sugar

1 Place the lemon juice, lemon zest and caster sugar in a small saucepan and stir over low heat for 5 minutes, or until the sugar is dissolved. Remove from the heat and leave to cool.
2 Add 500 ml (17 fl oz/2 cups) water to the juice mixture and mix together well. Pour the mixture into a shallow

30 x 20 cm (12 x 8 inch) metal container and place in the freezer until the mixture is beginning to freeze around the edges. Scrape the frozen sections back into the mixture with a fork. Repeat every 30 minutes until the mixture has even-size ice crystals. Beat the mixture with a fork just before serving. To serve, spoon the lemon granita into six chilled glasses.

Stir the juice, zest and sugar over low heat until the sugar has dissolved.

Scrape the frozen edges of the mixture back into the centre.

Beat the granita mixture with a fork just prior to serving

YOGHURT CAKE WITH SYRUP

Preparation time: 20 minutes
Total cooking time: 1 hour
Serves 8–10

185 g (6¼ oz) unsalted butter, softened
250 g (9 oz/1 cup) caster (superfine) sugar
5 eggs, separated
250 g (9 oz/1 cup) plain Greek-style yoghurt
2 teaspoons grated lemon zest
½ teaspoon vanilla extract
280 g (10 oz/2¼ cups) plain (all-purpose) flour
2 teaspoons baking powder
½ teaspoon bicarbonate of soda (baking soda)
whipped cream, to serve

Syrup
250 g (9 oz/1 cup) caster (superfine) sugar
1 cinnamon stick
4 cm (1½ inch) strip lemon zest
1 tablespoon lemon juice

1 Preheat the oven to 180°C (350°F/ Gas 4) and lightly grease a 20 x 10 cm (8 x 4 inch) loaf (bar) tin.
2 Place the butter and sugar in a bowl and beat until light and creamy. Add the egg yolks gradually, beating well after each addition. Then, stir in the yoghurt, lemon zest and vanilla extract. Then, with a metal spoon, fold in the sifted flour, baking powder and bicarbonate of soda.
3 Whisk the egg whites in a clean, dry bowl until stiff, and fold into the mixture. Spoon into the prepared tin and bake for 50 minutes, or until a

skewer comes out clean when inserted into the centre of the cake. Cool in the tin for 10 minutes, then turn out onto a wire rack to cool.
4 Meanwhile, to make the syrup, place the sugar and cinnamon stick in a small pan with 185 ml (6 fl oz/¾ cup) cold water. Stir over medium heat until

the sugar is dissolved. Bring to the boil, add the lemon zest and juice, then reduce the heat and simmer for 5–6 minutes. Strain.
5 Pour the syrup over the cake and wait for most of it to be absorbed before serving. Cut into slices and serve warm with whipped cream.

Stir the yoghurt, lemon zest and vanilla into the egg yolk mixture.

Using a metal spoon, gently fold the egg whites into the mixture.

Simmer the syrup, then remove the cinnamon stick and lemon zest.

CHOCOLATE RICOTTA TART

Preparation time: 20 minutes + chilling
Total cooking time: 1 hour
Serves 8–10

185 g (6 oz/1½ cups) plain (all-purpose) flour
100 g (3⅓ oz) cold butter, chopped
2 tablespoons caster (superfine) sugar
1 tablespoon butter, melted

Filling
1.25 kg (2½ lb) ricotta cheese
125 g (4 oz/½ cup) caster (superfine) sugar

2 tablespoons plain (all-purpose) flour
125 g (4 oz) chocolate, finely chopped
2 teaspoons coffee extract
4 egg yolks
40 g (1⅓ oz) chocolate, extra
½ teaspoon vegetable oil

1 Make sweet shortcrust (pie) pastry by sifting the flour into a large bowl and adding the butter. Rub the butter into the flour with your fingertips, until fine and crumbly. Stir in the sugar. Add 3 tablespoons cold water and cut with a knife to form a dough, adding a little more water if necessary. Turn out onto a lightly floured surface and gather together into a ball. Brush a 25 cm (10 inch) spring-form tin with

melted butter. Roll out the dough to line the tin, coming about two-thirds of the way up the side. Cover and refrigerate while making the filling.

2 To make filling, mix together the ricotta, sugar, flour and a pinch of salt until smooth. Stir in the chocolate, coffee essence and yolks until well mixed. Spoon into the chilled pastry shell and smooth. Chill for 30 minutes, or until firm. Preheat the oven to 180°C (350°F/Gas 4).

3 Put the tin on a baking tray. Bake for 1 hour, or until firm. Leave to cool before removing the sides from the tin. Melt the extra chocolate and stir in the oil. With a fork, flick thin drizzles of melted chocolate over the tart. Cool completely before cutting.

Have cool hands and use just your fingertips when rubbing butter into flour.

Do not knead the dough or it will become tough—just gather it together into a ball.

Mix together the melted chocolate and oil and flick over the tart.

Cut the egg yolks into the dry ingredients with a knife.

Put the raisins in a bowl, pour over the orange juice and leave to soften.

FRUITY NUT PASTRIES

Preparation time: 1 hour + chilling
Total cooking time: 20 minutes
Makes 40

310 g (9¾ oz/2½ cups) plain
　(all-purpose) flour
165 g (5½ oz) butter, chopped
125 g (4 oz/½ cup) caster
　(superfine) sugar
2 eggs plus 1 yolk, beaten
2 teaspoons lemon juice
1 egg yolk, lightly beaten, extra
1 tablespoon demerara sugar

Fruit and nut filling
125 g (4 oz) dried figs
75 g (2½ oz) raisins
2 tablespoons fresh orange juice
75 g (2½ oz) walnuts, finely
　chopped
100 g (3⅓ oz) blanched, roasted
　almonds, finely chopped
2 tablespoons marmalade
1½ tablespoons grated
　orange zest
¼ teaspoon ground cloves
1 teaspoon ground cinnamon

1 Sift the flour into a bowl and rub in the butter with your fingertips. Stir through the sugar, then add the eggs and yolk and cut through with a knife to combine; add enough lemon juice to form a dough. Gather together into a ball, cover with plastic wrap and refrigerate for about 30 minutes.

2 To make fruit and nut filling, chop the figs, cover with boiling water and leave for 15 minutes to soften. Put the raisins in a bowl, cover with orange juice and leave for 15 minutes to soften. Drain the figs and raisins and combine in a bowl with the remaining filling ingredients.

3 Preheat the oven to 180°C (350°F/ Gas 4). Cut the dough in half to make it easier to work with. Roll out each half to about 5 mm (¼ inch) thick on a lightly floured surface and cut rounds, using an 8 cm (3 inch) cutter. Spoon 1 full teaspoon of filling into the centre of each round, brush the edges lightly with water and fold over to enclose the filling.

4 Place on a lightly greased oven tray, brush with extra egg yolk and sprinkle with demerara sugar. Make

Divide the dough in half to make it easier to handle. Cut out rounds with a cutter.

Place the filling in the centre of the pastry round and then fold over to enclose.

cuts across the top of each pastry. Bake for 20 minutes, or until lightly browned.

STUFFED FIGS

Preparation time: 20 minutes
Total cooking time: 5 minutes
Makes 15

50 g (1⅔ oz) blanched almonds
15 soft dried figs
4 tablespoons mixed peel
100 g (3⅓ oz) marzipan,
    chopped

1 Preheat the oven to 180°C (350°F/ Gas 4). Place the almonds on an oven tray and bake for 5 minutes, until lightly golden. Leave to cool.
2 Remove the hard stem ends from the figs. Cut a cross in the top of each fig halfway through to the base and open out like petals.
3 Place the mixed peel and almonds in a food processor and process until fine. Add the marzipan and process in short bursts until fine and crumbly.

4 With your hands, press 2 teaspoons of marzipan filling together to make a ball. Place a ball inside each fig and press back into shape around it. Serve at room temperature with coffee.

COOK'S FILE

Variation: Dip the bases of the figs into melted chocolate.
Storage time: Store figs in a single layer in a covered container in the refrigerator for up to 2 days.

Cut away the hard stem end from the bottom of each fig.

Cut a cross in the top and open out each fig like the petals of a flower.

Place a ball of marzipan filling in each fig and then remould the fruit around it.

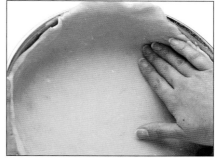

Press the pastry into the base with your fingertips.

Line with baking paper and then fill with dried beans or rice to bake blind.

SICILIAN CHEESECAKE

Preparation time: 45 minutes + chilling
Total cooking time: 1 hour 25 minutes
Serves 8

250 g (8 oz/2 cups) plain
   (all-purpose) flour
160 g (5¼ oz) butter, chopped
3 tablespoons caster (superfine)
   sugar
1 teaspoon grated lemon zest
1 egg, lightly beaten

Ricotta filling
60 g (2 oz/½ cup) raisins,
   chopped
4 tablespoons Marsala
500 g (1 lb) fresh ricotta
125 g (4 oz/½ cup) caster
   (superfine) sugar
1 tablespoon plain (all-purpose)
   flour
4 eggs, separated
125 ml (4 fl oz/½ cup) cream

1 Lightly grease a 26 cm (10½ inch) round spring-form tin. Sift the flour and a pinch of salt into a large bowl and rub in the butter. Add the sugar,

zest, egg and a little water if necessary and, using a knife, cut through until a rough dough forms. Press together into a ball.

2 Roll out the dough on a lightly floured surface to line the base and sides of the tin; chill for 30 minutes. Preheat the oven to 190°C (375°F/ Gas 5). Prick the pastry base, line with baking paper and fill with dried beans or rice. Bake for 15 minutes, then remove the beans/rice and paper, and bake for another 8 minutes, or until pastry is dry. If the base puffs up, gently press down with the beans in the paper. Allow to cool. Reduce the oven to 160°C (315°F/Gas 2–3).

3 To make filling, put the raisins and Marsala in a small bowl, cover and leave to soak. Push the ricotta through a sieve. Beat the ricotta and caster sugar with a wooden spoon until combined. Add the flour and egg yolks, then the cream and undrained raisins and mix well. In a small bowl, beat the egg whites until soft peaks form and gently fold into the ricotta mixture in two batches.

4 Pour the filling into the pastry case and bake for 1 hour, or until just set. Check during cooking and cover with

Push the ricotta through a sieve and then beat together with the sugar.

Fold the beaten egg white into the ricotta mixture with a metal spoon.

foil if the pastry is overbrowning. Cool a little in the oven with the door ajar to prevent sinking. Serve warm with whipped cream.

MAHALLABIA

Preparation time: 15 minutes + 1 hour
refrigeration
Total cooking time: 40 minutes
Serves 4

500 ml (17 fl oz/2 cups) milk
75 g (2½ oz) caster (superfine)
sugar
2 tablespoons cornflour
(cornstarch)
2 tablespoons ground rice
(see Note)

75 g (2½ oz) ground almonds
1 teaspoon rosewater (see Note)
2 tablespoons flower blossom
honey (see Note)
2 tablespoons shelled pistachios,
chopped

1 Place the milk and sugar in a
saucepan and stir over medium heat
until the sugar has dissolved.
2 Combine the cornflour and ground
rice with 3 tablespoons water and mix
to a paste. Add to the milk and cook,
stirring occasionally, over low heat for
20 minutes. Add the almonds (the

mixture will be quite thick) and cook
for 15 minutes, then add the rosewater.
Spoon into four small shallow dishes
and chill for 1 hour. Drizzle with honey
and sprinkle with pistachios to serve.

COOK'S FILE

Note: Ground rice and rosewater are
available from health food stores. If
flower blossom honey is not available,
use normal honey.

*Combine the cornflour, ground rice and
water and mix to a paste.*

*Stir in the ground almonds (the mixture
will be quite thick).*

*Spoon the mixture into four small shallow
serving dishes.*

HALVAS FOURNO

Preparation time: 30 minutes
+ 45 minutes cooling
Total cooking time: 30 minutes
Makes 12

115 g (4 oz) unsalted butter,
    softened
125 g (4½ oz/½ cup) caster
    (superfine) sugar
125 g (4½ oz/1 cup) semolina
110 g (3¾ oz/1 cup) ground
    roasted hazelnuts
2 teaspoons baking powder
3 eggs, lightly beaten
1 tablespoon finely grated
    orange zest
2 tablespoons orange juice
whipped cream or honey-
    flavoured yoghurt, to serve

Syrup
750 g (1 lb 10 oz/3 cups) sugar
4 cinnamon sticks
1 tablespoon orange zest, very
    thinly sliced
4 tablespoons lemon juice
125 ml (4 fl oz/½ cup) orange
    blossom water

Topping
60 g (2¼ oz/½ cup) slivered
    almonds
70 g (2½ oz/½ cup)
    roasted hazelnuts, coarsely
    chopped

1 Preheat the oven to 210°C (415°F/ Gas 6–7). Grease a 23 cm (9 inch) square baking tin and line the base with baking paper. Cream the butter and sugar in a bowl until smooth. Stir in the semolina, ground hazelnuts and baking powder. Fold in the eggs, zest and juice until well combined. Spoon into the tin, smooth the surface and bake for 20 minutes, or until golden and just set. Leave in the tin to cool.

2 Meanwhile, to make the syrup, place sugar and 830 ml (29 fl oz/ 3⅓ cups) water in a saucepan. Add the cinnamon sticks and heat gently, stirring, until the sugar has dissolved. Increase the heat and boil rapidly without stirring for 5 minutes. Pour into a heatproof measuring jug then return half to the saucepan. Boil for 15–20 minutes, or until thickened and

reduced to about 170 ml (5½ fl oz/ ⅔ cup). Stir in the orange zest.

3 Add the lemon juice and orange blossom water to the syrup in the jug. Pour over the cake in the tin. When absorbed, upturn the cake onto a large flat plate. Slice into 4 equal strips, then slice each strip diagonally into 3 diamond-shaped pieces. Discard the end scraps, but keep the pieces touching together.

4 To make the topping, combine the almonds and hazelnuts and scatter over the cake. Pour the thickened syrup and orange zest over the combined nuts and leave to stand for 30 minutes. Transfer the slices to plates and serve with whipped cream or honey-flavoured yoghurt.

Fold the eggs, orange zest and orange juice into the semolina mixture.

Add the juice and orange flower water to the syrup and pour over the cake.

Beat together the egg yolks and sugar until thick and pale.

Fold the beaten egg whites into the cream mixture with a metal spoon.

Dip the biscuits into the coffee mixture and arrange in the serving dish.

Layer the remaining biscuits in the dish and spread over the cream mixture.

TIRAMISU

Preparation time: 30 minutes + chilling
Total cooking time: Nil
Serves 6–8

750 ml (26 fl oz/3 cups) strong
  black coffee, cooled
3 tablespoons dark rum
2 eggs, separated
3 tablespoons caster (superfine)
  sugar
250 g (8 oz) mascarpone
250 ml (9 fl oz/1 cup) cream,
  whipped
16 large savoyardi (sponge
  finger) biscuits
2 teaspoons dark cocoa powder

1 Put the coffee and rum in a bowl. Using electric beaters, beat the egg yolks and sugar in a small bowl for 3 minutes, or until thick and pale. Add the mascarpone and beat until just combined. Fold in the whipped cream with a metal spoon.
2 Beat the egg whites until soft peaks form. Fold quickly and lightly into the cream mixture with a metal spoon, trying not to lose the volume.
3 Dip half the biscuits, one at a time, into the coffee mixture; drain off any excess and arrange in the base of a deep serving dish. Spread half the cream mixture over the biscuits.
4 Dip remaining biscuits and repeat the layers. Smooth the surface and dust liberally with cocoa powder.

Refrigerate for 2 hours, or until firm, to allow the flavours to develop. Delicious served with fresh fruit.

ESPRESSO GRANITA

Preparation time: 20 minutes
+ freezing
Total cooking time: 5 minutes
Serves 6

185 g (6 oz/¾ cup) caster
(superfine) sugar
1½ tablespoons cocoa powder
1.25 litres (5 cups) freshly
made, strong espresso coffee
whipped cream, to serve

1 Put the sugar and cocoa powder in a large pan, gradually add 125 ml (4 fl oz/½ cup) water and mix until smooth. Bring to the boil, stirring until the sugar dissolves. Reduce the heat and simmer for 3 minutes.
2 Remove from the heat and add the fresh coffee. Pour into a shallow container or tray and allow to cool completely. Freeze until partially set and then stir with a fork to distribute the ice crystals evenly. Freeze again until firm.

3 Using a fork, work the Granita into fine crystals and return to the freezer for 1 hour before serving. Spoon into glasses and serve immediately, with whipped cream.

COOK'S FILE

Hint: The mixture does tend to freeze rock-hard which is why it should be put into a shallow tray and broken up when partially frozen.

Put the sugar and cocoa powder in a large pan and gradually add the water.

Remove the pan from the heat and pour in the fresh coffee.

Use a fork to work the granita into fine crystals, then re-freeze for 1 hour.

ALMOND SEMIFREDDO

Preparation time: 30 minutes +
  4 hours freezing
Total cooking time: Nil
Serves 8–10

300 ml (10½ fl oz) cream
4 eggs, at room temperature,
  separated
85 g (3 oz/⅔ cup) icing
  (confectioners') sugar
3 tablespoons amaretto
80 g (2¾ oz/½ cup) blanched
  almonds, toasted and chopped

8 amaretti biscuits, crushed
fresh fruit or extra amaretto,
  to serve

1 Whip the cream until firm peaks form; cover and refrigerate. Line a 10 x 21 cm (4 x 8½ inch) loaf (bar) tin with plastic wrap so that it overhangs the 2 long sides.
2 Place the egg yolks and icing sugar in a bowl and beat until pale and creamy. Whisk the egg whites in a separate bowl until firm peaks form. Stir the amaretto, almonds and amaretti biscuits into the egg yolk mixture, then carefully fold in the

cream and the egg whites until well combined. Carefully spoon into the tin and cover with the overhanging plastic. Freeze for 4 hours, or until frozen but not rock hard. Serve in slices with fresh fruit or a sprinkling of amaretto.

COOK'S FILE

Note: Semifreddo means semi-frozen, so if you want to leave it in the freezer overnight, remove it and place it in the refrigerator for 30 minutes to soften slightly before serving.

Place the amaretti biscuits in a plastic bag and crush with a rolling pin.

Beat the egg yolks and sugar together with electric beaters.

Carefully spoon the mixture into the lined loaf (bar) tin.

STRAWBERRIES WITH BALSAMIC VINEGAR

Preparation time: 10 minutes +
  2 hours 30 minutes marinating
Total cooking time: Nil
Serves 4

750 g (1 lb 10 oz) small ripe
  strawberries
3 tablespoons caster (superfine)
  sugar

2 tablespoons balsamic vinegar
125 g (4½ oz/½ cup)
  mascarpone

1 Wipe the strawberries with a clean damp cloth and carefully remove the green stalks. If the strawberries are large, cut each one in half.
2 Place all the strawberries in a large glass bowl, sprinkle the caster sugar evenly over the top and toss gently to coat. Set aside for 2 hours to macerate, then sprinkle the balsamic vinegar over the strawberries. Toss them again, then refrigerate for about 30 minutes.
3 Spoon the strawberries into four glasses, drizzle with the syrup and top with a dollop of mascarpone.

COOK'S FILE

Note: If you leave the strawberries for more than 2 hours, it is best to refrigerate them.
Hint: Thick cream or crème fraîche can be used instead of mascarpone.

Hull the strawberries after wiping clean with a damp cloth.

Sprinkle the caster sugar evenly over the strawberries.

Use good-quality balsamic vinegar to sprinkle over the strawberries.

ALMOND CITRUS TART

Preparation time: 40 minutes + chilling
Total cooking time: 1 hour
Serves 6–8

250 g (8 oz/2 cups) plain
    (all-purpose) flour, sifted
3 tablespoons caster (superfine)
    sugar
125 g (4 oz) butter, softened
1 teaspoon finely grated
    lemon zest
2 egg yolks

Filling
350 g (11¼ oz) fresh ricotta,
    sieved
4 tablespoons caster (superfine)
    sugar
3 eggs, well beaten
1 tablespoon grated lemon zest
80 g (2¾ oz/½ cup) blanched
    almonds, finely chopped
3 tablespoons flaked almonds
icing (confectioners') sugar,
    to dust

1 Combine the flour, sugar and a pinch of salt in a large bowl. Make a well in the centre and add the butter, zest and yolks. Work the flour into the centre with the fingertips of one hand until a smooth dough forms (add a little more flour if necessary). Wrap in plastic wrap and chill for 1 hour.

2 To make filling, use electric beaters to beat the ricotta and sugar together. Add the eggs gradually, beating well after each addition. Add the zest, beating briefly to combine, and then stir in the chopped almonds.

3 Preheat the oven to 180°C (350°F/ Gas 4). Brush a 20 cm (8 inch) deep fluted flan (tart) tin with melted butter.

4 Roll out the pastry on a lightly floured surface and line the prepared tin, removing the excess pastry. Pour in the filling and smooth the top. Sprinkle with the flaked almonds and bake for 1 hour, or until set.

5 Cool to room temperature and carefully remove the sides from the tin. Dust with icing sugar to serve.

For perfect pastry, use just your fingertips to bring the dough together.

Add the grated lemon zest and beat briefly to combine.

Roll a rolling pin over the lined tin to remove any excess pastry.

LEMON SYRUP CAKE

Preparation time: 20 minutes
Total cooking time: 45 minutes
Serves 8

125 g (4 oz/1 cup) plain
   (all-purpose) flour
¾ teaspoon baking powder
¼ teaspoon bicarbonate of soda
   (baking soda)
50 g (1⅔ oz) unsalted butter
125 g (4 oz/½ cup) caster
   (superfine) sugar

2 eggs
4 tablespoons milk
3 tablespoons ground almonds
2 tablespoons grated lemon zest

Syrup
100 g (3⅓ oz) caster (superfine)
   sugar
4 tablespoons fresh lemon juice

1 Preheat the oven to 180°C (350°F/ Gas 4). Grease and line a 20 cm (8 inch) spring-form tin. Sift the flour, baking powder, bicarbonate of soda and a pinch of salt into a bowl.

2 In a separate bowl, beat the butter, sugar and eggs until light and creamy. Fold in the flour mixture, then gently stir in the milk, almonds and lemon zest. Spoon into the tin and bake for 30–35 minutes, or until a skewer comes out clean. Make holes in the top of the cake with the skewer.

3 To make syrup put the sugar and lemon juice in a small pan and stir over a low heat until syrupy; keep warm. Pour the syrup over the hot cake. Cool on a wire rack.

Fold in the flour mixture, then gently stir in the milk, almonds and lemon zest.

Use a skewer to make holes in the top of the cake so it absorbs the syrup.

Pour the syrup over the hot cake, so that it is absorbed. Cool before turning out.

245

HONEY NUT ROLLS

Preparation time: 25 minutes
Total cooking time: 35 minutes
Serves 8

250 g (8 oz/2 cups) plain
  (all-purpose) flour
3 tablespoons caster (superfine)
  sugar
100 g (3⅓ oz) cold butter
4 tablespoons honey, warmed
3 tablespoons chopped almonds
3 tablespoons chopped pecans
1 teaspoon ground cinnamon
4 tablespoons mixed peel,
  chopped
3 tablespoons chopped mixed
  almonds and pecans, extra

1 Preheat the oven to 180°C (350°F/ Gas 4). Put the flour, sugar, butter and a pinch of salt in a bowl. Rub in the chopped butter until crumbly. Add 2–3 tablespoons cold water and cut through, until the mixture forms a dough. Gather into a ball.

2 Cut the dough in half and roll each piece into a strip about 40 x 10 cm (16 x 4 inches). Spread 3 tablespoons honey over the dough and sprinkle with nuts, cinnamon and mixed peel. Roll up lengthways into two long sausage shapes and cut these in four. Place on a greased baking tray.

3 Glaze with the remaining honey, sprinkle with mixed nuts and make diagonal slashes in the top. Bake for 35 minutes, or until golden brown. Serve warm with whipped cream.

Roll out each piece of dough into a long narrow strip.

Spread with honey, sprinkle with nuts, cinnamon and peel and then roll up.

Sprinkle with mixed nuts and then make a few diagonal slashes in the top.

Cut the slab sponge cake into 12 curved pieces with a sharp knife.

Put the thin ends of the cake slices in the centre so they fit together neatly.

Spoon the chocolate and hazelnut cream into the centre cavity and pack firmly.

Make a cardboard template and enlist help to give the Zuccotto a fancy finish.

ZUCCOTTO

Preparation time: 1 hour + chilling
Total cooking time: Nil
Serves 6–8

1 slab sponge cake, about 30 x
    25 cm (12 x 10 inches)
4 tablespoons Kirsch
3 tablespoons Cointreau
4 tablespoons rum, Cognac,
    Grand Marnier or maraschino
500 ml (17 fl oz/2 cups) cream
90 g (3 oz) dark roasted almond
    chocolate, chopped
165 g (5½ oz/¾ cup) finely
    chopped mixed glacé fruit
100 g (3⅓ oz) dark chocolate,
    melted
70 g (2⅓ oz) roasted hazelnuts,
    chopped
cocoa powder and icing
    (confectioners') sugar, to
    decorate

1 Line a 1.5 litre (6 cup) pudding basin with damp muslin (cheesecloth). Cut the cake into 12 curved pieces with a sharp knife. Work with one strip of cake at a time, lightly brushing it with the combined liqueurs and arranging the pieces closely in the basin. Put the thin ends in the centre so the slices cover the base and side. Brush with the remaining liqueur to soak the cake. Chill.

2 Beat the cream into stiff peaks, then divide in half. Fold the almond chocolate and glacé fruit into one half. Spread evenly over the cake in the basin, leaving a space in the centre.

3 Fold the cooled melted chocolate and hazelnuts into the remaining cream and spoon into the centre, packing firmly. Smooth the surface, cover and refrigerate overnight to allow the cream to firm slightly.

4 Turn out onto a serving plate and decorate by dusting generously with cocoa powder and icing sugar. You can make a cardboard template to help you dust separate wedges neatly, although you may need help holding it in place. Serve immediately, as the cream mixture will soften quickly.

ICE CREAM CASSATA

Preparation time: 30 minutes + chilling
and overnight freezing
Total cooking time: Nil
Serves 8–10

250 g (8 oz) glacé fruit (such as
  cherries, apricots or
  pineapple), finely chopped
4 tablespoons slivered almonds,
  finely chopped
4 tablespoons Cointreau or
  orange-flavoured liqueur
2 litres (8 cups) good-quality
  vanilla ice cream, softened
  slightly
185 g (6 oz/1¼ cups) unsalted
  pistachio nuts, shelled and
  finely chopped

1 Cover the chopped glacé fruit and almonds with the liqueur and soak for 10 minutes. Put a 2.25 litre (9 cup) pudding basin in the refrigerator. While the pudding basin is chilling, divide the softened ice cream in half and fold the pistachio nuts through one half. If it begins to melt, return the ice cream to the freezer until it is firm enough to spread.
2 When the basin is very cold, line it with a layer of the pistachio ice cream to three-quarters of the way up the side (use a spoon, dipped in warm water occasionally, to help spread it evenly). Place in the freezer to re-set.
3 Combine the remaining ice cream with the soaked glacé fruit and almonds. Mix until well combined. (Return to the freezer if the ice cream has softened too much to spread.) Remove the basin from the freezer and spoon in the ice cream and fruit mixture. Smooth the surface and return to the freezer overnight, or until completely set.
4 Turn out onto a chilled platter and cut into wedges to serve.

COOK'S FILE

Storage time: Will keep frozen for up to one month.

Use a sharp knife to finely chop the glacé fruit and slivered almonds.

Fold the pistachio nuts into half of the softened ice cream.

Line the chilled basin with pistachio ice cream, using a warm spoon to spread it.

Spoon the fruit ice cream into the centre and return to the freezer to set.

CHILLED ORANGE CREAMS

Preparation time: 30 minutes + chilling
Total cooking time: 5 minutes
Serves 6

125 ml (4 fl oz/½ cup) juice of blood oranges
3 teaspoons gelatine
4 egg yolks
125 g (4 oz/½ cup) caster (superfine) sugar
315 ml (10 fl oz/1¼ cups) milk
1 teaspoon finely grated blood orange zest
250 ml (8 fl oz/1 cups) cream

1 Put a large bowl in the freezer and chill. Put a few drops of almond or light olive oil on your fingertips and lightly grease the insides of six ½ cup (125 ml/4 fl oz) moulds. Put the orange juice in a small bowl and sprinkle with gelatine; set aside.

2 Whisk the yolks and sugar in a small bowl until thick. Heat the milk and zest in a pan and gradually pour onto the egg mixture while whisking. Return to the pan and stir until the custard coats the back of the spoon—do not allow it to boil. Add the gelatine mixture and stir to dissolve.

3 Pour the mixture immediately through a strainer into the chilled bowl. Cool, stirring occasionally, until beginning to thicken. Whip the cream into soft peaks and fold into the custard. Spoon into the moulds and chill to set. Serve with cream, if liked.

COOK'S FILE

Variation: Blood oranges have a short season but they give the best colour. You could use navel or Valencia oranges, or mandarins.

Put the blood orange juice in a small bowl and sprinkle with gelatine.

Stir the custard until it will coat the back of a spoon.

Pour the custard mixture through a strainer into the chilled bowl.

Whip the cream into soft peaks and then fold into the custard with a metal spoon.

249

Index

Published in 2011 by Murdoch Books Pty Limited.

Murdoch Books Australia
Pier 8/9, 23 Hickson Road, Millers Point NSW 2000
Phone: +61 (0)2 8220 2000 Fax: +61 (0)2 8220 2558
www.murdochbooks.com.au

Murdoch Books UK Limited
Erico House, 6th Floor North, 93–99 Upper Richmond Road
Putney, London SW15 2TG
Phone: + 44 (0) 20 8785 5995 Fax: + 44 (0) 20 8785 5985
www.murdochbooks.co.uk

Publisher: Lynn Lewis
Senior Designer: Heather Menzies
Project Manager: Liz Malcolm
Designer: Kylie Mulquin
Editor: Justine Harding
Production: Alexandra Gonzalez

National Library of Australia Cataloguing-in-Publication Data

Title: Mediterranean.
ISBN: 978-1-74266-266-4 (pbk.)
Series: Step-by-step.
Notes: Includes index.
Subjects: Cooking, Mediterranean.
641.591822

Printed by 1010 Printing International Limited. PRINTED IN CHINA.